WITHDRAWN

D1192014

ONLY IN
MUNICH

Duncan J. D. Smith

ONLY IN
MUNICH

A Guide to Unique Locations,
Hidden Corners and Unusual Objects

Photographs by
Duncan J. D. Smith

**The
Urban
Explorer**

I dedicate this book with love and thanks to Roswitha,
without whom the following pages could not have been written,
also to the memory of our dear friend Martina

Above: Jugendstil frieze depicting Adam and Eve on Ainmillerstrasse (see no. 81)

Page 2: One of Erasmus Grasser's Morisco Dancers in the Münchner Stadtmuseum
(Munich City Museum) on St.-Jakobs-Platz (see no. 19)

Contents

Outer Suburbs – East (Bogenhausen; Berg am Laim; Trudering – Riem; Ramersdorf – Perlach; Obergiesing; Untergiesing – Harlaching)

Introduction

"Munich, between art and beer,
is like a village located between hills"

Heinrich Heine, poet (1797–1856)

Straddling the River Isar north of the Bavarian Alps, Munich is Germany's third largest city (after Berlin and Hamburg), but not without reason has it been dubbed the country's "Secret Capital".

Badly bombed during the Second World War – because of its position as capital of the Nazi movement – it has since been meticulously restored to its nineteenth century appearance, allowing the city to shine once again. Consequently, sites relating to its infamous Third Reich history, the fleeting *Räterepublik* of 1919, and the city's role as centre of the post-war Federal Intelligence Service, are ignored by many visitors in favour of Munich's world famous beer cellars, and enviable cultural and sporting facilities.

But there is much more to Munich besides this, from Gothic fragments of the medieval walled town and architectural extravagances of the Wittelsbach dynasty*, to modern curiosities such as a haven for surfing in the city centre and a concrete church sunk deliberately into a rubbish dump! It is with such places in mind that this new guide has been written, for those who want to take the time to discover something more of the place for themselves.

It only takes a few minutes of planning, and a glance at a decent street map**, to escape the crowds and the orchestrated tours to discover a somewhat different Munich. Based on personal experience, walking the city's twenty-five borough districts *(Stadtbezirke)*, the author points the fellow explorer in a new and unusual direction. This is the Munich of abandoned cemeteries and secret gardens; historic breweries and quiet Gothic corners; quirky museums and atmospheric church crypts; idiosyncratic shops and historic hotels; colourful markets and ancient customs; not to mention a recently restored Art Nouveau swimming Pool and a museum celebrating the humble potato! Munich remains, however, a city with a dark past, its myriad memorials to the victims of Nazi aggression still bearing grim witness to terrible times.

As would be expected, many of these less well-known locations are to be found in Munich's former walled town *(Altstadt)*, and in what are today the inner suburbs of Ludwigsvorstadt – Isarvorstadt, Maxvorstadt, Schwabing-West, and Au – Haidhausen. However, a similar number lie *outside* these long-established areas of occupation, in the outer suburbs ranged concentrically around the city centre, both east of the Isar, as well as in those far out to the south-west and north-west. Using Munich's extensive transport network of underground trains *(U-Bahn)*, suburban trains *(S-Bahn)*, trams *(Strassenbahn)*, and buses *(Autobus)*, the explorer can quite quickly reach all the places described within the following pages – and that's without detracting whatsoever from the sense of personal discovery that each of these places has to offer. Indeed, directions have been kept to a minimum so as to leave the visitor free to find their own particular path.

Whether searching for literary haunts in Schwabing, tracking down the former airport where the Munich air disaster occurred, marvelling at the world's oldest *kayak*, descending into the crypt of the Church of St. Michael, or searching for the remains of Hitler's secret headquarters in Pullach, it is hoped that the visitor will experience a sense of having made the discovery for themselves.

Duncan J. D. Smith, Munich & Vienna

* The dates given after the names of Bavaria's rulers are the actual years they reigned- for, whereas those given after important non-ruling personalities relate to their birth and death.
** Most street maps of Munich cover the central area and inner suburbs; the excellent Falk Stadtplan Extra Map also includes the outer districts, as well as tram, bus, met- ro and rail routes throughout the city.

(After each entry there is a selection of others within walking distance. An alphabetical list of opening times of places mentioned in the text can be found at the back of the book.)

One of the last fragments of Munich's medieval town wall, on Jungfernturmstrasse

1 Ancient Gates, Forgotten Walls

Altstadt – Lehel, a tour beginning with the fragment
of old city wall on Jungfernturmstrasse
U3, U4, U5, U6 Odeonsplatz; Tram 19

If it weren't for the presence of three ancient gateways – Karlstor, Sendlinger Tor, and Isartor – visitors might be forgiven for thinking that Munich never had a city wall. That it once did, and an extensive one at that, is made clear by a visit to the Bavarian National Museum (Bayerisches Nationalmuseum) at Prinzregentenstrasse 3, where there is a fascinating wooden model of Munich, carved in 1572 by Jakob Sandtner. It shows clearly the densely-built city, squeezed inside a medieval city wall. (A copy made in the late 1920s in lime wood can be found in the Münchner Stadtmuseum (Munich City Museum) on St.-Jakobs-Platz.)

By order of Charles Theodore, Elector of Bavaria (1777–1799), this wall was demolished in 1791 to enable Munich to expand. The moat along Sonnenstrasse was filled with rubble but the three gates were left standing, as was one short stretch of masonry on Jungfernturmsstrasse, its name recalling a tower that once stood here. This rare survival today provides the perfect location to get the map out and reflect on the forgotten history of Munich's city walls.

Much of the topography of Munich at the time of its founding in 1158 is now lost, the numerous streams criss-crossing the land, for example, having long since been culverted or re-directed. Fortunately there are contemporary documents surviving that describe the early settlement and its protective wall, erected in 1175 by Henry 'the Lion', Duke of Saxony and Bavaria (1156–1180), of the Welf dynasty. The wall enclosed an area defined approximately by Schäfflerstrasse and Sparkassenstrasse to the north, and Rosental and Färbergraben to the south, the latter two street names denoting the former presence of a defensive ditch. It was pierced by several gates and punctuated by towers, one of which, the Ruffini-Turm, is remembered in a wall plaque at Rindermarkt 10. Inside the wall stood predecessors of the Frauenkirche and of the Church of St. Peter (Peterskirche), the latter built around 1050 by the Benedictine monks from whom Munich takes its name (see no. 23).

Under Ludwig II, 'the severe' (1253–1294), of the Wittelsbach dynasty, Munich was raised to the status of a town and he chose it as his capital. For this reason he had Munich's first castle, known today as the Alter Hof (Old Court), built in the northeastern corner (see no. 8). During the reigns of Ludwig and his successor Ludwig IV, 'the Bavarian' (1294–1347), a Holy Roman Emperor responsible for reuniting Bavaria in 1340 after the First Partition (1253–1340), Munich grew to five times its original size. This made it necessary to build a new wall around the town, which was constructed in 1301–1337. This wall more or less followed the course of today's inner city ring road (Altstadtring), including Thomas-Wimmer-Ring, Frauenstrasse, Blumenstrasse, Sonnenstrasse, and Maximiliansplatz. Except for the addition of various towers (including the one on Jungfernturmstrasse, erected in 1493 and demolished in 1804) this wall remained unchanged until its demolition in 1791.

Munich's three remaining gates formed a part of this final wall (although there were others too, for example the one remembered in the street name Angertorstrasse). Karlstor, at the end of Neuhauser Strasse, is first mentioned in 1302 as Neuhauser Tor but has been known as

A wooden model of medieval Munich and its walls in the Münchner Stadtmuseum (Munich City Museum)

Karlstor since the 18th century, in honour of Elector Charles Theodore. Surviving casemates were unearthed in 1970, during excavations for the nearby Stachus Shopping Centre. Karlstor has been considerably remodelled, as has Sendlinger Tor (1318), at the end of Sendlinger Strasse, which once opened onto the trade route to Italy. The third remaining gate, Isartor (1337), is the only gate in its original state and today contains the eccentric Valentin Karlstadt Musäum (see no. 14). Some fragments of the adjoining wall were uncovered during building work in the area, at Thomas-Wimmer-Ring 1, Lueg ins Land, and the corner of Pflugstrasse and Marienstrasse, where there is a plaque.

In 1385, after a series of public uprisings against the Wittelsbachs, the Alter Hof

The Karlstor dates back to the 14th century

was abandoned in favour of a new moated castle, the Neue Veste, *outside* the wall on the north-eastern edge of the town. Only in 1476 did the Wittelsbachs feel confident enough to integrate the castle into the town fortifications. Not completed until 1570 the Neue Veste was abandoned almost immediately and work began replacing it with the more fashionable Munich Residenz (see no. 8).

Other places of interest nearby: 2, 3, 4, 5, 8

2 Three Very Different Fathers!

Altstadt – Lehel, the Archbishops' Palace (Erzbischöfliches Palais)
at Kardinal-Faulhaber-Strasse 7 (not open to the public)
S1, S2, S3, S4, S6, S7, S8 Marienplatz; U3, U6 Marienplatz;
U3, U4, U5, U6 Odeonsplatz; Tram 19

On Kardinal-Faulhaber-Strasse, in the northwestern corner of Munich's Old Town (Altstadt), there stands the Palais Holnstein. Since 1818 it has been the residence of the archbishops of Munich and Freising, hence its more common name of Archbishops' Palace (Erzbischöfliches Palais). However, the building was commissioned originally by Charles Albert, Elector of Bavaria (1726–1745), for his mistress Sophie Caroline von Ingelheim, Countess von Holnstein. In the tympanum can still be seen the coat of arms of Count von Holnstein, the illegitimate son fathered by Charles Albert: the clear division across it indicated the count's unfortunate family status. Erected between 1733 and 1737 the palace was designed by the Dutch court architect François de Cuvilliés (1695–1768), who was instrumental in bringing the Late Baroque (Rococo) style not only to the Wittelsbach court at Munich but also to Central Europe as a whole. With interior decoration by Johann Baptist Zimmermann it is the city's finest Rococo-style palace.

Directly over the doorway of the palace is a bas-relief depicting the Virgin surrounded by cherubs: many would consider this a more suitable motif for the period between 1977 and 1982, when the building served as the residence for Archbishop Joseph Alois Ratzinger, later Pope Benedict XVI. A native of Bavaria he was born in the market town of Marktl and studied theology in Munich. The Pope stayed here again during his papal visit to Munich in September 2006.

Moving westwards now along Prannerstrasse we arrive in Maximiliansplatz, where there is a monument to a rather different father figure. Standing in the square is a memorial to the German chemist Baron Justus von Liebig (1803–1873), the 'Father of the Fertiliser Industry'. Aged just twenty-one Liebig became a professor at the University of Giessen, and established the world's first school of chemistry. Whilst there he devised the modern laboratory-oriented teaching method, for which he is regarded as one of the greatest chemistry teachers of all time. School laboratories today still feature the vapour condenser that he popularised, known as a Liebig Condenser.

After receiving an appointment from the King of Bavaria in 1852

Liebig moved to the University of Munich, where he remained for the rest of his life making major contributions to agricultural, biological and organic chemistry. His unique contribution to the fertiliser industry was the discovery of nitrogen as an essential plant nutrient – hence the development of nitrogen-based fertilisers – and the formulation of the so-called Law of the Minimum, which describes the effect of individual nutrients on crops. A replica of one of Liebig's laboratories can be found in the chemistry section of the Deutsches Museum on Museumsinsel.

Liebig made his name in other spheres too, including the implementation of a process for silvering that greatly improved the effectiveness of mirrors (see no. 21). Together with Belgian engineer George Giebert, Liebig also developed an efficient method of

The Palais Holnstein on Kardinal-Faulhaber-Strasse, once the residence of Pope Benedict XVI

producing beef extract from carcasses. In 1865 they founded the Liebig Extract of Meat Company, marketing the extract as a cheap, nutritious alternative to real meat. Some years after Liebig's death, in 1899, the product was trademarked as Oxo, by which name the humble beef stock cube is known around the world today.

Other places of interest nearby: 1, 3, 4, 8

3 An Experiment in Communism

Altstadt – Lehel, the pavement memorial to Kurt Eisner at
Kardinal-Faulhaber-Strasse 14
U3, U4, U5, U6 Odeonsplatz; Tram 19

Outside the former Bavarian State Department, in the Palais Mont-gelas at Kardinal-Faulhaber-Strasse 14, there is what looks like a murder scene. The shape of a fallen man is outlined not in chalk but in steel. This unusual pavement memorial recalls the socialist statesmen Kurt Eisner (1867–1919), assassinated here because of his politics. Given short shrift in many guidebooks, Eisner's story tells us much about how Munich, and then Germany, fell eventually into the hands of the Nazi regime.

During the First World War, as the Allied blockade of Germany led to food and fuel shortages in Munich, Kurt Eisner joined the Independent Social Democratic Party of Germany (USPD). In 1918 he was convicted of treason for inciting a strike of munitions workers, and was sent to the city's Stadelheim Prison. By the time he was released, Germany had been defeated.

During the war Ludwig III, King of Bavaria (1913–1918) had grown increasingly unpopular, in part because of his blind loyalty to Prussia. Munich became the scene of tense political unrest and on 7th November 1918, the first anniversary of the Russian October Revolution, Eisner declared the Free State of Bavaria (Freistaat Bayern), with himself as prime minister. In so doing he brought to an end the monarchy of the Wittelsbach dynasty, which had ruled Bavaria for more than seven centuries. The end of the monarchy in Berlin was announced two days later, making way for the Weimar Republic.

The main aim of these new republics was to rapidly conclude a peace treaty and to bring about a thoroughgoing democratic and socialist renewal of state and society. However, although Eisner advocated a socialist government, he distanced himself from the Russian Bolsheviks, declaring that his government would protect property rights. Despite this he was unable to allay the bourgeois-conservative camp's fears of a communist revolution and was defeated in the February 1919 election. On 21st February 1919 he was gunned down on his way to the Bavarian Parliament to tender his resignation. Eisner's assassin was one Anton Graf von Arco auf Valley (1897–1945), a right-wing reserve lieutenant, who when questioned about his motives claimed the dead man was everything von Arco himself wasn't: an anarchist, a Bolshevist, and a Jew.

An outline in the pavement on Kardinal-Faulhaber-Strasse marks where the statesman Kurt Eisner was gunned down

The murder caused an escalation in unrest in Bavaria, and, with news of a soviet revolution in Hungary, communists and anarchists seized power. They proclaimed the Bavarian Soviet Republic *(Bayerische Räterepublik)*, a Soviet-style republic of workers' and soldiers' councils, with its capital in Munich. Lenin, who had lived in Munich himself some years before, at Kaiserstrasse 46, sent a congratulatory telegram. The new republic was ruled by USPD members and anarchists but their lack of experience did little to restore order. The regime collapsed within six days and was replaced by a second, more radical Communist republic.

Lawlessness continued and on 29th April the republic's own Red Army *(Rote Armee)* executed eight men as right-wing spies, including Prince Gustav von Thurn und Taxis. On 1st May 1919, taking this as a pretext, the Social Democrats used government troops and *Freikorps* to end the *Räterepublik* and arrest its leaders. Munich's brief experiment in Communism was over.

Law and order was restored by specially-created right-wing militias, who when they themselves were outlawed in 1921 began embracing extremist groups such as Hitler's National Socialist German Workers' Party (Nationalsozialistische Deutsche Arbeiterpartei). With Bavaria's moderate forces now seriously weakened the National Socialists could only grow in strength.

Other places of interest nearby: 1, 2, 4, 5, 8

4 Europe's Last Original *Tiki* Bar

Altstadt – Lehel, Trader Vic's bar and restaurant
in the Hotel Bayerischer Hof at Promenadeplatz 2–6
S1, S2, S3, S4, S6, S7, S8 Marienplatz; U3, U6 Marienplatz;
Tram 19; Bus N40

Munich's Bayerischer Hof on Promenadeplatz is a classic *Grand Dame* hotel of the type found in most large European cities. Luxurious and resolutely Old Europe its five-star charm has long appealed to the rich and famous, from royalty to Hollywood stars. Yet there is something in the basement of this hotel that will not be found in any other hotel in Europe: the oldest surviving example of a Polynesian *tiki*-style bar and restaurant.

So-called '*Tiki* Culture' began in the United States in 1934, with the opening of 'Don the Beachcomber', a Polynesian-themed bar and restaurant in Hollywood. The proprietor was a young man from Louisiana called Ernest Raymond Beaumont-Gantt, who had sailed throughout the South Pacific; later he legally changed his name to Don Beach. His eclectically-styled restaurant featured Cantonese cuisine and exotic rum punches, with a decor of flaming torches, rattan furniture, Hawaiian floral *leis*, and brightly coloured fabrics. Any real historical connection to *Tiki*, the first man in Polynesian creation mythology, was tenuous right from the start.

In the same year, Victor Jules Bergeron Jr. (1902–1984) opened a small bar and restaurant with the unpromising name of Hinky Dink's, across the road from his parents' grocery store in Oakland, California. Three years later he too adopted an exotic *tiki* theme and as the popularity of his establishment spread he re-named it Trader Vic's. Having spent just $700 getting started it would pave the way for the world's first successful themed restaurant chain, with branches around the globe.

The golden age of the Trader Vic's empire came in the wake of the Second World War, when American soldiers returning home brought with them stories and souvenirs from the South Pacific. Author James Michener won the 1948 Pulitzer Prize for his collection of short stories, *Tales of the South Pacific*, which in turn was the basis for *South Pacific*, the phenomenally successful 1949 musical by Rodgers and Hammerstein. Hawaiian statehood in 1959 fuelled further interest in exotic islands. Throughout the late 1950s and early 1960s continental America fell in love with a romanticised version of what such places were like

Polynesian style in Trader Vic's bar beneath the Hotel Bayerischer Hof on Promenadeplatz

and 'Tiki Culture' began to infuse every aspect of the country's visual aesthetic, from home accessories and dress, to music, cinema and architecture.

Short of visiting the islands themselves the average American could experience Hawaii and Polynesia by frequenting one of the many tiki hut bars and restaurants that sprang up across the land. Amidst the bamboo fittings and blowfish lampshades the de rigueur drink was most definitely the Mai Tai, a cocktail of white and dark rums, orange curaçao, sweet Orgeat syrup, and lime juice, served up with compulsory fruit trimmings and a paper umbrella. Still popular today its invention has been claimed by both Victor Bergeron in 1944, as well as his amicable rival Don Beach in 1934. Either way the name is derived from the Tahitian word Maita'i, meaning 'good'.

The Munich branch of Trader Vic's is a relatively late addition to the empire, opening in 1972, the year the city hosted the Olympics. It is now considered by experts to be the last such venue with 'original' decor, all subsequent openings seen as modern reinventions of the genre. With the current resurgence in popularity of retro kitsch, (including a revival of 'Tiki Culture') it is to be hoped that Trader Vic's in Munich will long continue to provide a fascinating and surprising cultural counterpoint to the more conservative charms of the Hotel Bayerischer Hof in which it can be found.

Other places of interest nearby: 1, 2, 3, 5, 6, 7

5   Once Hitler's Night Club

Altstadt – Lehel, the Künstlerhaus at Lenbachplatz 8
S1, S2, S3, S4, S6, S7, S8 Karlsplatz; U4, U5 Karlsplatz;
Tram 16, 18, 19, 20, 21, 22, 27, 28

Munich during the second half of the 19th century was a city to rival Vienna and Berlin in terms of cultural ferment. From 1873 onwards the focus of this activity was the Allotria Society, an artists' association whose avowed aim was to bring Munich's noble patricians and wealthy captains of industry together in one place, so that they might mingle with the city's great artistic practitioners. The dream was eventually realised in 1893, when Luitpold, Prince Regent of Bavaria (1886–1912) laid the foundation stone of the Künstlerhaus, or House of Artists, on the southern side of Lenbachplatz.

As befits a building in which culture, business and society were to converge, the architect Gabriel von Seidl (1848–1913) was commissioned to design an exuberant building in mock northern German Renaissance style, characterised by stepped gables and bronze ornamentation; attached to the main building are wings set around an inner courtyard.

The interior was predominantly the work of Munich painter Franz von Lenbach (1836–1904), who not only decorated the rooms with Italian Renaissance and Art Nouveau schemes, but was also responsible for organising much of the fund-raising necessary to realise the building in the first place.

Prince Regent Luitpold was on hand again in 1900 to officially open the building, after which Lenbach, together with the artists Friedrich August von Kaulbach (1822–1903) and Franz von Stuck (1863–1928), laid on a series of glamorous cultural events in celebration. Thereafter the building fulfiled its original purpose until June 1938, when the Nazi regime requisitioned the building and dissolved the Künstlerhaus Association that had hitherto administered it.

It was during the conversion of the Künstlerhaus into what would effectively be a nightclub for Nazi officials that Hitler inspected the rooms selected to be his private suite. Noticing that one of the windows faced Germany's third largest synagogue, opened in 1887 on Herzog-Max-Strasse, he ordered the building to be torn down immediately (see no. 29). Accordingly, on 8th June the synagogue authorities were given a mere 24 hours to evacuate the premises before demolition began. With-

in six days the synagogue had vanished and the site had been converted into a car park.

Hitler decreed that the Künstlerhaus would be Munich's official meeting place for Nazi artists, film-makers, sculptors, and writers. Parties were held in a luxuriously appointed hall, at one end of which the chorus and dancers of the Gärtnerplatz Theatre gave performances. The parties usually began around midnight and could last until ten o'clock the next morning, although Hitler usually departed for his apartment on Prinzregentenplatz long before then (see no. 53). Behind the scenes, however, the Künstlerhaus soon gained a tawdry reputation as a hotbed of intrigue and orgies. Especially sinister was a file kept

A traditional lithographic printing company, Steindruck München, now operates inside the Künstlerhaus

by the management detailing the physical attributes of several hundred females, the prettiest of whom could be quickly summoned for the Führer's delight.

During an air raid on 14th July 1944 the Künstlerhaus suffered considerable damage. After the war it was requisitioned by American troops, and returned to its rightful owners, the Künstlerhaus Association, in 1954. Following reconstruction the building was re-opened by Duke Albert of Bavaria and Mayor Jochen Vogel on 1st October 1961. Of its original interior only the ornately plastered vestibule and the so-called Venetian Room still remain intact.

In the century since the Künstlerhaus first opened its doors, the relationship between artist and society has changed considerably, being no longer the domain solely of the wealthy and aristocratic. In 1991 the building came under new management and the decision was taken to broaden its appeal. Moving away from the association's original motto of *Nobis et Amicis* (For Ourselves and Our Friends), which is inscribed over its doorway, the Künstlerhaus now plays host to a wide variety of public art exhibitions, conferences, and other multicultural events.

A fascinating permanent fixture in the Künstlerhaus is the Steindruck München printing workshop, which uses the traditional lithographic process pioneered in 1797 by Alois Senefelder (see no. 38). The heavy limestone plates, on which the image is hand-drawn before printing, can be seen from the street through the workshop's large arched windows. Senefelder's original press can be found in the printing department of the Deutsches Museum on Museumsinsel.

Other places of interest nearby: 3, 4, 6, 7, 33

6 A Descent into Munich's Crypts

Altstadt – Lehel, the crypt of the Church of
St. Michael (Michaelskirche) at Neuhauser Strasse 6
S1, S2, S3, S4, S6, S7, S8 Karlsplatz; U4, U5 Karlsplatz;
Tram 16, 18, 19, 20, 21, 22, 27, 28

Concealed beneath several of Munich's city centre churches can be found vaulted burial chambers, or crypts (from the Greek word *kryptós* meaning 'hidden'). Containing various members of the Wittelsbach dynasty, who ruled Bavaria from 1180 until 1918, they are atmospheric locations.

Not surprisingly the best known royal crypt *(Fürstengruft)* lies under the Frauenkirche (Cathedral Church of Our Lady) on Frauenplatz, a triple-naved brick building that is the largest Gothic structure in southern Germany. Built in just twenty years (1468–1488) – a record at the time – its iconic twin towers were crowned with onion domes instead of steeples due to lack of funds. Unfortunately, as a result of bomb damage in 1944, the crypt had to be completely renovated (1952), its re-built brick walls and modern lighting robbing the place of its former sepulchral atmosphere. Entered, as is normal, from the rear of the church the crypt contains the remains of several important Bavarian rulers, their coffins placed in wall niches marked with inscribed stones. Most important are those of Ludwig IV, variously Duke of Bavaria, King of Germany and Holy Roman Emperor (1294–1347) – a black marble monument to whom stands just inside the main door of the church – and Ludwig III, the last King of Bavaria (1913–1918).

More atmospheric is the crypt beneath the Baroque Church of St. Cajetan, known more commonly as the Theatinerkirche, at Theatinerstrasse 22. Together with a monastery for the Theatine order (named after the ancient Italian city of Theate, modern Chieti), the church was built in 1663–1690 and was the first large Baroque building to be built north of the Alps. Again the crypt is entered from the rear of the church and contains further important tombs. They include the founder of the church Ferdinand Maria, Elector of Bavaria (1651–1679), and his Italian wife Henriette Adelaide of Savoy; their son Maximilian II Emanuel, Elector of Bavaria (1679–1726), and his Polish second wife Teresa Kunigunde Sobieska; Charles Albert, Elector of Bavaria (1726–1745), who fought unsuccessfully against the Habsburg Maria Theresa in the Austrian War of Succession and was briefly Holy Roman Emperor; the

Inside the crypt beneath the Theatinerkirche

popular Luitpold, Prince Regent of Bavaria (1886–1912), who deposed his nephew King Ludwig II (after he was declared insane in 1886) and then ruled as regent for his mentally ill nephew Otto I, King of Bavaria (1886–1913); and King Otto of Greece (1833–1862), second son of Ludwig I, King of Bavaria (1825–1848) and the first modern king of Greece until he was overthrown in a military coup; his sarcophagus is decorated like a Classical Greek temple. Maximilian II, King of Bavaria (1848–1864) and his Prussian wife Marie Friederike Franziska Hedwig are buried in a side chapel in the church proper.

The most atmospheric of Munich's crypts is located beneath the choir of the Church of St. Michael (Michaelskirche) at Neuhauser Strasse 6. The church was built in the 1580s for the Jesuit order, in an effort to bolster their presence as leaders of the Counter Reformation. Reminiscent of the Il Gesù Church in Rome it is the mightiest Renaissance church north of the Alps, its barrel-vaulted nave the largest after that of St. Peter's itself. Compared with the fine Late Baroque (Rococo) interior of the church the crypt is dark and musty, the coffins visible rather than concealed within the walls. Amongst the thirty Wittels-

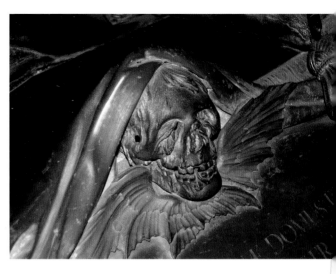

Detail of a sarcophagus in the crypt of St. Michael's (Michaelskirche) on Neuhauser Strasse

bachs interred here are Maximilian I, King of Bavaria (1799–1825, until 1806 as Elector Maximilian IV Joseph), whose daughter married Eugene de Beauharnais, the son of Napoleon's wife Josephine from her first marriage.

The most famous incumbent, however, is undoubtedly Ludwig II, King of Bavaria (1864–1886), the eccentric "Swan King" famed for his love of fairytale castles and the music of Richard Wagner. Following Ludwig's mysterious death at Lake Starnberg, south of Munich, an elaborate funeral was held and his remains interred in the crypt. In accordance with Bavarian tradition, however, his heart was placed in a silver urn and sent to the *Gnadenkapelle* (Chapel of Mercy) in Altötting, where it can still be found alongside those of his father and grandfather. Ludwig was succeeded by his brother Otto I, King of Bavaria (1886–1913), who is also buried in the crypt.

Other places of interest nearby: 4, 5, 7, 33

7 Hunting and Fishing Bavarian Style

Altstadt – Lehel, the German Hunting and Fishing Museum
(Deutsches Jagd- und Fischereimuseum) at Neuhauser Strasse 2
S1, S2, S3, S4, S6, S7, S8 Karlsplatz; U4, U5 Karlsplatz;
Tram 16, 18, 19, 20, 21, 22, 27, 28

On the corner of Ettstrasse with busy Neuhauser Strasse there stands a former Augustinian church, built in the late 13th century and notable for becoming the first building in Munich to be decorated in the Baroque style. In 1911 it was converted into a concert hall and its buttressed Gothic apse scooped out to form an entrance. A clue as to where this entrance leads today is given by the vigorous bronze sculpture of a wild boar on the pavement outside. Beyond is one of Munich's more unusual – and certainly most unusually located – museums: the German Hunting and Fishing Museum (Deutsches Jagd- und Fischereimuseum).

Billed as the largest collection of field sports equipment in the world, the museum was opened in 1938 by wealthy Nazi Party member SS Brigade Commander Christian Weber. He was one of a large number of Nazis who used their position after Hitler's accession as chancellor for blatant personal gain. As well as occupying the splendid Residenz, the former home of the Wittelsbach dynasty, Weber chose to indulge his passion for horses by becoming President of the Federation of German Riding Stable Owners and Thoroughbred Breeders. He also sponsored the 'Brown Band', the most valuable equestrian trophy in Germany, which he staged at Riem Racecourse (Galopprennbahn Riem) at Graf-Lehndorff-Strasse 36. A member of the Reichstag, Weber's wealth by the end of the war was estimated at a million Reichsmarks.

The museum was originally installed in the north wing of Schloss Nymphenburg, the Baroque summer palace commissioned by Ferdinand Maria, Elector of Bavaria (1651–1679). Closed during the Second World War the museum was not reopened until 1966, when it was relocated to the former church in which it resides today. At the heart of the collection, which illustrates German hunting and fishing practices from the Stone Age up to the present day, is the celebrated antler collection of Maximilian Count Arco-Zinneberg (1811–1885), the greatest of all Bavarian hunters. Almost as overwhelming is the thousand-strong stuffed animal and bird collection.

Of greater interest perhaps are the examples of traditional equipment once used by hunters and fishermen, including medieval rifles, fishing tackle, and canoes, all displayed against the magnificent backdrop of the former church; the collection of wooden sleighs suitably carved into the shapes of animals occupies the building's gilded former organ loft. There are also hunting trophies, oil paintings, and a series of charming miniature dioramas inhabited by tiny lead figures. The photo of an ornithologist clipping the wings off a bird for analysis might disturb some visitors but it is suitably balanced by an exhibit illustrating today's more eco-friendly recording techniques.

An example of the curious Wolpertinger in the German Hunting and Fishing Museum (Deutsches Jagd- und Fischereimuseum) on Neuhauser Strasse

To finish on a lighter note there is a tongue-in-cheek display devoted to the Wolpertinger *(Crisensus bavaricus)*, a hypothetical creature supposedly living in the alpine forests of Bavaria. This cryptid has the body parts of several creatures – usually wings, antlers and fangs – attached to the body of a small furry mammal, such as a rabbit or squirrel. Stuffed Wolpertingers are often displayed as tourist souvenirs in the countryside, each village peddling its own set of tales about local sightings. Like the American Jackalope, the Wolpertinger is thought by cryptozoologists to have been inspired by sightings of wild rabbits infected with the *Shope papillomavirus*, which causes the growth of antler-like tumours on a rabbit's head.

Other places of interest nearby: 3, 4, 5, 6, 17

8 Extraordinary Rooms in the Residenz

Altstadt – Lehel, the Antiquarium in the Residenz
at Max-Josef-Platz 3
U3, U4, U5, U6 Odeonsplatz; Tram 19

The Munich Residenz is a vast palace complex built between 1569 and 1842 in the northeastern corner of the city's Old Town (Altstadt). It was the political and cultural centre of the dukes, the electors, and finally the kings of Bavaria and occupies the former site of the so-called Neue Veste, a castle erected here in 1385 (see no. 1). As a residence, seat of government, and art repository, the history of the Residenz is intimately tied up with that of Bavaria's ruling dynasty, the Wittelsbachs, each of whom furnished and extended the palace in the artistic style prevailing at the time. Consequently, the 130 rooms and ten courtyards that make up the Residenz today reflect the main stages of European culture (Renaissance, Baroque, Rococo, and Classical). Three of them, which help make up what is known today as the Alte Residenz (Old Residence) fronting Residenzstrasse, can be singled out for their extraordinary and unusual design.

The first, the Grottenhof (Grotto Courtyard), is encountered on the ground floor and is one of the first areas to be entered during a round tour of the Residenz. It was constructed between 1581 and 1589 as part of a summer palace for William V, Duke of Bavaria (1579–1597). The grotto after which it is named occupies one side of the courtyard and is encrusted with seashells, crystals, and volcanic tufa. Emerging from the walls are a series of figures, by turns humorous and grotesque, including a gilded bronze statue of Mercury. The curious fountains raise many a visitor's eyebrow!

From the Grottenhof we enter the Antiquarium (Hall of Antiquities), the largest and most lavish secular Renaissance interior north of the Alps. The oldest surviving part of the Residenz this breathtaking room is 66 metres long. It was built in 1569–1571 to display the antiquities' collection of Albert V, Duke of Bavaria (1550–1579), thus making it one of the earliest museum halls in existence. Between 1581 and 1600 Albert's successors, William V, Duke of Bavaria (1579–1597) and his son Maximilian I, Duke (later Elector) of Bavaria (1597–1651), transformed the Antiquarium into a banqueting hall. They lowered the floor, erect-

The matchless Renaissance Antiquarium in the Munich Residenz

ed a balustraded dais at each end, installed a fireplace, and added the distinctive paintings to the barrel-vaulted roof. Of particular interest are the 102 rondels in the vaults above the windows, and on the window jambs, being views of towns, markets and palaces in what was then the Duchy of Bavaria. The busts and other sculptures on display include both original works of classical antiquity and Renaissance copies. Some formed part of Duke Albert's collection, whilst others were added in the 17th and 18th centuries. After being reduced to rubble during an Allied bombing raid on 18th March 1944 the Antiquarium was painstakingly rebuilt and is today considered a masterpiece of architectural reconstruction.

A third extraordinary space in the Residenz is the Reiche Kapelle (Ornate Chapel), situated on the second floor and overlooking the Grotto Courtyard. Dedicated in 1607 it was the private place of worship of Maximilian I, Duke (later Elector) of Bavaria (1597–1651) and his second wife, Elisabeth of Lorraine (hence their clearly visible initials). It was also here that Maximilian stored his collection of saintly relics. The Catholic Church considered such relics as sacred intermediaries between man and God making this tiny chapel the spiritual centre of the entire Residenz. It was decorated accordingly, its walls clad with

stucco panels polished to look like marble *(Scagliola)* and its ceiling adorned with gilt reliefs on a blue ground resembling lapis lazuli. In the centre of the ceiling is a lantern with stained glass windows. The focal point of the chapel is an altar bearing extremely fine silver reliefs created by the Augsburg goldsmiths Hans Schebel and Jacob Anthoni.

Looking into the Reiche Kapelle (Ornate Chapel) in the Munich Residenz

After leaving the Residenz peep inside the Hofapotheke (Court Pharmacy) at Residenzstrasse 1, which still contains its original apothecary jars. Notice also the line of bronze cobblestones on nearby Viscardigasse, installed as a reminder of the route once taken by those wishing to avoid giving the Nazi salute at the Feldherrnhalle, where a monument to Hitler's failed Beer Hall Putsch once stood. The street was dubbed Drückebergergassl (Dodgers' Alley).

Other places of interest nearby: 1, 2, 3

9 Curiosities in an English Garden

**Altstadt – Lehel, the English Garden (Englischer Garten) on
Prinzregentenstrasse
U3, U6 Odeonsplatz; U4, U5 Lehel; Tram 18**

Munich's famous English Garden (Englischer Garten) is one of the
largest city parks in the world. Stretched out along the west bank of the
River Isar, from the city centre northwards to the very edge of the city,
it covers 3.73 square kilometers and contains 578 kilometres of paths.
It is extremely popular, with an estimated 300 000 people visiting on a
fine summer's day. They come here to pursue a wide variety of leisure
activities, including cycling, jogging, football, horse riding, and even
surfing, on the chilly waters of the River Eisbach (see no. 65). Others are
students from the adjacent Ludwig Maximilian University (Ludwig-
Maximilians-Universität), who study beneath the trees, whilst many
more come to just laze in the sun.

Then there are those (this author included) who come to uncover
the story behind this historic garden, and to explore the unusual structures hidden along its winding paths. For these people it is best to approach the garden from the south, through the entrance on Prinzregentenstrasse. Just inside, on the lefthand side, stands the so-called
Rumford Memorial, a neo-Classical monument by the sculptor Ludwig
von Schwanthaler (1802–1848) (see no. 31). Erected in 1795 the memorial features a bas-relief depicting on one side *Bavaria* favoured by
Abundance, and more interestingly a portrait of Benjamin Thompson,
Graf von Rumford (1753–1814) on the other. Thompson was a Massa-
chusetts-born Anglo-American army officer, government administra-
tor, and physicist, who as War Minister spent eleven years reorganising
the Bavarian army for Elector Charles Theodore (1777–1799). In 1789 he
had the marshy land around the Isar drained and developed as military
gardens, in which soldiers could be trained in agriculture and survival.
Thompson designated the area east of these gardens as the first public
park in Europe, which was opened in 1792. It was called the English
Garden not after Rumford but because it was designed in the manner
of 18th century English landscape parks, by royal gardener Friedrich
Ludwig von Sckell (1750–1823). The military gardens were eventually
incorporated into the English Garden in 1800.

Whilst in Munich Thompson also established workhouses for the
poor, and facilitated the cultivation of the potato, in honour of which he

The Rumford Memorial recalls the creator of the English Garden (Englischer Garten)

was made Count Rumford (an imposing statue of Rumford clutching his design for the English Garden stands opposite the State Museum of Ethnology (Staatliches Museum für Völkerkunde) at Maximilianstrasse 42).

Continuing on from the Rumford Memorial, a path to the left crosses the swift-flowing, blue-green waters of the Eisbach, down which groups of children are happily swept during the summer months. At the end of the path there is a tiny island on which stands a charming Japanese teahouse, erected to commemorate the Munich Summer Olympics in 1972. It is the work of the Urasenke Foundation, a venerable organisation of internationally-minded tea ceremony masters.

Returning to the main path continue onwards until another left turn leads through trees to a small artificial hillock made of construction waste from the Residenz. On the top stands the Monopteros, a neo-Classical structure in the form of a circular Greek temple designed by Bavarian court architect Leo von Klenze (1784–1864). It was erected in 1836 by order of Ludwig I, King of Bavaria (1825–1848), an ardent admirer of the Classical world (see no. 39). On a clear day there is a fine view over the city from here, with the Alps visible in the distance. Beyond the hillock stretches the Schönfeldwiese, popular with naked sunbathers. This pastime, which has been legal since the 1960s, even has its own name: Freikörperkultur (Free Body Culture).

Returning to the main path yet again, continue onwards to reach the most surprising feature in the garden: the Chinese Tower (Chinesischer Turm). This 23 metre-high, five-storey pagoda was erected as a viewing tower and bandstand by the military architect Josef Frei, when the garden opened in 1789. Frei based his design on the Great

Pagoda in the Royal Botanic Gardens in London. Destroyed during the Second World War the tower was re-built from scratch in 1952, complete with golden bells hanging on the eaves of its multiple wooden rooves. Spread out beneath it is Munich's second largest beer garden, with seats for 7000 patrons. Also located here is a wonderful children's carousel constructed originally in 1823 and replaced in 1912. Still in use today, after restoration in 1980, it is the work of the Schwabing sculptor Joseph Erlacher, ably assisted by the artist August Julier. Alongside the usual horses can be seen more unusual creatures such as an ibex, stork, flamingo, and swan.

The neo-Classical Monopteros stands on a low hill in the English Garden (Englischer Garten)

Finally, north of the pagoda, beyond the neo-Classical Rumford-Haus (1791), is the Kleinhesseloher See, an artificial lake which is fed by the Eisbach and the Schwabinger Bach. Created in 1802 the lake can be explored by means of rented paddleboats, although alighting on its three small islands is not permitted because of their importance to wildfowl. On the lakeside there stands a memorial to the garden's designer, Friedrich Ludwig von Sckell, as well as the Seehaus, another popular beer garden, which is the perfect place to take refreshment before plunging into the less-frequented, northern reaches of the English Garden, known as the Hirschau. Incorporated into the garden in 1799 it includes a small amphitheatre contructed in 1985, to replace an 18th century predecessor that is now lost.

Other places of interest nearby: 10, 11

10 The Nativity as Art

Altstadt – Lehel, the Crib Collection (Krippensammlung) in the
Bavarian National Museum (Bayerisches Nationalmuseum)
at Prinzregentenstrasse 3
U4, U5 Lehel; Tram 18

The building housing the Bavarian National Museum (Bayerisches Nationalmuseum) on Prinzregentenstrasse is an architectural wonder. Intended to embody the notion of a 19th century artistic shrine, it was designed by Gabriel von Seidl (1848–1913) and constructed in 1894–1895.
The mixture of architectural styles employed on the outside of the building was intended to reflect the rich variety of collections within, which
themselves were displayed in galleries specifically designed for them.
This is still apparent in the collection of Gothic religious art on the first
floor, which is displayed in a vaulted gallery resembling a church.

Although the museum encompasses art from Classical antiquity up
to the 19th century, its core remains the private religious art collection of
the Wittelsbach dynasty, which Maximilian II, King of Bavaria (1848–

One of the many Italianate cribs in the Bavarian National Museum's Crib Collection
(Krippensammlung)

1864) donated to the country in 1855. Unusual objects abound, from the altar piece depicting a skeleton riding a lion (symbolising Death on the prowl) to a Scandinavian box made of bronze and Mammoth tusk ivory. Most unusual of all, however, is the museum's exhibition of cribs (Krippensammlung), considered the largest and most important collection of its kind anywhere in the world.

The Nativity, or birth of Jesus, has been a major subject in Christian art since the 4th century, appearing in media as diverse as illuminated manuscripts, stained glass windows, oil paintings, and stone sarcophagi. The most novel form is the crib (or crêche) in which two-dimensional or sculptured figures are arranged against a realistic backdrop. Based on Biblical narratives this is either a barn or a cave, in which the Infant Jesus lying in a manger is placed centre-stage, together with Mary and Joseph. A donkey and an ox often accompany the trio reflecting a verse from Isaiah 1:3: "the ox knoweth his owner, and the ass his master's crib", the two animals representing the Israelites and the Gentiles respectively. Optional figures include the shepherds with their sheep, and the Magi bearing gifts. Above the crib is sometimes depicted the Star of Bethlehem, as well as a heralding angel. Once constructed the crib is brought out each year and displayed in churches, town squares, and private houses during the Christmas period.

The origin of the crib as a distinct European folk art form is thought to date back to 1220 and the return of St. Francis of Assisi to Italy from a journey through Egypt and the Holy Land. According to his biographer, Thomas of Celano, Francis saw three-dimensional nativity scenes there and was asked in 1223 to construct something similar for the Italian town of Greccio. This first European crib, installed in a cave where Francis preached at Christmas Eve mass, probably consisted of little more than a straw-filled manger, an ox and a donkey.

From the 19th century onwards the crib became a much more elaborate affair, as anyone will find whilst visiting the Bavarian National Museum's Crib Collection (Krippensammlung). This former private collection of Bavarian, Tirolian, and Italian cribs is today displayed in the labyrinthine vaulted cellars of the museum and is sure to surprise and delight adults and children alike. Each one a miniature world the cribs are designed like tiny stages, their players artfully illuminated in the atmospheric gloom. The effect is quite magical.

Some of the cribs are noteworthy for depicting Jesus' birthplace as an ivy-clad Romanesque or Classical ruin, set against a backdrop that looks less like Palestine and more like the Bavarian or Italian countryside, in much the same way as Dutch or German paintings of the

A crib depicting Jerusalem as a 19ᵗʰ century European city

Nativity often incorporate European street scenes. Most impressive is an enormous paper crib created by Wenzel Fieger in 1890, comprising a mossy hillside grazed by countless sheep, cattle and deer. Some cribs even contain Baroque churches in their settings, with characters dressed in European silk finery. Another common theme is the crib as a grotto, adorned with crystals and stalactites.

Although the first true European crib was set up by the Jesuits of Prague in 1562 (and in Munich in 1597 in the Church of St. Michael (Michaelskirche) at Neuhauser Strasse 6, it is Italy that remains the spiritual home of the crib. The collection affirms this with the presence of several magnificent Neapolitan cribs and other quasi-Biblical scenes, the latter including a lively Italian street scene and a model of Jerusalem in the form of a grand 19ᵗʰ century European city. Near to the exit is a cabinet containing a collection of delicately-carved everyday objects used to decorate the cribs, including miniaturised crockery, musical instruments, loaves of bread, and bowls of fruit.

Those wishing to construct their own crib should visit the Crib Market (Kripperlmarkt) on Rindermarkt, one of Munich's numerous Christmas markets (*Christkindlmärkte*) staged during Advent. The earliest record of a Christmas market in Munich is that of the Nicholas Market on Kaufingerstrasse in 1642. The biggest today is on Marienplatz, with others on Wittelsbacher Platz, Weissenburger Platz, Sendlinger-Tor-Platz, Theresienwiese, Rotkreuzplatz, Praterinsel, Forum Münchner Freiheit and in the Englischer Garten. They are renowned for their *Christbäume*, *Lebkuchen* and *Glühwein*.

Other places of interest nearby: 9, 11

11 The World's Oldest *Kayak*

Altstadt – Lehel, the State Museum of Ethnology (Staatliches Museum für Völkerkunde) at Maximilianstrasse 42
U4, U5 Lehel; Tram 18, 19

The grand building at Maximilianstrasse 42, which was built in 1859–1865, housed originally the Bavarian National Museum (Bayerisches Nationalmuseum). From 1900 until 1923 it was used by the German Museum (Deutsches Museum) but since 1926 it has been home to the State Museum of Ethnology (Staatliches Museum für Völkerkunde), the second largest collection of such material in Germany after Berlin. The heart of the collection dates from 1782, when exotic cultural 'curiosities' in the collections of Bavaria's rulers were brought together and displayed in the Munich Residenz.

Although the collection today contains approximately 150 000 items, only a representative selection are displayed, enabling the visitor to take away a series of valuable and insightful impressions of traditional, non-European cultures.

Spread across two floors, the collections are arranged geographically, each of which has its fair share of highly unusual objects. The Indian and East Asia collection on the first floor, for example, contains a small votive *stupa* of the Pala-Sena period, at the back of which is a peephole leading down to a miniaturised *stupa* within; there is also a *Shivalinga* shrine from South India here, and a finely-carved wooden Jain shrine. The Islamic collection on the same floor contains the reconstructed façade of a mosque, and a Punjabi garden scene, with pavilion and a pair of the most intricately carved wooden doors. In the adjacent Oceania col-

An Oceanic ceremonial mask in the State Museum of Ethnology (Staatliches Museum für Völkerkunde) on Maximilianstrasse

The world's oldest kayak is made of sealskin and dates back to the 16th century

lection are displayed fish traps from Papua New Guinea, as well as a Micronesian warrior's shark-tooth spear and Porcupine Fish helmet.

On the second floor can be found the North American collection including objects from the sub-Arctic, such as a waterproof Eskimo child's *anorak* made from paper-thin seal intestine. Pride of place here goes to a simple sealskin *kayak* displayed on the balcony, which is not only the earliest identifiable object in the museum but also the oldest existing *kayak* in the world. It is thought to have arrived in Holland in 1577, together with another complete with its owners (!): a man, his wife, and their child. The family were probably brought to Europe during this time by polar explorers, to be exhibited as curiosities. It was the Count of Hanau who presented one of the *kayaks* to William V, Duke of Bavaria (1579–1597). A *kayak*, incidentally, differs from a canoe in that it is powered by a double-bladed paddle and its occupant is surrounded by a watertight seal.

Two more collections cover South America, with its Peruvian anthropomorphic ceramics and colourful fabrics, and Africa, with a collection of striking wooden Congolese statues and samples of the ever-intriguing bronzes of Benin.

Other places of interest nearby: 9, 10, 12

12 Hotel Secrets, Secret Hotels

Altstadt – Lehel, a tour beginning at the Hotel Vier Jahreszeiten
Kempinski at Maximilianstrasse 17 (note: the Old Bar is open to
the public but is not a tourist attraction)
S1, S2, S3, S4, S6, S7, S8 Marienplatz; U3, U6 Marienplatz,
U3, U4, U5, U6 Odeonsplatz; Tram 19

Some of Munich's famous hotels contain secrets, whilst other less well
known ones are secrets in themselves. Here are a handful of them.

The Hotel Vier Jahreszeiten Kempinski at Maximilianstrasse 17
was opened in 1858 under the auspices of Maximilian II, King of Bavaria (1848–1864). For half a century it vied with the Bayerischer Hof
as the preferred hotel for visiting heads of state; the King of Siam once
stayed here along with his 1320 suitcases! Today, however, the 303-room
luxury hotel, which enjoys a prime location amongst Munich's highest
concentration of designer brand stores, holds a dark secret. It was here
in 1918–1919 that the shadowy Thule Society (Thule-Gesellschaft), a
nationalist, anti-semitic, and anti-Bolshevik organisation, with the
swastika as its emblem, met frequently in the hotel's Old Bar. The society's members, several of whom held prominent public offices, were
determined to undermine the socialist government in Munich in favour of a racially pure, nationalist dictatorship. To promote their ideas
amongst the working classes they initiated and financed the foundation of the German Workers' Party (Deutsche Arbeiterpartei or DAP),
which Adolf Hitler joined in late 1919 after attending one of their meetings at the Sterneckerbräu beer hall at Tal 54 (now number 38). In 1920
the DAP was re-named the National Socialist German Workers' Party
(Nationalsozialistische Deutsche Arbeiterpartei or NSDAP), providing
the springboard for Hitler's future political career.

The story of the Nazi Party in Munich is taken up again by the
Hotel Torbräu at Tal 41. Occupying a building dating back to 1490
(making it the oldest hotel in Munich) the Torbräu is where the history
of Heinrich Himmler's notorious SS began. In May 1923, when the Torbräu was a beer hall and bowling alley, twenty two Nazi Party members
met in the hotel's back room and swore unconditional loyalty to their
leader. This was the birth of the so-called 'Stosstrupp (Shock Troop)
Adolf Hitler', a bodyguard unit, which alongside Ernst Röhm's *Sturmabteilung* (Stormtroopers) would participate in Hitler's abortive Beer
Hall Putsch of 1923. Following Hitler's release from prison in 1924 he

The mysterious Thule Society (Thule-Gesellschaft) once met in the Hotel Vier Jahreszeiten Kempinski

ordered the formation of a new elite guard unit, one no longer controlled by the SA, which in 1925 became the Schutzstaffel (SS) (Protective Squadron). Lead from 1929 onwards by Heinrich Himmler (1900–1945) the organisation would eventually be responsible for the deaths of some twelve million people considered inferior by the Nazi regime.

In complete contrast, the only secret at the Splendid-Dollman Hotel is its quiet location. Tucked away at Thierschstrasse 49, in the old quarter of Lehel, it offers the perfect Old Town (Altstadt) hideaway. The hotel is housed in an elegant former 19th century townhouse replete with open fire, cosy library, a small garden, and charming rooms furnished traditonally with antiques.

Another storied Munich hotel is the Am Siegestor at Akademiestrasse 5, located alongside the triumphal arch after which it is named. Standing close to the heart of the university district this neo-Renaissance house was completed in 1886, originally as a part of the nearby Academy of Fine Arts (Akademie der Bildenden Künste). The design of its façade was approved personally by Ludwig II, King of Bavaria (1864–1886). Damaged during the Second World War it re-opened as a hotel in 1950, at which time an elevator was installed; still in use, it is one of the oldest working elevators in Munich.

We finish with the former Hotel Max München at Amalienstrasse 12, which during the 1960s was called the Hotel Dachs, after the family who owned it. Undoubtedly the hotel's most celebrated guest was guitar legend Jimi Hendrix, who checked in on 16th May 1967 and spent the night in room 43. The registration document (Anmeldeschein) filled out by "James Hendrix, Musician" can be found today amongst the 3000 other pieces of music memorabilia in the Munich Rock Museum inside the Olympiaturm at Spiridon-Louis-Ring 7, adjacent to the Olympic stadium.

Other places of interest nearby: 11, 13

13   A Celebration of Alpinism

Altstadt – Lehel, the Alpine Museum of the German Alpine Club
(Alpines Museum des Deutschen Alpenvereins) at Praterinsel 5
U4, U5 Max-Weber-Platz; Tram 16, 19

Munich may well be Germany's third city in terms of size, but when it comes to geography it takes first place, standing some 50 kilometres north of the glorious Bavarian Alps. Little surprise then that one of Munich's best small museums is devoted to Germany's love affair with mountains.

The decision to create an alpine museum for the German-Austrian Alpine Association was made in 1907, following the establishment of Italian and Swiss alpine museums, in Turin (1875) and Berne (1905) respectively. Munich was selected not only for its geographical setting but also because the city made a fine late-19th century building available free of charge. Standing amongst trees on the south-western shore of Praterinsel – one of several small islands in the Isar – the building had previously been used as a café.

Unfortunately, Munich's Alpine Museum was badly damaged during the Second World War, resulting in the destruction of many valuable artefacts, notably topographer Xaver Imfeld's magnificent scale model of the Jungfrau (adorned with 60 000 model trees), which had been exhibited at the 1900 World's Fair in Paris. As a result the German-Austrian Alpine Association was split into two separate organisations, the Austrian exhibits having previously been removed to safety in Innsbruck, where they remain to this day. It was not until 1996 that the German Alpine Club (Deutscher Alpenverein or DAV) reopened the museum on Praterinsel, re-naming it the Alpine Museum of the German Alpine Club (Alpines Museum des Deutschen Alpenvereins).

Everything a small museum should be, the collection today documents the history and science of German alpinism, not only through displays of artefacts and geological specimens, but also by means of associated aesthetics, including maps, paintings, and photographs. Several permanent displays are open to the public, one of which details the earliest ascents of Europe's high mountains during the 18th and 19th centuries. Amongst the old fashioned climbing equipment, field guides, and scientific instruments there is a magnificent Solnhofen lithographic plate once used for printing detailed alpine maps.

Another display is devoted to the Schlagintweit brothers, Hermann

Old fashioned climbing equipment in the Alpine Museum of the German Alpine Club (Alpines Museum des Deutschen Alpenvereins) on Praterinsel

(1826–1882), Adolf (1829–1857) and Robert (1833–1885). Natives of Munich the trio came to the attention of Prussian naturalist and explorer Alexander von Humboldt (1769–1859), who recommended they undertake a three-year expedition on behalf of the British East India Company, to study the earth's magnetic field in Central Asia. Their 29 000 kilometre-long journey commenced in 1854 and took them through the Deccan and up into the Himalayas and Karakoram, where Hermann and Robert became the first Europeans to cross the Kunlun mountains of western China. They also established a new altitude record during an abortive attempt to climb Mount Kamet, India's third highest mountain. The pair returned to Germany in 1857, leaving behind Adolf, who shortly afterwards was executed on suspicion of spying. With them they brought back rock samples, biological specimens, ethnographic artefacts – and some 750 watercolours! Three hundred of these are held by the museum, a selection of which are used to illustrate the lives of the brothers.

The museum's other rooms illustrate the many and varied artistic representation of mountains, from vast romantically-lit oil paintings of the 19th century, and Alfons Walde's stylised skiers, to images from the German *Bergkino* genre of the 1920s. There are also exhibits illustrating the effect of politics on alpinism, notably the imposition of a separate Jewish section within the association as early as 1924, and the stylised use of mountain imagery by the Nazis in their propaganda programme. Interesting too is the effect of industrialisation on the Alps, with the arrival of mountain railways and mass tourism.

Munich's Alpine Museum additionally offers alternating special exhibitions, as well as access to the world's largest alpine library. And the museum continues outside, too, in the form of a teaching garden containing 350-million-year-old geological specimens that show how the Alps were formed: children seem to especially enjoy this part of the museum, whilst their parents relax with a drink from the café. On departing don't miss Michael Friedrichsen's wonderful aluminium sculpture *The Wanderer*, depicting a life-sized alpinist intently studying his map (see front cover).

Other places of interest nearby: 12, 14, 23, 24

14 Germany's Answer to Charlie Chaplin

Altstadt – Lehel, the Valentin Karlstadt Musäum inside the Isartor on Isartorplatz
S1, S2, S3, S4, S6, S7, S8 Isartor; Tram 16, 18

The life of the comedian, actor, and cabaret performer Karl Valentin (1882–1948), remembered fondly as the "Charlie Chaplin of Germany", began in Munich on 4th June 1882. He was born Valentin Ludwig Fey at Entenbachstrasse 63 (now Zeppelinstrasse 41), in the district of Au, where a wall plaque marks the spot. After elementary school he became a carpenter's apprentice but quickly grew bored; in 1902 he famously "hung up his profession on a nail in the wall" and became a folk singer instead. That nail can be found today in the entrance to the Valentin Karlstadt Musäum, which keeps alive the memory of one of the city's most gifted entertainers.

A visit to this most eccentric of museums is a must for anyone with a sense of humour: even without one it is a good opportunity to explore the towers of the 14th century Isartor, in which the museum has been housed since 1959. Nothing is normal here, from the spelling of 'Musäum' and the opening times (11.01am, for example), to the admission fees (99 year-olds are admitted free if accompanied by their parents!). On the first floor there is an exhibition illustrating the life and work of Valentin (pron. *Fal-in-teen*), who toured the cabarets and beerhalls of northern Germany honing his comedic skills until his breakthrough in 1908. The success of his sketch *The Aquarium* lead to a stint at the popular beergarden of the Frankfurter Hof, where in 1911 he met his future professional partner, Liesl Karlstadt (real name Elisabeth Wellano) (1892–1960). Her life is illustrated on the second floor of the museum. Over the next thirty years the pair would present some 400 of Valentin's comedy routines. So inseparable were they in the public eye that it was often assumed that they were married, although in reality Valentin married his parents' maid and had two daughters.

This large ear for the short sighted is typical for the Valentin Karlstadt Musäum!

Props once used by Karl Valentin displayed in the Valentin Karlstadt Musäum

The recurring theme of Valentin's writing is the helplessness of modern man in his day-to-day struggle against hypocrisy and pomposity. With his trademark spindly legs, Pinocchio-like nose, and linguistic dexterity Valentin cast himself as a laughing philosopher, whose job it is to highlight the faults in his fellow man using Karlstadt as his comic foil. Of their many popular sketches, several of which were filmed in black-and-white, favourites include *Sonntag in der Rosenau*, *Im Photoatelier*, *An Bord*, *Buchbinder Wanninger*, and *Der Theaterbesuch*. The pair also appeared in the film *Mysterien eines Friseursalon (Mysteries of a Barbershop)*, written by Bertolt Brecht and now considered one of the most important works in the history of German filmmaking. It was Brecht who compared "the clown Valentin" so favourably to Chaplin.

Crossing over from the south tower into the north, an intimate collection of Valentin's personal effects can be found, including his wig, glasses, prosthetic nose, makeup box, and typewriter. Also here is a room dedicated to the golden age of the Bavarian music hall, including its many colourful characters and venues. It was against this backdrop that Valentin and Karlstadt found success well beyond the bounds of Munich and Bavaria: in Berlin, Vienna, and Zurich. However, Valentin would always gravitate back to his native Munich, where he felt his material worked best.

Dotted around the various rooms of the museum are many amusing exhibits, of which Valentin and Karlstadt would undoubtedly have approved. They include a sculpture of melted snow, a marble cake made of marble, an oversized human ear for the short-sighted, a clock

The grave of Liesl Karlstadt in the Bogenhausen Cemetery (Friedhof Bogenhausen)

showing the exact time yesterday, an iron handkerchief, a gentleman's stand-up collar lying down, and a ghost drum that can only be heard at night. There is also a fur-covered, winter toothpick, which Valentin himself invented.

Considered precursors of the Theatre of the Absurd, Valentin and Karlstadt's last performance together (after a break in 1941–1946) came on 31st January 1948, the year of Valentin's death. Although he was buried outside Munich, in Planegg, Liesl Karlstadt's grave, with its red-painted heart, can be found in the city's tiny, rose-filled Bogenhausen Cemetery (Friedhof Bogenhausen) at Bogenhausener Kirchplatz 1. Known also as the Cemetery of St. George (Friedhof St. Georg), after the Late Baroque (Rococo) church whose congregation it serves, this is undoubtedly the prettiest cemetery in Munich.

Before leaving the museum be sure to visit the café at the top of the south tower, furnished in eclectic late 19th century style, and renowned for its *Weißwürste, Brezen* and beer. The cosy circular room is crammed with over 400 curious objects, covering the floor, wall, and ceiling, most of which are in some way connected with the rich history of Munich and Bavaria.

Other places of interest nearby: 15, 16, 23, 28

15 Raising the Maypole

Alstadt – Lehel, the maypole (Maibaum) in the
Viktualienmarkt between Petersplatz and Frauenstrasse
S1, S2, S3, S4, S6, S7, S8 Marienplatz; U3, U6 Marienplatz;
Bus 52, 62

Most visitors will at some time walk through Munich's Residenz, with its magnificent Antiquarium, one of the finest Renaissance rooms in Europe (see no. 8). Few, however, will notice amongst the stone busts and ornate plasterwork a fresco by Hans Donauer the Elder (1540–1596) depicting the town of Starnberg (it is on the lefthand side of the last window on the left). In the fresco can be seen a large house to the right, behind which stands a maypole *(Maibaum)*. Painted in 1590 it is probably the earliest known artistic representation of one.

The erecting of maypoles has been a popular tradition in Bavaria since the 16th century, although the roots of the tradition stretch back to the time of the Germanic tribes, who were active across Europe in the wake of the fall of the Roman Empire. Undeniably pagan in origin the maypole is generally considered a phallic symbol, associated with the worship of the fertility god Freyr. It might also be related to the pagan worship of the sacred tree of life, as well as representing a symbolic axis linking the world of the living with the underworld. Much of this ancient mythic potency is lost today, the raising of maypoles on May 1st being an opportunity for community get-togethers heralding the arrival of summer.

In the villages and small towns around Munich maypoles are still raised the traditional way, by a combination of ropes, long sticks (called *Schwalben*), and brute force, providing a spactacle in itself. In Munich itself, however, even that has changed, a law stating that for safety reasons the task must be achieved using a mechanised crane. This is the case with the maypole in the centre of the Viktualienmarkt, which must be checked annually for safety reasons and replaced every five years.

Fortunately, a certain amount of tradition in preparing the maypole for erection remains wherever the custom is found. It is usually the task of the men to select, fell, and transport a suitable tree, which must be at least 30 metres high. Traditionally brought to the erection site by horse-and-cart the job is done today by tractor. Once on site the tree is stripped of its branches and bark, cleaned, and planed where necessary. The pole is then painted with white and blue lozenges in imitation of the flag of the Free State of Bavaria, as well as the crest used by the Wittelsbach dynasty during their six hundred year reign. Finally, the women decorate the pole with a wreath at the top, and figurative painted panels attached to the sides. First instigated in the 18th century these panels were used to announce the various trades and crafts carried on in the marketplace below, to those unable to read. A primitive form of advertising the panels today still often carry the names of local businesses and shops in the area (see Ferdinand-Miller-Platz and Wiener Platz). Rather more unusual is the Viktualienmarkt maypole, which has panels depicting the six great breweries of Munich (Augustiner, Hacker-Pschorr, Hofbrau, Löwenbrau, Paulaner, and Spaten), and the maypole in the Hellabrunn Zoo (Tierpark Hellabrunn), which carries images of wild animals.

After preparing the maypole it is important to guard it because young men from neighbouring villages traditionally attempt to steal them unnoticed on April 30th. Unwritten rules decree that no force be used and that the maypole must not

Munich's most famous maypole (Maibaum) towers over the Viktualienmarkt

be damaged. If successful, the maypole can be returned after friendly negotiations have taken place over a few beers, without the need to involve the local police.

After being blessed by the local priest the maypole is erected on May 1st and the community comes together for a day of drinking, eating, brass band music, and other entertainment. More than fifty such events *(Maibaumaufstellen)* occur annually across Munich and the region of Upper Bavaria. The most traditional ones in Munich are in former village centres, such as Margaretenplatz in Sendling and Pfanzeltplatz in Perlach.

Other places of interest nearby: 14, 16, 17, 18, 29

16 Good and Bad Memories in the Old Town Hall

Altstadt – Lehel, the Toy Museum (Spielzeugmuseum) in the
Old Town Hall (Altes Rathaus) at Marienplatz 15
S1, S2, S3, S4, S6, S7, S8 Marienplatz; U3, U6 Marienplatz;
Bus 52, 62

Inside the tower of the Old Town Hall (Altes Rathaus) on Marienplatz
is Munich's charming Toy Museum (Spielzeugmuseum), which illustrates the history of European and American children's toys from prehistoric times up to the 1950s. Spread across four of the tower's five
storeys (the fourth is reserved for use by the city's Bürgermeister, or
mayor), it is adviseable to take the elevator to the top and then slowly
descend by means of a spiral stone staircase, which is an adventure in
itself.

Of interest to both children and adults, the collection is wonderfully nostalgic and includes everything from dolls and dolls' houses,
clockwork figures, and teddy bears, to model aeroplanes, tin cars, carousels, and wooden farm animals. Of particular interest are the 19th
century Märklin-brand steam engines, and the miniature domestic
utensils (such as sewing machines, irons, and dinner services) used for
educational purposes. There is also a 1930s fort complete with miniature fighting cowboys and indians, and a wonderful zoo inhabited by
hand-painted animals. The many clockwork tinplate toys include forgotten novelties such as 'Pad-
dy's Dancing Pig' and 'Lehr-
mann's Crawing Beetle'. The
museum, which was opened
in 1983, is the brainchild of
toy collector Ivan Steiger,
whose daughter has opened
a similar museum in Prague.

Unfortunately, despite the
Old Town Hall having long
been the backdrop against
which Munich's council
strengthened the position
of its citizens, it was also the
venue for the anti-democratic

A model zoo in the Toy Museum (Spielzeugmuseum) in
Munich's Old Town Hall (Altes Rathaus)

The Toy Museum (Spielzeugmuseum) also contains these splendid clockwork steam trains

activities of the Nazi Party. It was in the banqueting hall *(Festsaal)* here on 9th November 1938, during the annual meeting to commemorate Hitler's abortive Beer Hall Putsch, that Propaganda Minister Joseph Goebbels unleashed Germany's most ferocious Jewish pogrom. At the meeting news broke that Ernst vom Rath, an official in the German embassy in Paris, had died of injuries sustained during an assassination attack by a Jew. Goebbels claimed that it was part of a Jewish conspiracy against Hitler and gave orders to start a pogrom against the Jews of Germany and Austria. Known as *Kristallnacht* (or Night of Broken Glass) the operation had been planned well in advance and saw Jewish synagogues, Jewish schools and businesses raided and burned down, the police and fire services doing little to intervene. By the following day more than ninety Jews were dead and the way was paved for the Holocaust.

Other places of interest nearby: 14, 15, 17, 18

17 A Legendary Cuckoo Clock

Altstadt – Lehel, the Glockenspiel at the New Town Hall
(Neues Rathaus) on Marienplatz
S1, S2, S3, S4, S6, S7, S8 Marienplatz; U3, U6 Marienplatz;
Tram 19; Bus 52, 62

Every morning at 11am and midday (as well as 5pm between March and October) visitors to Munich gather in Marienplatz. They do so to listen to Europe's fourth largest carillon, or chiming clock *(Glockenspiel)*, which is housed in the tower of the New Town Hall (Neues Rathaus). Depending on which tune is played on the clock's 43 bells, the performance lasts between twelve and fifteen minutes.

During the concert thirty two clockwork figures appear in the tower's ornate, triple-decker, oriel window, its copperwork weathered to a distinct green. In time to the music the life-sized figures

Munich's chiming clock (Glockenspiel) is high up on the New Town Hall (Neues Rathaus) on Marienplatz

re-enact two stories from the 16th century, often to the complete bemusement of onlookers below. To get a better understanding of the proceedings visit one of the upper floors of the excellent Hugendubel bookshop, directly opposite the tower. Through the large windows of the shop the figures can be seen more clearly. Those in the upper part re-enact the marriage of William V, Duke of Bavaria (1579–1597), founder of the Court Brewery in 1589 (including the world famous Hofbräuhaus) to Renata of Lorraine. In honour of the happy couple there is a jousting contest between a Bavarian knight (in white and blue) and one representing Lor-

An inscription inside the New Town Hall (Neues Rathaus)

Den Mitgliedern der US-Streitkräfte,die München am 30.April 1945 von der nationalsozialistischen Gewaltherrschaft befreiten. Die Landeshauptstadt München am 30.4.1992

raine (in red and white): the Bavarian knight is always victorious, of course!

The joust is followed in the lower part of the oriel window by the so-called *Schäfflertanz* (Dance of the Coopers). The coopers' guild first organised the dance in 1517 to signal the all clear to the cowering populace after a terrible visitation of the plague. To express his relief William IV, Duke of Bavaria (1508–1550) ordered that the dance be re-enacted every seven years during the city's pre-Lent carnival season *(Fasching)*, which occurs between Epiphany (January 6th) and Ash Wednesday. (The next dance is scheduled for 2012.)

The end of the performance is marked by the appearance of a golden bird, which chirps three times in the opening at the top of the oriel window. That's not quite all, however, since around 9pm in the twin bays directly beneath the clock face there appear two further figures. One is a nightwatchman sounding the curfew on his horn, the other the Angel of Peace blessing the Münchner Kindl, a bronze figure of a child and the symbol of the Bavarian capital. It can also be seen on top of the town hall tower.

The New Town Hall itself was constructed between 1867 and 1909 in Flanders Gothic style. Its façades are adorned not only with decorative details but also with sculptures alluding to Bavarian history and legend. Just inside the main entrance are a series of inscriptions, the most important of which is one marking the liberation of Munich from the grip of Nazism by the 7th US army, on 30th April 1945; it was added on 30th April 1992. Above the inscription are the crests of Munich's twin towns, namely Edinburgh, Cincinnati, Harare, Kiev, Sapporo, Bordeaux, and Verona. Other inscriptions on the wall opposite refer to the building itself (a new wing added in 1899–1909, and the renovation of the *Glockenspiel* in 1904), national events (the *Turnfest* German Gymnastics Festivals of 1923, 1958, and 1998), and international events (the Olympic Games 1972 and the European Games 2004).

Other places of interest nearby: 7, 15, 16, 18

18 Obatzter, Weißwürste, and Schmalznudeln

Altstadt – Lehel, a tour finishing at Café Frischhut
at 8 Prälat-Zistl-Strasse
S1, S2, S3, S4, S6, S7, S8 Marienplatz; U3, U6 Marienplatz;
Bus 52, 62

Germany in general – and Bavaria in particular – is known for its hearty kitchen, with signature pork dishes such as *Schweinshaxe* (roast pork knuckle) and *Schweinsbraten* (sliced braised pork in beer gravy) an iconic part of the traditional dining scene. There is much more, however, to the region's culinary landscape, especially in Munich, where there can be found numerous idiosyncratic shops purveying several local specialities.

A good place to start is in either of the city's two major delicatessens, which between them stock everything the gourmet could wish for. The venerable Käfer at Prinzregentenstrasse 73 was founded in 1930 and is worth visiting for its labyrinthine architectural layout alone. Inside there is a bakery selling a wide selection of German breads, ideal for making *Brotzeit* ('bread time') snacks between meals; neighbouring departments will gladly supply an array of fillings from traditional smoked sausage to *Obatzter*, a spicy Bavarian cream cheese first made in the 1920s from old camembert revitalised with butter, beer and paprika. For those with a sweet tooth there is a praline counter, and in the cellar there are stored a hundred thousand bottles of fine wine.

Equally venerable is Dallmayr, Munich's other major delicatessen, at Dienerstrasse 14–15. Founded 300 years ago as a grocer's store it became a supplier to the Royal Bavarian Court in 1900. Since 1933 it has purveyed its own brand of coffee (Prodomo), which is dispensed from hand-painted Nymphenburg porcelain containers and weighed on traditional scales. Be sure to look out for the cherub-adorned fountain containing live crayfish!

At the other end of the shopping spectrum are the city's street markets and small independent stores. The most famous of Munich's markets is the Viktualienmarkt, a permanent fixture between Petersplatz and Frauenstrasse, offering a vast array of local produce (for example Schrobenhausen asparagus) and a fascinating history to go with it (see no. 27). Very popular with tourists it can get busy, so when you've had

Bavarian white sausages (Weißwürste) should always be consumed before noon

enough try exploring the side streets for some of Munich's more workaday retailers.

As elsewhere in Europe, many food shops have been taken over by retail chains, the exceptions being small butcher's shops, bakeries and confectioners, each offering traditional products at reasonable prices – and with good old-fashioned service to match. Take a peek into the row of butchers' shops in the brick arcades behind the Church of St. Peter (Peterskirche) at Rindermarkt 1 and you will see the ubiquitous Bavarian *Weißwürste*. Eaten as a pair these white veal sausages are steamed and served in a bowl of hot water, accompanied by sweet, grainy mustard, a *Breze* (beer pretzel), and a glass of *Weißbier*. Before the days of refrigeration they were eaten fresh in the morning, as either a second breakfast or a pre-lunch snack, but *never* later. This accounts for the Munich saying that "the sausage should not hear the clocks sound noon."

If you've a sweet tooth visit the hundred year-old Café Frischhut on the other side of the Viktualienmarkt, at Prälat-Zistl-Strasse 8. It is renowned for its deep-fried yeast dough *Schmalznudeln* and long plaited *Stritzeln*, as well as golden-brown *Rohrnudeln*, which are square yeast cakes baked in the oven, and filled with either plums or raisins. A steady stream of regulars can be seen scurrying away with them in paper bags.

Other places of interest nearby: 15, 16, 17, 19

19 The Historic Home of the Dancing Moors

Altstadt – Lehel, the Münchner Stadtmuseum (Munich City Museum) at St.-Jakobs-Platz 1
S1, S2, S3, S4, S6, S7, S8 Marienplatz; U3, U6 Marienplatz;
U1, U2, U3, U6 Sendlinger Tor; Bus 52, 62

The fascinating story of how Munich grew from a 12th century river-side salt-trading settlement to a 20th century commercial and cultural metropolis is nowhere better told than in the Münchner Stadtmuseum (Munich City Museum) at St.-Jakobs-Platz 1. Part of the museum building plays a small part in the story itself, having been constructed in 1410 as a granary, and converted later into an arsenal (*Zeughaus*) and stables (*Marstall*).

In March 1848, inspired by news from Paris, Bavarians demanded government reform, and it is said that some Munich citizens armed themselves with antiquated weapons from the arsenal. In reality, with the exception of scattered outbreaks of peasant violence in Franconia and Swabia, the revolution in Bavaria was a non-violent one, and a far-reaching set of demands was presented peaceably to Ludwig I, King of Bavaria (1825–1848). Under pressure from his advisors because of popular criticism over his private life, and unwilling to preside over political changes he considered incompatible with monarchy, Ludwig abdicated in favour of his son, Maximilian II (1848–1864). The Bavarian parliament subsequently passed a wide-ranging series of laws providing for the abolition of restrictions on land ownership, reform of the court system, freedom of the press, and a more liberal electoral law. It would be the dawn of a golden age for Munich, heralding the construction of many of its finest buildings, and the establishment of the city as a major centre for the arts and sciences.

Some years after the revolution it was decided to convert the arsenal into a local history museum, with major efforts being made at the time to accumulate artefacts relating to the city's history. One and a half thousand objects were soon amassed, to which a purchased collection of etchings with a Munich theme was added. In 1888 the collection was opened to the public as the Museum of History, a name it retained until 1954, when it was re-branded the Münchner Stadtmuseum (Munich City Museum). By this time four additional wings had been added to contain the ever-growing collection.

One of Erasmus Grasser's expressive Morisco Dancers in the Münchner Stadtmuseum (Munich City Museum) on St-Jakobs-Platz

To mark the city's 850th anniversary in 2008 a selection of the museum's most important exhibits were newly displayed across five galleries under the banner of *Typisch München! (Typically Munich!)*, each gallery illustrating a different historical era. The first of these galleries, the Morisken-Saal, illustrates the story of 'Old Munich' (1158–1806), from its founding through to its accession as capital of the Kingdom of Bavaria. It contains the museum's most unusual exhibit, namely the so-called Morisco Dancers (Moriskentänzer). These ten figures were carved from lime wood in 1480 by the renowned woodworker Erasmus Grasser (c.1450–c.1518). Depicted in the most expressive poses the figures are notable examples of bourgeois Gothic art, and were once used to adorn a ballroom in the Old Town Hall (Altes Rathaus) on Marienplatz. Completed in 1474 a set of copies are displayed there today. The *Morisco* (or Morris) dance was imported from Moorish Spain and spread throughout Europe by itinerant singers and musicians. According to the city's financial records from 1480 Grasser was paid to produce a total of sixteen Morisco figures: the whereabouts of the missing six remains a subject for conjecture amongst historians.

The story of Munich is continued in the museum's four other galleries as follows: the Königssaal ('New Munich' (1806–1858) – the capital of the Kingdom of Bavaria is transformed into 'Athens on the Isar'), the Monachiasaal ('The City of Munich' (1858–1958) – from municipal emancipation to the rebuilt city celebrating its 800th anniversary), the Feuchtwangersaal ('Kasperl's Class Struggle' – the political, cultural and economic upheavals of the 1920s), and the Arenasaal ('Munich, the

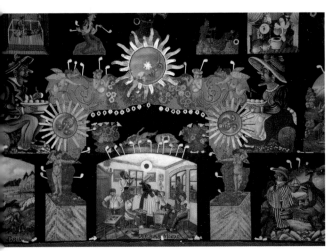

A traditional rifle-range in the fairground collection of the Münchner Stadtmuseum (Munich City Museum)

Metropolis' (1972–2008) – from the Olympics to Munich's current designation as Germany's 'Media Capital').

There are also several independently-operated thematic collections housed in the museum, including a fascinating musical instruments collection (with its Javan gongs, ivory Congolese trumpets, and European harps), a puppetry collection (including a glass cabinet bursting with hand-crafted puppet heads), and a highly atmospheric fairground collection (which includes a rifle-range and a morbid waxworks sideshow). Other important collections are devoted to the era of National Socialism in Munich, photography, and film (samples of which are screened Tuesday-Sunday in the in-house cinema).

Further examples of Erasmus Grasser's expressive figurative carving include the oak choir stalls of the Frauenkirche on Frauenplatz, a statue of St. Peter on the high altar of the Church of St. Peter (Peterskirche) at Rindermarkt 1, and a figure of the *Madonna Enthroned* in the Church of Maria Ramersdorf (see no. 59).

Other places of interest nearby: 15, 17, 18, 20

20 Gothic Corners of Old Town

Altstadt – Lehel, a tour beginning with the
Ignaz-Günther-Haus at Oberanger 15/St.-Jakobs-Platz 20
S1, S2, S3, S4, S6, S7, S8 Marienplatz; U3, U6 Marienplatz;
U1, U2, U3, U6 Sendlinger Tor; Bus 52, 62

Gothic architecture, characterized by the use of the pointed arch, ribbed vault and ornamental stonework, originated in France in the mid-12th century and persisted in Western Europe until the mid-16th century. It is no surprise then that Munich's own Gothic architectural heritage is located predominantly within the former walls of the city's medieval Old Town (Altstadt) (see no. 1). Tracking it down takes the explorer away from the busy main roads and along more atmospheric back streets.

Our tour begins in St.-Jakobs-Platz, within sight of the Münchner Stadtmuseum (Munich City Museum) and its fine collection of Gothic stone- and woodwork. In the far corner of the square at St.-Jakobs-Platz 20 there stands the easily-missed Ignaz-Günther-Haus. Now a private office (rather than an advertised tourist attraction) this rare example of a Late Gothic residential house may be visited during weekday office hours by knocking politely on the door. Inside, the house retains its original tiny lightwell with fountain, and a grand first floor reception room with 16th century wooden ceiling. The house is named after Ignaz Günther (1725–1775), one of Europe's finest Late Baroque (Rococo) sculptors, who lived here from 1761 until his death. In 1754 Günther became court sculptor to the Wittelsbachs, and his work can be found in the Church of St. Peter (Peterskirche) at Rindermarkt 1, the Frauenkirche on Frauenplatz, and in the upper church of the Bürgersaalkirche at Neuhauser Strasse 14. Günther was also responsible for the statue of the Virgin Mary *(Hausmadonna)* on the Oberanger side of the house, the original of which is now in the Bavarian National Museum (Bayerisches Nationalmuseum) at Prinzregentenstrasse 3.

A second domestic building with origins in the Middle Ages can be found a couple of streets away, at the corner of Hackenstrasse and Hotterstrasse. The Hundskugel lays claim to being Munich's oldest *Gasthaus*, dating back to 1440 (see page 232). Its Hackenstrasse façade comprises two distinct elements, namely a half gable and a conventional roof, whilst its cosy interior features low, timbered ceilings. A sign outside the building depicts a group of dogs playing with a ball, hence

The Late Gothic Ignaz-Günther-Haus occupies a corner of St.-Jakobs-Platz

the building's curious name; it is thought to represent the working classes ('the dogs') enjoying a bowling alley that was once located hereabouts.

At the far end of Hackenstrasse is Kreuzstrasse, where at number 10 stands All Hallows' Church (Allerheiligenkirche am Kreuz) erected in 1485. Like other Gothic churches its interior was reworked during the Baroque period leaving only a few clues as to its Gothic origins, in this case fan vaulting over the nave, and fragments of a fresco of Christ with a halo.

We move eastwards now to Sterneckerstrasse 2, and the building which today contains the Beer and Oktoberfest Museum (Bier- und Oktoberfestmuseum). Another of Munich's oldest buildings it was erected in 1327 after the great fire. Beer aside the building contains some fascinating Gothic details, including niches to denote party walls, open fireplaces, painted ceilings, and an unusual staircase leading from ground floor to roof in one continuous flight.

Turning to the city centre we visit Burgstrasse 5, the former offices of the City Writers' Guild (Stadtschreiberei) from 1552–1612. The town council purchased this plot in 1510 and built the present building here in 1551. Of particular interest is the Late Gothic side entrance, with its curving doorframe, and the staircase tower inside the courtyard beyond.

Another rare example of medieval secular architecture lies at the top end of Burgstrasse in the Alter Hof (Old Residence) (1253–1255), the original fortified residence of the Wittelsbachs before their move

The Eiles-Hof is a medieval courtyard hidden away between Residenzstrasse and Theatinerstrasse

to the so-called Neue Veste (later Residenz) in the 14th century. Its most distinctive feature is also a staircase tower, known as the Monkey Tower, it is said because a monkey once carried the young Ludwig IV (1282–1347), later Holy Roman Emperor, to the top of it!

Not far away, running between Residenzstrasse 13 and Theatinerstrasse 40–42, there is a modern shopping passage in the middle of which is the mid-16th century Eiles-Hof, the last surviving arcaded courtyard of medieval Munich. The arched cloisters with Late Gothic openwork balustrades formed part of a monastery here between 1714 and 1803.

Our tour finishes at the Church of the Saviour (Salvatorkirche) at Salvatorplatz 17, constructed in the 1490s and still retaining much of its Gothic details and atmosphere (see no. 76). One can, however, continue the journey *outside* Old Town by visiting the likes of St. Wolfgang's Church at Pippinger Strasse 499, the last intact Gothic village church in Munich.

Other places of interest nearby: 18, 19, 21, 22

21 The History of Emergencies

Altstadt – Lehel, the Munich Fire Brigade Museum
(Münchner Feuerwehrmuseum) at An der Hauptfeuerwache 8
U1, U2, U3, U6, U7 Sendlinger Tor; Bus 52,62

The German municipal architect Carl Hocheder (1854–1917) is best remembered in Munich for the Müller Baths (Müllersches Volksbad) on Rosenheimer Strasse (see no. 23). Unknown by comparison is the city's main fire station (Haupfeuerwache), which was built to his design at An der Hauptfeuerwache 8 in 1902–1904. The building's façade has eight ground-floor doorways, large enough to enable vehicles to pass through. The keystone of each opening is carved with the god of wind in the act of blowing out fires. Also on the façade is a sculpture of St. Florian, the patron saint of firefighters, pouring water onto a burning building. The saint is encountered again to the rear of the building, where a doorway in the courtyard leads into the Munich Fire Brigade Museum (Münchner Feuerwehrmuseum). In the entrance hall there is a statue of the saint surrounded by a collection of painted glass icons, traditionally placed in the home to protect against fire.

Opened in 1979 to mark the centenary of the Munich Fire Brigade the ground floor rooms of this fascinating small museum are filled with artefacts illustrating the development of the Munich fire service, from earliest times until today. In one room there is a collection of bright red fire alarms, once a feature of the city's streets, together with the telephone exchanges where the alarm would be received. Another room contains portable hand-powered pumps, a horse-drawn fire tender, and an array of accessories such as hosepipes, firemen's axes, brigade insignia, helmets, and vintage brass trumpets for sounding the alarm. Also here is a reconstruction of the tiny firewatching room that once existed in the tower of the Church of St. Peter (Peterskirche) on Rindermarkt (see no. 31). Dating back to 1850 it contains a so-called pyroscope, once used to measure the intensity of heat emanating from a fire. This curious, trumpet-shaped instrument was invented by the German physicist Carl August von Steinheil (1801–1870), who was also involved in the early development of photography, telegraphy, and the manufacture of telescopes, the latter benefitting greatly from a silvering process pioneered by his friend Baron Justus von Liebig (1803–1873) (see no. 2).

The collection continues in the basement with a reconstruction of a Second World War house cellar, strengthened against air raids; surrounding it are sirens, portable house extinguishers, and uniforms carrying the Nazi swastika. Also in the basement is a collection of 20th century firefighting equipment (including both liquid and dry extinguishers), and an exhibition illustrating the most common causes of fire. The museum concludes with an exhibit illustrating Munich's U-Bahn fire just outside the Königsplatz station in September 1983, the centrepiece of which is the actual burnt out remains of train 7149.

Architectural detail on the Munich Fire Brigade Museum (Münchner Feuerwehrmuseum) at An der Hauptfeuerwache

The story of Munich's emergency services is continued in the Münchner Sanitätsmuseum (open by appointment only, www.brk-museum.de), which coincidentally occupies the old Sendling fire station at Boschetsrieder Strasse 33. This collection illustrates the less well-known but no less important history of the Bavarian Red Cross (Bayerisches Rotes Kreuz). Munich's first voluntary medical corps was set up in 1875, with a permanent watch station opened in 1894 at Marstallstrasse 4, near the Residenz, from where men using a wheeled stretcher (the so-called *Handmarie*) were dispatched to transport the ill and injured to safety. By the turn of the century, larger premises had been acquired at nearby Hildegardstrasse 12, with posts established at the railways stations, and in 1906 the first vehicle was acquired. The organisation amply demonstrated its medical worth during this time, in disasters as varied as the collapse of the Corneliusbrücke (1902), a tram car collision on Am Gasteig (1911), the fire at the Glaspalast (1931), and even an elephant running amok during a street procession (1889)!

Considered a vital element in Munich's emergency response strategy, representatives of the Bavarian Red Cross were eventually to be found in theatres and cinemas, on sports fields and in factories. Despite being banned in the immediate aftermath of the Second World War because of its political status under the Nazi Party, the Red Cross

A collection of fire alarms in the Munich Fire Brigade Museum (Münchner Feuerwehrmuseum)

quickly reaffirmed its importance during a Corpus Christi procession through the city in May 1945. In September of the same year the US Army approved the creation of a new Bavarian Red Cross, which is still in existence today.

Other places of interest nearby: 18, 19, 20, 22

22 Count Pocci's Miniature Theatre

Altstadt – Lehel, the Munich Puppet Theatre (Münchner Marionettentheater) at Blumenstrasse 32
U1, U2, U3, U6, U7 Sendlinger Tor; Bus 52,62

There is a longstanding and venerable tradition of stringed puppetry in Germany and Austria, much of it derived from the 16th century Italian tradition of masked improvised comedy *(commedia dell'arte)*. Throughout the 18th century puppet theatres were considered established elements of travelling fairs, their performances often based on popular legends and fairytales. Even renowned European composers, such as Gluck, Haydn, de Falla, and Respighi, composed adult operas specifically for puppet theatres.

By the 20th century, however, there was an increasing interest in creating puppet theatres for children, and two men were in the vanguard. The first was Joseph Leonhard Schmid (1822–1912), who founded a permanent puppet theatre in Munich in 1858 in the belief that it could be used not only to entertain children but also to educate them, especially in the matter of morality and religion. Known affectionately as 'Papa Schmid' he presided over the construction in 1900 of the Munich Puppet Theatre (Münchner Marionettentheater) at Blumenstrasse 32, near the Sendling Gate (Sendlinger Tor).

The second man was Count Franz Pocci (1807–1876), a Bavarian court official, composer and dramatist, who sponsored Schmid and wrote some forty children's plays for his puppet theatre during the mid-19th century. Count Pocci was also an accomplished artist, renowned for his remarkable shadow puppets and his illustrations for the fairy tales of the Brothers Grimm and Hans Christian Andersen. Pocci's work greatly influenced Professor Anton Aicher, who founded the Salzburg Marionette Theatre in 1913.

The Munich Puppet Theatre is today considered the oldest permanent puppet theatre in the German-speaking world. Constructed in the style of a tiny neo-Classical palace it is sometimes billed as Munich's smallest opera house, and is certainly one of the most unusual of the city's theatrical venues. On one side of the building there is a cosy little ticket office open most mornings from where details of forthcoming performances can be had. They invariably include afternoon fairytales for the children, as well as performances featuring Kasperl

Even the ticket office is manned by puppets at the Munich Puppet Theatre (Münchner Marionettentheater) on Blumenstrasse

Larifari, Count Pocci's most enduring character. The German equivalent of the British character known as Mr. Punch, Kasperl plays a prominent part in numerous plays, such as *Die Kleine Hexe (The Little Witch)*.

In the evenings there are puppet performances of popular operas, such as Mozart's *Don Giovanni* and *Die Zauberflöte (The Magic Flute)*, and Offenbach's *Hoffmann's Erzählungen (Tales of Hoffmann)*, in line with Papa Schmid's intention that adults should also be catered for in his puppet theatre. The production values of all the performances are equal to those of a conventional theatre, making a visit here a special experience for young and old alike. In front of the building there is a bronze cabinet featuring a bas-relief of Count Pocci together with a tiny bowing Kasperl, whilst the wall facing Blumenstrasse carries a commemorative plaque to 'Papa Schmid'.

Munich boasts a further two puppet theatres. The Marionettenstudio Kleines Spiel at Neureutherstrasse 12 was founded in the late 1940s, its young puppetmasters performing works by Ben Jonson and Bertolt Brecht among others, for an adult audience each thursday night. The other is Otto Bille's Marionettenbühne at Bereiteranger 15, an old-fashioned puppet theatre popular with children.

Those wishing to learn about the history of puppetry should visit the Museum für Antike Puppen at Gondershauser Strasse 37, and the puppet collection at the Münchner Stadtmuseum (Munich City Museum) at St.-Jakobs-Platz 1 (see no. 19). To purchase handmade puppets, including those of Kasperl, visit Die Puppenstube at Luisenstrasse 68 (see no. 42).

Other places of interest nearby: 19, 20, 21, 29

23 The *Jugendstil* Bathing Temple

Au – Haidhausen, the Müller Baths (Müllersches Volksbad)
at Rosenheimer Strasse 1
S1, S2, S3, S4, S6, S7, S8 Rosenheimer Platz; Tram 15, 25

At the turn of the 20th century Germany's artists responded boldly to the success of French *Art Nouveau* with their own interpretation called *Jugendstil*, the centre of which was in Munich (see no. 81). Revelling in the same new-found freedom of artistic expression, the movement boldly turned its back on the staid historicist trends that had dictated art and architecture during the previous decades. *Jugendstil* manifested itself not only in domestic housing but also in several significant public buildings, including the Protestant Church of Christ the Redeemer (Erlöserkirche) at Ungererstrasse 13, designed by Theodor Fischer and erected in 1899–1901, and the Munich Chamber Theatre (Münchner Kammerspiele im Schauspielhaus) at Maximilianstrasse 34–35. The latter, constructed in 1900–1901 to a design by Richard Riemerschmid, is one of the few surviving *Jugendstil* theatres in Germany and features a glorious interior whose lines have been typically softened with swirling floral motifs.

Undoubtedly Munich's most unusual *Jugendstil* building is the Müller Baths (Müllersches Volksbad) at Rosenheimer Strasse 1 on the east bank of the Isar in Haidhausen. The complex was built in 1897–1901 to a design by the German municipal architect Carl Hocheder (1854–1917) and financed by Karl Müller, a civil engineer and philanthropist, whose name they bear. Even if you are not a keen swimmer the recently restored baths should still be seen to appreciate what at the time were considered the finest in all Germany.

The Müller Baths is a veritable bathing temple: a visual and sensual treat for visitors. The exterior is both striking and beautiful, with its exotic combination of neo-Baroque clock tower, Moorish style domes, and *Jugendstil* stucco ornamentation. Inside, the men's and women's pools were originally strictly divided, the former beneath a barrel-vaulted roof, the latter under a large cupola. Now open to both sexes the most impressive pool remains the men's, with a stuccoed ceiling that would not look out of place in a church. The whole building reflects the new concepts of hygiene that were coming into vogue during the late 19th century, together with an awareness of the bathing traditions of the ancient Romans. Today, the baths include several relax-

The magnificent
clocktower of
the Müller Baths
(Müllersches Volksbad)
on Rosenheimer
Strasse

ation areas, therapeutic baths, a steam room, and even a dog grooming centre in the basement!

After leaving the Müller Baths it's worth pausing for a moment on the nearby Ludwigsbrücke to reflect on the origin of Munich itself. It was in 1156 that Henry 'the Lion', Duke of Saxony and Bavaria (1156–1180), of the Welf Dynasty, ordered the demolition of a toll bridge over the Isar, built by the Bishop of Freising, just north of where Munich's airport now stands. As the only bridge over the Isar it had enabled the bishopric to grow rich by levying customs duties from merchants using the Salzstrasse, the salt route connecting Salzburg with western Germany and France, which had existed since Roman times.

Henry secured this lucrative business for himself by building a new bridge in his own duchy to the south, on the site of today's Ludwigsbrücke. He called the place 'Ze den Munichen' (dialect for 'by the monks') after a pre-existing settlement of Benedictines, which had been founded in the year 1000 on the present-day site of the Church of St. Peter (Peterskirche) at Rindermarkt 1. On 14th June 1158 Frederick I Barbarossa, Holy Roman Emperor and King of Germany recognised Henry's actions and awarded market rights to the newly-founded settlement, which eventually took the name München (Munich); a monk has appeared on the town's coat of arms since 1253. In 1180 Henry was dispossessed of his lands for refusing to follow the emperor's army and Bavaria fell to Otto I (1180–1183) of the House of Wittelsbach, which was to remain the ruling house until 1918. Munich itself came under the jurisdiction of the Bishop of Freising until it too came into the possession of the Wittelsbachs in 1240.

Jugendstil carving on the Müller Baths (Müllersches Volksbad)

The oldest buildings in this historic area today are an ensemble of 18th century houses south of the Ludwigsbrücke on Lilienstrasse. Behind them runs the fast flowing Auer Mühlbach, one of the last of the numerous streams that once traversed the Munich area (see no. 1).

Other places of interest nearby: 13, 14, 24, 28

24 A Place for Contemplation

Au – Haidhausen, the Church of St. Nicholas at Gasteig
(St. Nikolai-Kirche am Gasteig) at Innere Wiener Strasse 1
S1, S2, S3, S4, S6, S7, S8 Rosenheimer Platz; Tram 15, 25

If one wanted to find a quiet corner in central Munich, a special place for private contemplation away from the crowds, that place might be the little Church of St. Nicholas at Gasteig (St. Nikolai-Kirche am Gasteig) at Innere Wiener Strasse 1. Although it is located alongside a busy road, as well as the huge Gasteig München cultural centre (itself built partially on the site of the Bürgerbräukeller from where Hitler staged his Beer Hall Putsch in 1923) the church manages to retain a magical air of tranquillity.

The church was built around 1200 and is mentioned in 1315 as being part of a leper hospital, located for obvious reasons *outside* the walls of Old Town (Altstadt), on the east bank of the Isar. In the 16th century it was re-built in the Late Gothic style, and then remodelled again during the Renaissance and Baroque periods, during which time it received its whitewashed walls and onion dome, recalling the churches of rural Bavaria. After suffering damage during the Second World War the church was renovated once more, and a late Baroque altar from Garmisch installed. Although the nave of the church is gated outside service hours, visitors are still able to enter the church and enjoy the solitude it offers.

The Church of St. Nicholas at Gasteig (St. Nikolai-Kirche am Gasteig) on Innere Wiener Strasse is always a peaceful place

The same applies to the so-called Altöttinger Lorettokapelle, which adjoins the church. Built originally in 1678 the chapel was re-built in 1820, and then in 1926 an arcaded ambulatory was added to the outside of the chapel in imitation of the famous *Gnadenkapelle* (Chapel of Mercy) at Altötting, one of the most visited shrines in Germany. Inside the chapel are glass-fronted cabinets crammed with votive candles given in thanks to St. Anthony and St. Jude, patron saints of the lost and desperate.

On the roadside in front of the church is a Crucifixion group that once formed part of a Baroque wayside Calvary, an 18th century expression of religious devotion rendered in stone as ordered by the Council of Trent during the Counter Reformation. The crucifix itself is modern, the original having been destroyed during the war.

Alongside the Church of St. Nicholas at Gasteig (St. Nikolai-Kirche am Gasteig) is the so-called Altöttinger Lorettokapelle

Another Munich church that offers peace in the city is the Old Catholic Church of St. Willibrord (Alt-Katholische Kirche St. Willibrord). This little, brick-built church, which is partially obscured by trees, stands on a slip of land between An der Hauptfeuerwache and busy Blumenstrasse. Founded in the early 19th century it serves the English-speaking Catholic community. St. Willibrord (658–739), incidentally, was the first Bishop of Utrecht.

Other places of interest nearby: 13, 24, 25

25 Coffee With the Locals

Au – Haidhausen, a tour beginning with the Johannis-Café
at Johannisplatz 15
U4, U5 Max-Weber-Platz; Tram 15, 19, 25

It is sometimes said that Munich – like Berlin, Vienna, and the other great cities of Central Europe – has a café society as varied as life itself. In some respects this is true, although it could also be maintained that the golden age of the coffeehouse was extinguished by the Second World War. So whilst perhaps not quite the crucibles of intellectual ferment they once were, Munich's cafés are still plying their trade, and it makes for an unusual thematic tour to track down a handful of the more interesting ones.

We begin at the tiny Johannis-Café at Johannisplatz 15, which has become something of an institution in the former working class district of Haidhausen, despite being only a little over ten years old. Open daily from late morning until early the next it is referred to as a *Tagescafé* and attracts an eclectic audience. As well as the long hours and convivial 'living room' atmosphere, with its faded wallpaper and eclectic art, the family-run café offers a handful of pavement seats and some hearty snacks, including meatloaf with fried egg *(Leberkäs mit Ei)*, sausage with potato salad *(Würstel mit Kartoffelsalat)*, beefburgers *(Fleischpflanzerl)*, and spicy Bavarian cream cheese *(Obatzter)* served with pretzels *(Brezeln)* and radishes. Its most famous late morning habitué is songwriter and singer Gog Seidl-Carusa, whose eponymous paean to the Johannis-Café can be found on the jukebox. Upon leaving the café you might care to visit Haidhausen's French Quarter, so-called because its small cluster of streets and squares are named after French cities (e.g. Pariser Platz and Orleansstrasse) and are arranged in a radiating pattern like those in Paris.

Our next stop is the Café am Beethovenplatz, which has been installed on the ground floor of the Hotel Mariandl since it was built in 1899 at Goethestrasse 51. The neo-Gothic building was used as a food distribution point for the city's outer suburbs during the Second World War, after which it served the occupying American forces as the Femina Nightclub. Since then it has reverted back to its original function as a traditional coffeehouse, with the added interest of hosting classical music concerts, making it Munich's oldest *Konzertcafé*.

A coffeehouse popular for *Kaffee und Kuchen* is the modern yet

genteel Café Kreutzkamm at Maffeistrasse 4 in the heart of Old Town (Altstadt). The café was opened originally in Dresden by Heinrich Kreutzkamm in 1825 but after that was destroyed by bombing in 1945 Kreutzkamm's great grandson opened another of the same name in Munich. A popular confection here is almond-scented *Baumkuchen* ('tree cake'), shaped like a stack of doughnuts, which when sliced reveals alternating dark and light concentric rings, like the cross-section of a tree.

There are two other traditional coffeehouses in the city centre. The Café Arzmiller is hidden away at Theatinerstrasse 22, behind the Theatinerkirche. The cakes and pastries here (including *Herrenschnitte*, *Nusstorte*, and *Apfeltorte*) are worthy of a Viennese coffeehouse, and the café's leafy courtyard is a delightful place to escape the crowds in summer. Opposite the Theatinerkirche stands the venerable Café Tambosi (originally Café Annast) at Odeonsplatz 18. Again Viennese in style it dates back to the late 18th century, making it the oldest coffeehouse in Munich.

Equally good cakes, and some mouthwatering chocolates, are available at the Café Luitpold at Brienner Strasse 11, several streets to the north. Opened on 1st January 1888 this was once ranked amongst the world's most spectacular coffeehouses, along with the Café de la Paix in Paris, the Kranzler in Berlin, and the Sacher in Vienna. The highlight of its sumptuously decorated interior, which also included a ballroom, fountains, and billiard rooms, was a huge neo-Renaissance cupola and vaulted corridor (dubbed the Palace Café) beneath which 1200 people could be seated at any one time, amongst them writer Henrik Ibsen and artist Wassily Kandinsky. Unfortunately, the building was severely damaged in the Second World War and subsequently demolished, leaving only today's modern Palm Garden (Palmengarten) to hint at the lost opulence. For an impression of how the building once looked don't miss the Café Luitpold Collection (Sammlung Café Luitpold) in the corner; officially Munich's smallest museum it relates the colourful history of this once legendary café.

Our tour finishes in the elegant Café Altschwabing at Schellingstrasse 56. Opened in 1887 this venerable establishment reminds the visitor of the lost great age of the Munich coffeehouse, when it would have been used as a forum for creative discussion by the city's artists and intellectuals. Regulars here included the writers Frank Wedekind, Joachim Ringelnatz, and Stefan George, artists Wassily Kandinsky, Franz Marc, and Paul Klee, and the politician Lenin. Its most famous habitué was the writer Thomas Mann (1875–1955), who lived in Munich between 1891 and 1933 (see no. 51). Also a victim of Allied air raids the café's magnificent neo-Classical interior has now been lovingly restored, and today houses a restaurant, enticing passers-by to step inside and take a seat beneath the chandeliers. And if the setting is too grand why not try Kaffee, Espresso & Barista at Schörstrasse 11 with its more modest retro styling, vintage advertisements, and old fashioned coffee machines.

For a change to coffee try the unusual Friesische Teestube at Pündterplatz 2, where since 1975 proprietor Oswald Telfser has purveyed 140 types of tea in the cosiest of café surroundings, comprising a pair of carpeted rooms with armchairs and large Frisian-style wooden couches.

Not constructed as a café but today used as one, the unusual Golden Bar (Goldene Bar) in the Haus der Kunst (1937) on Prinzregentenstrasse is surely one of Munich's most curious rooms. It is adorned with pseudo-mosaics depicting maps of those parts of the world famous for producing beverages that might once have been purchased here. Hence there is a French wine cellar and a map of Great Britain featuring whisky and gin distillers. Ironically, within a few brief years Germany would be at war with both these countries.

Other places of interest nearby: 23, 24, 25

26 All that Remains of a Crystal Palace

Au – Haidhausen, the Glaspalastbrunnen on Weissenburger Platz
S1, S2, S3, S4, S6, S7, S8 Rosenheimer Platz; Tram 15, 25

Strolling through the Old Botanical Garden (Alter Botanischer Garten), which was laid out on a semi-circular plan in 1804–1814, between Elisenstrasse and Sophienstrasse, it is difficult to imagine that a huge glass and iron exhibition building once stood here. After the garden's original greenhouse was demolished, Munich's *Glaspalast* ('Glass Palace') was constructed as a venue for the First General German Industrial Exhibition (Erste Allgemeine Deutsche Industrieausstellung), which opened on 15th July 1854. Before burning down on 6th July 1931 the structure filled the entire northern half of the gardens.

Nothing remains of the *Glaspalast* today except for an ornate fountain, called the Glaspalastbrunnen, which miraculously survived the fire intact. Today it can be found adorning the centre of Weissenburger Platz, a beautifully-planted roundabout surrounded by pedestrianised streets. Visiting it makes for an opportunity to reflect on the history of one of Munich's greatest lost buildings.

The *Glaspalast* was commissioned by Maximilian II, King of Bavaria (1848–1864) and designed by the German architect August von Voit (1801–1870); he was also responsible for the original Neue Pinakothek art gallery on Theresienstrasse (demolished in 1949). Von Voit's inspiration was the Crystal Palace in London opened a couple of years earlier in 1851. This revolutionary building had been designed by the glasshouse pioneer Joseph Paxton (1803–1865), whose experiments with glass and iron now permitted large and durable structures to be erected quickly and easily. Although less than half the size of the Crystal Palace, the *Glaspalast* still measured a colossal 234 metres long and 67 metres wide, with a height of 25 metres in the middle.

The *Glaspalast* was subsequently used to host many large-scale art exhibitions and international trade fairs, one being the International Electrotechnical Exhibition (Internationale Elektrotechnische Ausstellung). This was the world's first exhibition to be electrically illuminated, made possible by the German engineer Oskar von Mil-

Weissenburger Platz is dominated by an elegant fountain called the Glaspalastbrunnen

ler bringing an overhead DC power line all the way to Munich from Miesbach, 50 kilometers away. The line was also used to power an artificial waterfall, in order to demonstrate further the possibilities of bringing power over long distances.

Like London's Crystal palace, the *Glaspalast* eventually fell victim to fire, the cause being later cited as arson although the motive remains unknown. At the time the structure was being used to host an exhibition of German Romantic paintings, more than 110 of which were destroyed: included were works by Casper David Friedrich, Moritz von Schwind, Karl Blechen, and Philipp Otto Runge. Plans to rebuild the *Glaspalast* were abandoned in 1933 when Hitler became Chancellor, the Nazis choosing instead to construct their own House of German Art (Haus der Deutschen Kunst) at Prinzregentenstrasse 1, which was completed in 1937 (see no. 44).

In 1914 new Botanical Gardens (Botanischer Garten) were laid out at Schloss Nymphenburg, and the Old Botanical Garden was converted into a municipal park. All that remains of the old garden is a solitary neo-Classical portal at the corner of Sophienstrasse and Elisenstrasse.

Other places of interest nearby: 25, 55

27 An Historic Fair

Au – Haidhausen, the *Auer Dult* on Mariahilfplatz
Tram 17 Mariahilfplatz; Bus 52

The Bavarian calendar is sprinkled liberally with religious festivals, colourful traditions, and historic markets and fairs, one of the oldest and most storied being the so-called *Auer Dult*. Although nowadays this traditional fair is orchestrated by the Munich Tourist Office its history can be traced far back into the Middle Ages.

The Germanic word *'Dult'*, meaning 'observance', originates in a religious celebration held in honour of a saint. Stalls were erected outside churches, from which goods were sold to parishioners and pilgrims, and over time these exclusively religious events were transformed into popular fairs.

In 1310, a fair associated with St. Jacob's Day, the *Jakobidult,* is recorded as taking place in Old Town (Altstadt), in a meadow now occupied by St.-Jakobs-Platz. In 1791 it was relocated to Kaufingerstrasse and Neuhauser Strasse, and then in 1796 Charles Theodore, Elector of Bavaria (1777–1799) bestowed the right to hold the fair twice-yearly in the district of Au, on the opposite side of the river. It is from this time that the name *Auer Dult* enters general parlance. Au, incidentally, which has a history dating back to 1340, was incorporated into Munich in 1854. Its original name, *Awe ze Gysingen*, means 'Land on Water' and it was here until the early 20th century that the city's poor lived, in cottages that can still occasionally be seen today.

Since 1905 the *Auer Dult* has been held three times a year on Mariahilfplatz, in the lee of the neo-Gothic Mariahilf Church (Mariahilfkirche). Completed in 1839 it is the first instance of the Gothic revival in Southern Germany. Each *Dult* lasts nine days, the *Maidult* in May, the *Jakobidult* in July, and the *Kirchweihdult* in October (see www.auerdult. de for exact dates). Although the fair was not held between 1943 and 1946, due to the Second World War, it has continued ever since.

Today, each fair attracts approximately 100 000 visitors, who are keen to peruse the wares of some 300 stallholders, the majority of whom offer household ornaments, kitchen implements, herbal remedies, and reasonably-priced antiques, with everything from chamber pots to hair care products. There are foodstalls too, as well as sideshows, and an ever-popular funfair featuring nostalgic carousels, shooting galleries, swing-boats, a miniature Ferris wheel, and the famous children's

A typical market stall at the thrice-yearly Auer Dult on Mariahilfplatz

puppet show *Kasperl von der Au*. When compared with Munich's boisterous Oktoberfest, the *Auer Dult* is really more of a folk festival, and all the more interesting for that. Visitors unable to attend the *Auer Dult* can get some impression of what they are missing by visiting the gift shop of the Münchner Stadtmuseum (Munich City Museum), where one of the original stalls is permanently on display.

Munich's oldest permanent outdoor market is the Viktualienmarkt, which is open daily on the southern edge of Old Town, on a square which carries its name. The square was established in 1807 by Maximilian I, King of Bavaria (1799–1825, until 1806 as Elector Maximilian IV Joseph), who decreed that the market move there after it outgrew its original home on Marienplatz. Today, 140 stalls are laid out across 22 000 square metres, selling predominantly fresh fruit, vegetables, flowers, meat, and poultry. The popular and historical backdrop of the market is emphasised not only by the presence of a beer garden and a maypole on the square, but also by the famed masked dance of the market women *(Marktfrauen)*, which is performed on Shrove Tuesday, the penultimate day of the city's pre-Lent carnival season *(Fasching)*.

Munich has other markets too, including the Elisabeth market (Elisabethmarkt) on Elisabethstrasse, both named after Empress Elisabeth of Austria, who was the cousin of Ludwig II, King of Bavaria. Inaugurated in 1880 it is a similar but more intimate experience than the Viktualienmarkt. And there are farmers' markets too, for example the one held on Mariahilfplatz each Wednesday morning, and fleamarkets, including Bavaria's largest, the Flohmarkt Riem, at the Neue Messe München (New Munich Trade Fair Centre).

Other places of interest nearby: 28

28 Under the Ground and Up in the Air

Ludwigsvorstadt – Isarvorstadt, the Deutsches Museum on Museumsinsel
S1, S2, S3, S4, S6, S7, S8 Isartor; U1, U2, U7 Frauenhofer-strasse; Tram 16, 18

The Deutsches Museum on Museumsinsel is one of the largest and most important technical museums in the world. Opened in May 1925 as the German Museum of Masterpieces of Science and Technology it illustrates every aspect of the development of technology, from glass blowing and tunnel construction, to paper-making and the invention of the moog synthesiser. To see everything the visitor would have to walk a 16 kilometre-long path that winds its way over six floors. Even then there would be more to see, since in 2002 the museum's collection of automobiles, motorcycles and railways was relocated to the Deutsches Museum Verkehrszentrum at Theresienhöhe 14a, and since 1992 an aeronautical display, the Deutsches Museum Flugwerft Schleißheim, has existed at Effnerstrasse 18 in Oberschleißheim. The latter includes some of the oldest surviving airfield buildings in the world.

For now, let us stay with the Deutsches Museum on Museumsinsel, and visit just three of its more unusual highlights. We begin in the mining department, located suitably in the museum's sprawling basement. Here can be found an impressively realistic and historically accurate reconstruction of several mining scenes, spread across an area of 3475 square metres, and involving 214 steps. The coal mining display, with its blackened workers, propped shafts, and heavy machinery, is interesting – but we are here to learn about salt mining.

Mineral salt has played a vital part in the history of civilisation, being originally extracted for nutritional and preservative purposes. Today, it is mined as a raw material for the chemical industry and for use in the production of artificial fertilisers. It is commonly released from underground beds by means of water and pumped to the surface as brine. However, during the 18th century pure rock salt was mined by pillar-and-chamber work. It is this older process that is so atmospherically depicted in the museum by means of a reconstruction of a salt mine at Wieliczka, near Kraków in Poland. Down here in the silence, illuminated only by make-believe oil lamps, one can almost hear the lifeless mannequins whispering to each other while they work.

A reconstruction of a Polish salt mine in the Deutsches Museum on Museumsinsel

By complete contrast we ascend now, not only to the first floor but to the skies. Suspended from the ceiling of the aviation hall is a single-seat Fokker Dr. 1 Triplane *(Dreidecker)*, one of the most recognisable fighter aircraft of the First World War. In terms of manoeuvrability and climbing ability, its short wing span (just 7 metres), and the impressive lift provided by its three wings, made it the perfect fighter interceptor of its time. The plane entered service in April 1917 but was replaced by the faster Fokker bi-plane in May 1918 because the air resistance created by its three wings forced it to fly at lower speeds. Of the 320 of these ground-breaking machines built none have survived, the one you are looking at being a magnificent replica. The red paint is identical to that of the aircraft flown by Manfred von Richthofen, the Red Baron (1892–1918), in which he died in April 1918 in northern France. Due to Richtofen's reputation as the most successful flying ace of the First World War the original aircraft was dismembered by souvenir hunters immediately afterwards.

Our third unusual exhibit, a full-scale reconstruction of the Altamira cave paintings, can be found on the second floor. Altamira is a hill in north-east Spain, where in 1879 a cave was discovered containing Stone Age wall paintings made nearly 15 000 years earlier. On the cave roof, the numerous depictions of animals, including bison, horse and deer, are among the earliest and finest examples of Palaeolithic art. The artist used natural pigments such as ochre, manganese, and charcoal, and in places utilised the undulating rock surface itself to impart a three-dimensional effect.

Unfortunately, the Altamira cave is no longer open to the public, in order to protect the paintings from fluctuating temperature and humidity. As a result of the closure the Deutsches Museum developed new techniques to create an exact replica of the ceiling displayed in the museum today. An associated exhibit on Stone Age technology, including the invention of tools and the discovery of fire, accompanies it.

A copy of the Red Baron's Fokker Triplane hangs from the ceiling of the Deutsches Museum

After leaving the museum, aviation enthusiasts might also like to visit Munich's International Airport (Flughafen München), where there is a visitors' park with its own S-Bahn station (Besucherpark). Here can be found an artificial hill, with an open-air viewing platform on top and several historic aircraft displayed around the base, including a Fokker Tri-Motor and a DC3.

Other places of interest nearby: 14, 23, 27, 29

29 Munich's Lost Synagogues

Ludwigsvorstadt – Isarvorstadt, a tour ending at
Reichenbachstrasse 27
U1, U2, U7 Fraunhoferstrasse; Tram 27

On 9th November 2006 Munich's Orthodox Jewish Community (Israelitische Kultusgemeinde München) moved premises from Reichenbachstrasse to the Ohel Jakob synagogue on St.-Jakobs-Platz, a part of the city's newly-built Jewish Centre (Jüdisches Zentrum). With anti-semitism again on the increase, and the Jewish Community's 9000-strong membership returned to the strength it was before Hitler became chancellor, the significance of this relocation back into the city centre is obvious. To place it in context, however, one must look at the changing fortunes of Munich's lost synagogues.

The first documented evidence for a Jewish community dates back to 1229, just seventy years after Munich's founding. Following several pogroms the community was expelled in 1442 by the Wittelsbach Duke Albert III (1438–1460), and the city's first synagogue was converted into a church. Not until 1763 did a new Jewish community re-emerge,

A memorial on Herzog-Max-Strasse marks where one of Munich's synagogues once stood

which in 1816 opened what is now called the Old Jewish Cemetery (Alter Israelitischer Friedhof) on Thalkirchner Strasse (see no. 67). In 1826 a Liberal Jewish synagogue was opened on Westenriederstrasse in the presence of Ludwig I, King of Bavaria (1825–1848).

Having gained the right to vote in 1848, and following the abolition in 1861 of limits on the number of Jews permitted in each district, there was a growing influx of Jews into Munich, bolstered in 1880 by Eastern Jews escaping pogroms in Russia. The existing synagogue was deemed too small and in 1882 King Ludwig II (1864–1886) granted land for a new one, Germany's third largest, on Herzog-Max-Strasse. To cater for Orthodox Jews another synagogue, the Ohel Jakob Synagogue, was opened at Herzog-Rudolf-Strasse 3 (formerly Kanalstrasse), followed by a second cemetery on Garchinger Strasse in 1910. A third synagogue was opened in 1931 at Reichenbachstrasse 27, this time for the Eastern Jewish congregation, which had settled around Gärtnerplatz half a century before.

Everything changed for the Jews with the accession of Hitler as chancellor in 1933. As the capital of the Nazi movement anti-semitism was stronger here than anywhere else and in June 1938 the synagogue on Herzog-Max-Strasse became the first in Germany to be demolished (a granite memorial was erected in 1969) (see no. 5). Nazi anti-semitism reached a peak on the night of 9th November 1938 *(Kristallnacht)*, when the synagogues on Herzog-Rudolf-Strasse and Reichenbachstrasse were attacked by Hitler's *Sturmabteilung* (Stormtroopers). Although the former had to be demolished, and is today remembered by a wall plaque, the latter survived albeit in an unusable condition. For a while afterwards a Jewish prayer room was set up at Lindwurmstrasse 125 but this too was torn down when it was claimed to be an obstacle in the way of an underground railway tunnel (see no. 82).

Orchestrated by the Office of Aryanisation at Widenmayerstrasse 27 those Jews that couldn't escape were placed in holding areas and then deported to the concentration camps, their businesses conficated without compensation (see the wall plaque marking the former site of the Uhlfelder department store at Rosental 16). Of Munich's approximately 9 000 Jewish residents in 1933, only 84 remained at the end of the war.

When the war was over Munich's remaining Jews congregated at the Reichenbachstrasse synagogue, which was re-inaugurated in 1947. It remained the headquarters of Munich's Orthodox Jewish Community until its relocation to St.-Jakobs-Platz in 2006. As Munich's single surviving Jewish synagogue from before the war there are plans afoot

The Ohel Jakob synagogue on St.-Jakobs-Platz

to restore it. The restrained exterior (the building scarcely differs from its neighbours) reflects the period in which it was built, when anti-semitism was rife. The interior, however, is another matter, with its marble walls and ornate fixtures and fittings.

Other places of interest nearby: 14, 15, 22, 28

30 In Praise of Strong Beer

Ludwigsvorstadt – Isarvorstadt, the Paulaner Bräuhaus at
Kapuzinerplatz 5
U3, U6 Goetheplatz; Bus 58

Such is the popularity of brewing and drinking beer in Munich that a museum devoted solely to its history, the Beer and Oktoberfest Museum (Bier- und Oktoberfestmuseum), has been opened in one of the city's oldest buildings (1340), at Sterneckerstrasse 2. This hasn't prevented many of the city's beer halls being oversubscribed with visitors but most manage to retain some charm and individuality. They include the Augustinerbräu at Neuhauser Strasse 27 with its shell-adorned Muschelsaal (Shell Hall), the legendary Hofbräuhaus at Platzl 9 and its collection of padlocked tankards (ownership of a key is an inherited privilege), the Augustiner-Keller at Arnulfstrasse 52 with its magnificent brick-built storage cellars, and Zum Flaucher at Isarauen 8 on leafy Flaucher Island, a hidden summer sanctuary for walkers and cyclists.

Inaugurated in 1810 the Oktoberfest is the most important date in Munich's brewing calendar (see no. 31). As the largest folk festival in the world it attracts more than six million people who drink a similar number of litres of beer! However, the Oktoberfest is not the city's only beer festival nor is it the oldest, since the origins of Munich's lesser-known *Starkbierzeit* (Strong Beer Season) date back to 1634. In this year the Italian monks of the Neudeck monastery in the suburb of Au, who had been invited to Munich by Maximilian I, Elector of Bavaria (1623–1651), brewed their first beer to sustain themselves during the rigours of the Lenten fast. Initially, the existing Munich breweries made sure the monks were prevented from selling their beer to the public but in 1745 one hostelry close to the monastery was finally permitted to sell it. On 2nd April 1751, the feast day of the monastery's patron St. Francis of Paola (1416–1507), the monks themselves were also allowed to sell their beer to the public. A strong so-called *Doppelbock* it proved popular and was dubbed 'Sankt-Vater-Bier'. Munich's *Starkbierzeit* tradition had been born.

Not until 1780 were the monks permitted to sell their beer wherever and whenever they liked, and production increased rapidly. The monks did not profit for long, however, since in 1799 Napoleon entered Munich and sold the monasteries off to local businessmen. In 1813 one Franz Xaver Zacherl purchased the Neudeck monastery and converted

The gleaming copper microbrewery of the Paulaner Bräuhaus on Kapuzinerplatz

it into a steam-powered brewery; a beer hall called the Salvatorkeller followed in 1861. During this period the date of the *Starkbierzeit* was moved from April to two weeks in March, and the beer's original name was contracted to 'Salvator' (Latin for saviour). In 1899 the brewery's new owners, the Schmederer brothers, renamed it Paulanerbräu and in 1928 the brewery merged with the Gebrüder Thomas brewery, creating Paulaner Salvator Thomas Bräu. It is today part owned by Heineken.

To experience the Paulaner story first-hand pay a visit to Zacherl's old beer hall, now the Paulanerkeller at Hochstrasse 77, high on the Nockherberg. It is today the venue for the annual *Starkbierfest* (Strong Beer Festival) held between Ash Wednesday and Good Friday (although admittedly all the big breweries today offer their own *Doppelbocks*).

Most interesting of all is a visit to the Paulaner Bräuhaus, a monumental building erected in 1899 at Kapuzinerplatz 5. Behind the bar can be seen the gleaming copper vats of a microbrewery set up in 1990. It is one of more than twenty similar ones established in places as far away as Beijing, Cape Town, and St. Petersburg. A tour of the microbrewery, which should be arranged in advanced (www.paulaner-brauerei.de), illustrates how sweet malted barley is crushed and then water added ('mashing'), during which starch is converted to sugar. The liquid is then pumped into the copper vats (the 'brewhouse'), heated to 100 °C, and hops added for refreshing bitterness. This unfermented liquid ('wort') is then pumped to the fermentation tanks, where the all-important yeast is added, and stored in cool cellars for up to four weeks. The fresh beer is then available for consumption.

31 The City from Above

Ludwigsvorstadt – Isarvorstadt, the Bavaria statue and the
Ruhmeshalle on Theresienwiese
U4, U5 Theresienwiese

There are several locations in Munich that offer magnificent overviews of the city. One of the best is the Church of St. Peter (Peterskirche) at Rindermarkt 1, which stands on the highest point of Old Town (Altstadt). A flight of 300 or so steps leads to the top of its tower, known as *Alter Peter* (Old Peter), from where there is a splendid view over the surrounding area. Not surprisingly a firewatching station existed here in the mid-19th century (see no. 21).

A similar view may be had from the tower of the New Town Hall (Neues Rathaus) at nearby Marienplatz 8 (see no. 17), as well as from the iconic twin towers of the 15th-century Frauenkirche at Frauenplatz 1 (which themselves can be viewed from the rooftop lounge of the Hotel Bayerischer Hof). By law no new building that might obscure the view of this iconic church is allowed, hence the vistas it offers remain unobstructed too. It is interesting to note that a lack of funds forced architect Jörg von Halsbach to abandon his original idea of Gothic towers in favour of the more delicate octagonal towers seen today, their onion domes the forerunners of all others in Bavaria.

For an unconventional but no less remarkable view of the city a trip should be made out to the Theresienwiese, where for almost two centuries Munich's world-famous Oktoberfest has been held during the fortnight before the first Sunday in October. The event first took place in 1810 and was staged around a great horse race and folk festival, held to commemorate the marriage of Crown Prince Ludwig, later Ludwig I, King of Bavaria (1825–1848), and Princess Theresa of Saxe-Hildburghausen; the festival grounds were subsequently named Theresienwiese ('Theresa's Meadow') in her honour.

The beer festival is not, however, the only attraction on Theresienwiese. On an elevated ridge stands the neo-Classical Ruhmeshalle (Hall of Fame), built in 1848–1853 to a design by the architect Leo von Klenze (1784–1864), who also designed the Propyläen on Königsplatz. In the tympana of the hall's side wings the sculptor Ludwig von Schwanthaler (1802–1848) has rendered allegories of the four Bavarian provinces (Bavaria, Palatinate, Swabia, and Franconia), whilst inside there are exhibited more than a hundred marble busts honouring Bavaria's great

St. Paul's Church as viewed from inside the head of the Bavaria statue on Theresienwiese

and good (the first female busts, of actress Klara Ziegler and author Lena Christ, were not installed until 2000).

In front of the Ruhmeshalle there is a grand staircase on which stands a gigantic statue. Again the work of the sculptor Schwanthaler it stands 18.5 metres high and weighs more than 70 tons. The bronze statue represents Bavaria as an Amazonian Germanic goddess, protecting the state with her sword, a lion at her feet. The statue was unveiled during the twenty-fifth Oktoberfest in 1850 and has been called *Bavaria* ever since.

Cast by Ferdinand von Miller the statue was a technological masterpiece in its day, predating New York's Statue of Liberty by some thirty years. Like its American cousin visitors are able to clamber up a 120-step spiral staircase inside the statue to a miniscule viewing platform inside the head, where just two people can sit huddled together. Four tiny windows afford views of both the surrounding Theresienwiese and the city beyond. (Warning: the inside of *Bavaria* is not for the claustrophic, and in hot weather it is almost unbearably humid.)

Typically the Nazis had their own plans for the Theresienwiese. Horse races were to continue, but on a far grander scale. A huge assembly hall was to be erected on the south side of the meadow, with a tribune capable of holding 12000 spectators. Exhibition buildings were planned to the west, and in the east there was to be a Classical-style sports forum. Like so many of the plans for Nazi Munich nothing ever left the drawing board.

32   A Pharaoh's Missing Coffin

Maxvorstadt, the State Museum of Egyptian Art
(Staatliches Museum Ägyptischer Kunst) in the Kunstareal
at Gabelsbergerstrasse 35
U2 Königsplatz; Tram 27

Munich's State Museum of Egyptian Art (Staatliches Museum Ägyptischer Kunst) opened in 1970 in the Residenz on Max-Joseph-Platz. Despite being a world-class collection the grand surroundings meant it was all too often bypassed by visitors in their rush to see the Residenz proper. This changed in 2013 when the museum relocated to Gabelsbergerstrasse in the Kunstareal (Maxvorstadt), a culture forum containing the Alte Pinakothek (including works by Dürer and Rubens), the Neue Pinakothek (Goya and Renoir), the Pinakothek der Moderne, and the Lenbachhaus Art Gallery (Galerie im Lenbachhaus) (see no. 35). The new museum building is a wonder in itself: located underground it is inspired by ancient Egyptian burial chambers with an entrance in the style of an Egyptian temple portal.

The origins of the collection stretch back to the 16th century, when Albert V, Duke of Bavaria (1550–1579) acquired a number of ancient

The gilded sarcophagus mask of New Kingdom Queen Sat-Djehuti in the State Museum of Egyptian Art (Staatliches Museum Ägyptischer Kunst)

A limestone statue of the 19th Dynasty high priest Bekenchons

Egyptian statues for his famous antiquities' collection (see no. 8). Not until the late 18th and 19th centuries did the rulers of Bavaria (notably Elector Charles Theodore and King Ludwig I) again purchase Egyptian artefacts, this time from collections in Rome on behalf of the Bavarian Academy of Sciences and the Glyptothek. The city's holdings were enhanced further in the 20th century through private donations, so that by the time the museum was established it was a worthy rival to similar collections in London, Paris, Berlin, and Turin. The resulting collection of sculptures, reliefs, paintings, and decorative artefacts represents the entire ancient Egyptian period, from prehistoric times down through the Old, Middle and New Kingdom pharaonic periods, to the Graeco-Roman Ptolemaic period. Represented too is the lost world of Nubia, as well as Coptic Egypt, and the Egyptianised art of Imperial Rome.

One artefact that will *not* be seen in the museum is the lower half of a coffin from Tomb KV55 in the Valley of the Kings at Thebes. Discovered in 1907 and sheathed entirely in gold the coffin is thought to have been made originally for a woman and then adapted for kingly use, although the new owner's cartouches were subsequently excised. That owner is now thought to have been the heretical Pharaoh Akhenaten (husband of Nefertiti and probable father of Tutankhamun), vilified for his suppression of Egypt's traditional gods, replacing them with a monotheistic faith under the one god, Aten. He also abandoned the old religious capital at Thebes and created a new one, Akhetaten, out in the desert at Tel el-Amarna. After Akhenaten's death around 1334 BC his city was abandoned and his country returned to polytheism, and the former capital at Thebes. In time Akhenaten's body found its way to the Valley of the Kings, where it was re-buried in Tomb KV55 in a re-used coffin, the ornamentation of which is quite incompatible with his religious beliefs.

Sometime between 1915 and 1931 the lower half of this intriguing coffin disappeared from the Egyptian Museum in Cairo, where it was being stored. Presumed lost forever it was spotted by the then director of the Munich museum in the early 1980s, in the private collection of a Swiss collector, who had himself obtained it in Italy. The Swiss collector agreed to hand the artefact over to the Munich museum for restoration. Later, during a trip to the Middle East, the former Bavarian President Edmund Stoiber agreed to return the coffin base to Cairo on condition that the upper half was first loaned temporarily to the Munich museum, where the reunited coffin attracted 50 000 visitors.

Despite this justified restitution, Munich's Egyptian museum still contains plenty of other equally fascinating objects, including a well-preserved papyrus copy of the *Book of the Dead*, letters written on stone tablets to Pharaoh Amenhotep IV (the name used by Akhenaten before making his sweeping religious reforms), a stunning sculpture of a falcon rendered in electrum (a naturally occurring alloy of gold and silver), and a beautifully-decorated 21st Dynasty coffin for Herit-Ubekhet, a temple musician from Karnak. Perhaps even more interesting are the objects from daily life, such as wooden cosmetic and writing implements, as well as funerary objects, such as canopic jars in which to store the organs of the deceased, and miniature figures called *shawabtis*, included in the tomb as workers in the afterlife.

No less accomplished than the artefacts of the Pharaonic period are those from the Roman period, especially the lifelike mummy portraits, the coffin of a five year-old Roman child (70–80 AD), and an unusual plaster crocodile mask. The collection closes with delicate fragments of figurative Coptic textiles (500 AD), and several Egyptian-style statues created in Egypt during the Roman Empire.

Other places of interest nearby: 37, 38, 39, 40, 41, 42

33 Where Eagles Dare to Perch

Maxvorstadt, the former Bavarian State
Tax Office at Sophienstrasse 6
S1, S2, S3, S4, S6, S7, S8 Karlsplatz; U4, U5 Karlsplatz;
Tram 16, 18, 19, 20, 21, 22, 27, 28

On 25th June 1945 the American military command in Munich ordered that the city, like all other cities in the former German Reich, be de-Nazified. As a result some one hundred streets which had been named after Nazi grandees reverted back to their original names (thus Hermann-Göring-Strasse once again became Azaleenstrasse). De-Nazification also meant that all overtly Nazi public sculpture be removed, and all structures associated with Nazi cult practices be removed. Whilst in the most obvious cases this was carried out thoroughly (e.g. the removal of the memorial to Hitler's Beer Hall Putsch of 1923 at the Feldherrnhalle in Odeonsplatz, the demolition of the Temples of Honour *(Ehrentempel)* on Königsplatz, and the removal of the bronze eagles from the façades of the nearby *Führerbau* and NSDAP administration building), others slipped the net. The existence of these escapees reminds the onlooker not only of the former function of certain buildings under the Nazis, and of the way in which the regime used buildings for propaganda purposes, but also of the piecemeal nature of the de-Nazification process (the granite slabs in Königsplatz, for instance, laid by the Nazis for their ceremonial parades, were not removed until 1988).

A good example can be found at Sophienstrasse 6, where between 1938 and 1942 a building complex was erected for the Bavarian State Tax Office. The building is still standing and sports a large Nazi-period eagle on its façade, albeit in its de-Nazified state, with the swastika *(Hakenkreuz)* erased from inside the oak wreath held in the eagle's talons. In the summer of 1945 the US Military Authority occupied the building, joined soon after by the so-called America House, which was established to re-educate the German people about Western democracy (the institution moved in 1948 into the former *Führerbau* on Königsplatz). Between May 1947 and January 1949 the Bavarian State Parliament held meetings here, and today the building is a regional finance office (Oberfinanzdirektion).

Of course, it should not be forgotten that the German coat of arms – a black eagle on a gold shield – is the oldest European national emblem still in use. Its origins can be traced back to the Germanic tribes of Europe (for whom the eagle was a symbol of strength, of the sun, and of the highest Norse god Odin), as well as to the Romans, who revered it as a symbol of their Emperor's invincibility. The eagle as the national emblem of Germany dates to the time of Charlemagne, the King of the Franks (768–814), who was crowned Emperor of the Romans in 800, claiming direct succession from the Emperors of Rome. In 1433 the Holy Roman Emperor Sigismund (1410–1437) adopted the double-headed eagle, which was used in various forms until 1867, when the Kingdom of Prussia adopted a single spread eagle once again. This was retained during the German Empire (1871–1918) and the Weimar Republic (1918–1933), until Hitler stylised it after the eagle of the Roman legions, adding the oak wreath and swastika. In 1950 the Federal Republic of Germany incorporated the

A Third Reich eagle still adorns the former Bavarian State Tax Office on Sophienstrasse

less militaristic Weimar Republic-era eagle into its coat of arms and it is this version, known henceforth as the Federal Eagle, which continues to serve as the state symbol of reunified Germany today.

In the case of the eagle on Sophienstrasse one must deduce that it was deemed enough to remove only the swastika and not the martial eagle itself, despite its distinctively lean Nazi appearance (compare it with the softer eagle representing the Bavarian Free State in the courtyard inside the building).

Other eagles in variously de-Nazified states can be found on the gateway into the former Funk Kaserne barracks on Frankfurter Ring, outside the former Reichsgeneral Ordnance Depot of the NSDAP at Tegernseer Landstrasse 210, over a doorway in the Bavarian National Museum (Bayerisches Nationalmuseum) at Prinzregentenstrasse 3, and inside the former Luftgaukommando (Regional Headquarters of the Luftwaffe) building across the road at number 24–28. The latter is also interesting for the sculpted steel helmets worked into the pediments and especially the swastikas incorporated in the iron grilles on

Swastikas still visible on a former Third Reich building on Prinzregentenstrasse

the Oettinger Strasse side of the building. The most controversial and immediately recognisable symbol of the Third Reich, it is shocking to still find the swastika *(Hakenkreuz)* so visible in what was once the 'Capital of the Nazi Movement' (Hauptstadt der Bewegung).

An even more ancient symbol than the eagle, the swastika first appeared as a decorative motif on Neolithic pottery and then as a Sanskrit sacred symbol (meaning 'something good') across the Hindu world. It was only subverted by Nazi theorists in support of their spurious Aryan racial ancestry of the German people from the ancient Greeks and Proto Indo Europeans. Known as the national emblem *(Hoheits(ab)zeichen)*, the powerful combination of swastika and martial eagle was used by the Nazi Party as a symbol of German strength and renewal.

Fortunately, this author has only been able to identify two other examples of the swastika in modern Munich, namely the curious *Hakenkreuzhäuser* (Swastika houses) at Hanfstaenglstrasse 16–20 and Donaustrasse 25–31, which can only be made out from the air.

Some commentators have suggested that the swirling Bavarian flags, painted on the ceiling of the famous Hofbräuhaus at Platzl 9, are also swastikas. Whatever the case, it was here on 24th February 1920 that Hitler launched the Nazi Party programme, and where on 13th August he made his "foundational speech" regarding what he termed the "Jewish Question" that would lead eventually to the Holocaust.

Other places of interest nearby: 5, 6, 34, 40, 41

34 An Easily Overlooked Monastery

Maxvorstadt, the Basilica of St. Boniface (Basilika St. Bonifaz)
at Karlstrasse 34
U2 Königsplatz; Tram 20, 21, 22

In 1806 Bavaria was granted the status of a kingdom and in 1808 the first large urban expansion of the city began under Maximilian I, King of Bavaria (1799–1825, until 1806 as Elector Maximilian IV Joseph). Called Maxvorstadt ('Max suburb') in the king's honour, this chequerboard grid of streets north-west of the city centre is still clearly evident today.

A modern church operates today inside the remains of the Basilica of St. Boniface (Basilika St. Bonifaz) on Karlstrasse

Laid out around Brienner Strasse, which acted as a Royal Route connecting the Residenz with Schloss Nymphenburg, the architectural focal point of Maxvorstadt is the Königsplatz forum, a formal open square defined by the Propyläen on the west, the Glyptothek to the north, and the National Collection of Antiquities (Staatliche Antikensammlungen) to the south. The ensemble was commissioned by Maximilian's successor, Ludwig I, King of Bavaria (1825–1848), whose passion for ancient Greece and Rome is reflected in its neo-Classical style (see no. 39).

Ludwig's architect of choice for the Propyläen and the Glyptothek was Leo von Klenze (1784–1864), the second most prominent proponent of the neo-Classical movement in 19th century Germany after Prussian court architect Karl Friedrich Schinkel. However, when it came to designing the southern side of Königsplatz, Ludwig, who was temporarily at loggerheads with Klenze, commissioned the architect Georg Friedrich Ziebland instead. The result was an exhibition hall completed in 1848, which was modelled on the design of a late Classical Greek temple. Between 1898 and 1916 the hall housed the gallery of the Munich Secession (the city's answer to the Art Nouveau movement), after which it was taken over by the New State Gallery (Neue Staatsgalerie), and then in 1967 by the National Collection of Antiquities.

Interesting as the exhibition hall and its contents are, it is the building immediately behind it which interests us here. Often overlooked in favour of the Königsplatz forum, the Basilica of St. Boniface (Basilika St. Bonifaz) was also commissioned by Ludwig and designed by Ziebland. Constructed between 1835 and 1848 as the parish church of Maxvorstadt the basilica's location is an interesting one. Although its entrance stands on Karlstrasse it is joined at the rear to the back of Ziebland's exhibition hall, illustrating contemporary ideas about architecture, in which religion was to be linked with art and science, a theme cultivated by the Benedictine monks to whom the basilica passed after Ludwig's death.

Unlike the buildings in Königsplatz, the basilica was executed in the style of an early Christian church, notably that of St. Apollinaire in Classe in Ravenna. Behind the entrance portico, which is supported by three Ionic columns, there are three arched doorways. The central one is flanked by statues of St. Peter and St. Boniface, and above the arch is an unusual portrait of the architect himself in medieval garb. Until it was severely damaged during an air raid in the Second World War, these doorways would have led into a vast double-aisled church 76 metres long, its walls adorned with beautiful wall paintings. Most notably it had a roof made from a forest of exposed timber beams supported on sixty-six monolithic columns.

Of the original basilica only the outer walls and twenty-two columns towards Karlstrasse survived the bombs. Fortunately, the white marble tomb of Ludwig I, King of Bavaria (1825–1848) was unscathed, as was the tombstone of his wife Theresa beside it. Subsequently, for financial reasons the building was stabilised but not restored, the lost northern half of the building being closed off with a new wall; in its place a pastoral care and education centre has been set up, with a dozen monks tending to the needs of the city's homeless. The remaining part

The Basilica of St. Boniface (Basilika St. Bonifaz) still contains the white marble tomb of Ludwig I, King of Bavaria

of the basilica has since been reorganised as an open-plan place of worship, which draws an enthusiastic audience each Sunday.

St. Boniface himself was a 7th century Anglo-Saxon missionary. Known as the 'Apostle of the Germans', he was sent to Germany and Frisia to establish Christianity and to nurture cultural development amongst the pagan Germanic tribes there, who had migrated into the area in the wake of the collapse of the Roman Empire. Before his murder at the hands of the Frisians, Boniface established the important bishoprics of Freising, Regensburg, Passau, and Salzburg. He is also credited by some with having invented the Christmas tree, being originally an evergreen fir that sprang miraculously from the roots of a felled pagan sacred tree called Thor's Oak.

Other places of interest nearby: 33, 35, 37, 38, 39, 40

35 In a Florentine Garden

Maxvorstadt, the Lenbachhaus Art Gallery
(Galerie im Lenbachhaus) at Luisenstrasse 33
U2 Königsplatz

Emerging from the U-Bahn station at Königsplatz can be disorientating: the surrounding buildings are predominantly Classical Greek in style rather than Germanic (see no. 39). The confusion continues if one walks a short distance northwards along Luisenstrasse, where on the lefthand side there stands the Lenbachhaus, a Florentine *palazzo* set in a Tuscan-style garden. Built between 1887 and 1891 this charming Italianate ensemble was commissioned by the renowned German portrait painter Franz von Lenbach (1836–1904). To understand why the artist chose to have his home built in the Italian idiom one must look at his life and the time in which he lived.

Franz von Lenbach was born in the Bavarian town of Schrobenhausen. As a teenager he was sent to the polytechnic at Augsburg, where his father intended he would follow in his own footsteps and become a master mason. Instead, the young Lenbach became entranced by painting, notably the animal studies of Johann Hofner (1832–1913), whose works he saw in the galleries of Augsburg and Munich. To improve his own technical abilities he spent much time as a copyist, and like Hofner he became a student of the Munich Historicist painter Carl Theodor von Piloty (1826–1886). In 1858 aged just 22 years old Lenbach accompanied Piloty on a study tour of Italy that affected him deeply. Several works from this important first journey still exist, including *The Goatherd* (1860), which can be seen in the Schack Gallery (Sammlung Schack) at Prinzregentenstrasse 9.

After Lenbach's return from Italy it was the wealthy art collector Friedrich von Schack (1815–1894) who lured Lenbach away from a Professorship at the Weimar Academy. Schack's main interest lay in contemporary Munich painters, and he often sponsored young artists who had not yet been recognised. Lenbach was just such a painter and Schack commissioned him to paint a large number of copies for his private collection. The task took Lenbach to Italy a second time in the same year to copy many Old Masters, as well as a trip to Spain in 1867–68, where he copied pictures in Madrid's Museo del Prado, as well as in the museums of Granada and the Alhambra. Little wonder then that his own home was constructed in a Mediterranean style. In tan-

The Lenbachhaus on Luisenstrasse resembles a Florentine palazzo

dem with his work for Schack, Lenbach also pursued a lucrative career as a portraitist and painted many of the most famous personages of the day. He exhibited frequently at exhibitions in Munich and Vienna, and in 1900 he was awarded a Grand Prix in Paris.

Franz von Lenbach died in 1904 and in 1924 his wife sold their former home to the City of Munich, for use as an art gallery. This is a function the building has served well having been designed by Gabriel von Seidl (1848–1913), architect of the Bavarian National Museum (Bayerisches Nationalmuseum) on Prinzregentenstrasse, and the Künstlerhaus on Lenbachplatz (see nos. 10 & 35).

Now called the Lenbachhaus Art Gallery (Galerie im Lenbachhaus) the building contains several fascinating collections of art, including some of Lenbach's own works displayed in rooms that he would still

recognise, adorned with their original silk wallpapers and gilded ceilings. Alongside are contemporary works by other Munich painters including von Piloty, as well as Carl Spitzweg (1808–1885), Franz von Stuck (1863–1928), Friedrich August von Kaulbach (1822–1903), Lovis Corinth (1858–1925), and Wilhelm Leibl (1844–1900). The gallery's real treasures, however, are undoubtedly the Expressionist works by the group *Der Blaue Reiter* (The Blue Rider), established in Munich in 1911 and including Wassily Kandinsky, Franz Marc, and Paul Klee.

A fountain in the Tuscan-style gardens of the Lenbachhaus

As an artist Franz von Lenbach may well have looked to the classical world for his inspiration, but his former home is certainly forward-looking in its ongoing function as one of Munich's more dynamic art galleries. The gallery is today home to a profound collection of works by contemporary international artists, including Richard Serra (b. 1939), Jenny Holzer (b. 1950), Joseph Beuys (1921–1986), Olafur Eliasson (b. 1967), Dan Flavin (1933–1996), Liam Gillick (b. 1964), Michael Heizer (b. 1944), Asger Jorn (1914–1973), Ellsworth Kelly (b. 1923), Anselm Kiefer (b. 1945), Gerhard Richter (b. 1932), and Andy Warhol (1928–1987). Young unknowns are promoted too, in the affiliated Kunstbau located near the Königsplatz U-Bahn station, where our journey began.

Other places of interest nearby: 32, 34, 36, 37, 38, 39, 40

36 Munich's Mysterious Patron

Maxvorstadt, the Church of St. Benno (St. Benno-Kirche)
on Ferdinand-Miller-Platz
U1 Maillingerstrasse; Tram 20, 21

An air of mystery hangs over Saint Benno (1010–1106), the patron saint of Munich. Little is known of his early life but it now seems unlikely that he was a descendant of Saxon noble family the Woldenburgs, as claimed by his hagiographers, nor that he was educated in the monastery of St. Michael in Hildesheim. It seems more probable that he was a canon of Goslar in Lower Saxony, and it is certain that in 1066 he was made Bishop of Meissen by Holy Roman Emperor Henry IV, King of Germany.

Benno appears to have supported the Saxon insurrection of 1073 prompting Henry to imprison him; he was only released in 1078 after agreeing to an oath of fidelity. It wasn't long before Benno broke his oath to the king because of what he perceived as an attempt to subordinate the power of the church to that of the state (in reality, Henry's entire reign was spent trying to create a balance between maintaining the loyalty of the powerful nobility and ensuring the continuing support of the pope). As a result in 1085 Benno was deprived of his bishopric by the Synod of Mainz.

Benno now aligned himself strategically with Guibert of Ravenna, who as the antipope Clement III was supported by Henry. After taking Benno's confession, Clement granted him absolution and wrote a letter of commendation to Henry, who restored Benno to his bishopric once again. It is said that Benno promised to use his influence to achieve an enduring peace with the Saxons but once again he reneged, returning in 1097 to the papal party and recognising Urban II as the rightful pope. With this Benno vanishes from recorded history.

Not surprisingly Benno enjoyed veneration in his native Saxony throughout the later Middle Ages, and the canons of Meissen, together with George, Duke of Albertine Saxony, campaigned to have him made a saint. The canons sought the prestige of a sainted local bishop, whilst the duke desired a model bishop to bolster the ongoing Reformation and its zeal for church reform. Their attempts were successful and in 1523 Pope Adrian VI made Bishop Benno a saint.

Even during this time, some four centuries after his death, Benno's place in history was shadowy, with him becoming a symbol for both

sides of the German reforming debate. Luther railed against Benno in his early tracts against saintly cults, whilst Catholic reformers turned him into the very model of orthodoxy. In 1539 Protestant mobs desecrated Benno's tomb in Meissen, after which his remains were moved to Munich, where the staunchly Catholic Wittelsbach dynasty made him patron saint of the city. (Benno's relics were first installed in 1576 in the Residenz and then moved to the Frauenkirche in 1580.)

Benno's story now moves forward another 350 years to the late 19th century, and a time when Munich was a rapidly expanding city. It was decided to build three new parish churches, one of which in the Maxvorstadt would be dedicated to Saint Benno. The young architect Leonhard Romeis (1854–1904) opted for a neo-Romanesque style church, used originally in the great Rhine cathedrals of the Middle Ages. This was a deliberate choice in order to stress continuity from the Holy Roman Empire into the recently-founded German Empire (the same style can be seen in the Catholic St. Maximilian's Church in Isarvorstadt, and St. Anna's Church in Lehel).

The Church of St. Benno (St. Benno-Kirche) can be found on Ferdinand-Miller-Platz and is easily identified by its pair of 64-metre-high

A modern sculpture outside the Church of St. Benno (St. Benno-Kirche) reflects a legend concerning the saint

towers, one of which carries an astronomical clock. The building takes the form of a cross-shaped basilica terminated by semi-circular apses, the walls pierced by sturdy neo-Romanesque arched windows and doorways. The foundation stone was laid on 16th June 1888, the feast day of St. Benno, and the building was completed in 1895. It was financed by an association specifically created for the construction of the city's new parish churches, as well as by private donations, including a generous one from Luitpold, Prince Regent of Bavaria (1886–1912) for the tabernacle on the high altar: it is adorned with bronze reliefs, including one of Benno himself. Although the church was badly damaged during air raids in 1944 it was restored subsequently in 1947–1953.

Outside the church there is an 11.6 metre-high column supporting a bronze statue of Benno, erected in 1910. More unusual, however, is a modern aluminium sculpture called *Fisch und Schlüssel* (Fish and Key) (2005) by Iskender Yediler. The work represents Benno's iconographic accoutrements, namely a fish with a set of keys in its mouth. Legend relates how Benno threw the keys of Meissen Cathedral into the Elbe after he lost his bishopric, only to retrieve them from the stomach of a freshly-caught fish upon his return. This explains not only why a fine stained glass window inside the church depicts Benno clutching a fish, as well as the fish-and-keys mosaic on the floor of the nave, but also why he has subsequently been made patron saint of fishermen.

Other places of interest nearby: 32, 35, 37, 38

37 Rocks from Mars, Crystals from Bavaria

Maxvorstadt, the Geological Museum
(Geologisches Museum) at Luisenstrasse 37
U2 Theresienstrasse; Tram 27

Munich boasts a pair of small geology museums, located just a few streets from each other in Maxvorstadt. One of them, the Mineralogy Museum (Museum Reich der Kristalle) at Theresienstrasse 41 (entrance on Barer Strasse), represents the public display of the Bavarian State Collection for Mineralogy (Mineralogische Staatssammlung), which originated with collections of rocks and minerals found in the 18th century. It is a low-key but glittering affair served up artistically in a darkened room. Most impressive of the exhibits are the specimens of light-emitting stones, the so-called *geodes* (crystal-lined volcanic bubbles preserved in stone), and the examples of petrified wood. Seemingly drab by comparison but no less thought-provoking are rock samples taken from Martian meteorites.

To understand the powerful physical forces that created such specimens a visit should next be made to the even smaller Geological Museum (Geologisches Museum) at Luisenstrasse 37. Academic in tone, the museum contains two permanent exhibitions running the length of a single room, namely "Bavaria's Rocky History" (Bayerns steinige Geschichte), which transports visitors back millions of years in time, and "Earth's Changing Crust" (Erdkruste im Wandel), which details the fundamentals of geology, including sedimentation, mountain building, volcanism, and plate tectonics. Although the labelling is only in German it is fun to open the draws beneath each cabinet and handle the samples they contain. At one end of the museum a door leads into the adjacent Palaeontology Museum (Paläontologisches Museum), which is fascinating not only for its fossils but also the stones which contain them (see no. 38).

The subject of plate tectonics, which is used today to explain the location and behaviour of volcanoes and earthquakes, has a fascinating history in itself. It is based on the theory of continental drift, as proposed by the German interdisciplinary scientist and meteorologist Alfred Lothar Wegener (1880–1930). Whilst browsing in the library at the University of Marburg, where he was teaching in 1911, Wegener became intrigued by the occurrence of identical fossils in geological strata separated by oceans. Accepted thinking posited that the continents were

Munich has two small
museums illustrating
the subject of geology

fixed and that they had formerly been connected by land bridges, across which creatures had migrated. Wegener, on the other hand, suggested that 180 million years ago today's continents had shifted away from a single supercontinent, which he called Pangaea (meaning 'all-lands').

From 1912 he advocated publicly this revolutionary theory of 'continental drift', supporting it with some controversial evidence. Most astonishing were land features such as mountain ranges in Africa and South America, which Wegener claimed could be lined up exactly, coal fields in Europe that matched similar ones in North America, and fossilised creatures found on either side of oceans across which they could never have swum. The evidence was circumstantial but it certainly pointed towards the former existence of a single primal landmass that had split apart.

Unfortunately for Wegener he was unable to think up a convincing mechanism to explain the drift, suggesting erroneously that centrifugal force moved the heavy continents to the equator as the earth spun. Consequently his theory was dismissed by many in the scientific community and he died in relative obscurity in Greenland in 1930.

Not until the discovery of the phenomenon of sea-floor spreading during the 1960s, the result of convection within the earth's mantle, was Wegener's hypothesis of continental drift resurrected and accepted, leading directly to the theory of plate tectonics. The unsung pioneer was thus vindicated and quickly recognised as a founding father of one of the great scientific discoveries of the 20th century. Wegener himself would no doubt have approved of the Geological Museum's Geo Forum, whose up-to-the-minute geology news bulletins are posted on a board at one end of the museum.

Other places of interest nearby: 32, 34, 35, 38, 39, 40

38 Fossilised Birds and Giant Deer

Maxvorstadt, the Palaeontology Museum (Paläontologisches
Museum) at Richard-Wagner-Strasse 10
U2 Königsplatz

The first thing to strike those visiting Munich's Palaeontology Museum (Paläontologisches Museum München), tucked away at Richard-
Wagner-Strasse 10, are the students scurrying along the adjacent
streets and corridors. This is because the surrounding buildings contain the lecture halls of the Ludwig-Maximilians-Universität. The students' comings-and-goings certainly add dynamism to what otherwise
might be mistaken for a minority-interest museum. On the contrary,
the Palaeontology Museum should interest everyone from dinosaur-
loving children to serious academics. Incidentally, if you visit first thing
in the morning you will probably have the place all to yourself, since it
opens at 8 am.

The building in which the museum has been housed since 1950 was
erected in 1899–1902 to a design by the German architect Leonhard
Romeis (1854–1904). As a proponent of the backwards-looking Historicist school Romeis drew on an eclectic range of precursors for inspiration, the building serving initially as the Royal College of Arts and
Crafts for Girls, hence the decorative motifs adorning the entranceway.

Inside, the building works surprisingly well as a museum, especially
the main exhibition hall, which occupies a glass-roofed arcaded courtyard. It is here that the largest and most popular exhibits are displayed,
including a fossilised Triceratops, a sabre-toothed tiger, a giant woolly
mammoth (with intact tusks), and a Pterodactyl suspended from the
ceiling.

Two examples of so-called 'megafauna' (giant animals) warrant
special attention here. The first is the skeleton of a Giant Deer *(Mega-
loceros giganteus)* found in an Irish peat bog and sporting the largest
pair of antlers of any deer. They measure five metres across and weigh
45 kilogrammes. Such antlers would preclude a forested habitat and
so it is thought the creature inhabited a steppe-like landscape similar
to the tundra, which stretched across Europe and into Asia during the
Late Pleistocene period. With the end of the Ice Age and the subsequent spreading of the forest the deer's habitat shrank until its last
refuge was Ireland, where it died out about 10 000 years ago (this has

The impressive fossilised skeleton of a Giant Deer in the Palaeontology Museum (Paläontologisches Museum) on Richard-Wagner-Strasse

given rise to the popular if misleading name of Irish Elk). The second example is the *Bradysaurus*, a lumbering herbivorous reptile from the richly-fossiliferous Karoo desert of South Africa. Distinguished by its curiously knobbly skull and bony skin it dates from the Permian period around 250 million years ago.

There is much more to the museum than just large animals, most notably the extensive first floor collection of delicate fossils from the fine-grained Solnhofen limestone of Bavaria. It was the author Alois Senefelder (1771–1834) who first used specially prepared blocks of this stone for the process of lithographic printing, which he invented in 1797 (see no. 5). The subsequent quarrying of limestone for lithographic plates yielded spectacular fossils dating back 150 million years, from the large sea-lily *Saccocoma* to the earliest bird known to man, *Archaeopteryx*. Thought to represent the missing link between saurian reptiles and birds *Archaeopteryx lithographica* is often held up as vindication of Darwin's theory of evolution. All ten known examples of *Archaeopteryx* hail from the Solnhofen area. The Munich example was discovered in 1991 and has been given the name *Archaeopteryx bavarica* because it appears to be a distinctly smaller sub-species. The bird was probably car-

ried by a storm to the warm and salty sub-tropical lagoons that flanked the northern edge of the so-called Tethys Sea, a primeval ocean which existed before the Mediterranean. Here its body sank and was gradually fossilised under layer-upon-layer of fine mud.

One exhibit that unfortunately can no longer be seen is the skeleton of the 94 million year old *Spinosaurus aegyptiacus*, which was destroyed during an air raid in 1944. This extremely rare dinosaur was first discovered in 1912 by the now-forgotten German palaeontologist Ernst Stromer (1870–1952) in Egypt's Bahariya Valley, an oasis 300 kilometres south-west of Cairo. With its 1.75 metre-long skull and spines up to 2 metres in length it is not surprising that it was chosen as the main antagonist in the blockbuster film *Jurassic Park III* (2001).

For those who still haven't had their fill of old stones there is a small Geological Museum (Geologisches Museum) next door, which can be reached either from the Palaeontology Museum or from its own entrance at Luisenstrasse 37 (see no. 37).

Other places of interest nearby: 34, 35, 37, 39, 40

39 Athens on the Isar

Maxvorstadt, the Glyptothek at Königsplatz 3
U2 Königsplatz; Bus 20, 21, 27

Ludwig I, King of Bavaria (1825–1848) was an ardent admirer of the Classical world and a passionate Philhellene, so much so that in 1825 he ordered that the original German spelling of the name 'Baiern' (Bavaria) be written henceforth as 'Bayern', using the Greek letter Ypsilon to denote the letter 'i'. The move was intended to demonstrate the close bonds between Bavaria and Greece, Ludwig's second son, Otto, having recently become the first ruler of the newly independent Greek state after the country's War of Liberation against Turkey (1821–1829).

Whilst still Crown Prince, Ludwig twice visited Rome and assembled a collection of Classical sculpture of international importance. In 1816 he commissioned the Bavarian court architect Leo von Klenze (1784–1864) to design a building in which his collection could be displayed to the public. Opened in 1830 on the north side of Königsplatz it is called the Glyptothek, after the Greek word *glypte*, meaning 'carved stone'. A walk through Ludwig's Glyptothek today is a rare pleasure, since its tranquil galleries are rarely crowded leaving a strong impression on the visitor.

Amongst the masterpieces here, such as the Barberini Faun and the Rondanini Alexander, are three rooms devoted to sculptures obtained by Ludwig from the Temple of Aphaia, which was erected

The Glyptothek on Königsplatz was deliberately designed in imitation of a Classical Greek temple

Sculptural fragments from the Greek island of Aegina, collected by Ludwig I, King of Bavaria

in c.510–480 B.C. on the Greek island of Aegina. Room VII contains the reconstructed west pediment of the temple, whilst Room IX contains the east, the theme of both pediment groups being the struggle of the mythical forefathers of Aegina to conquer the city of Troy in the two Trojan Wars, lorded over inevitably by the great goddess Athena. In between the two rooms, in Room VIII, are fragments from the roof decoration of the temple, together with objects found in the temple sanctuary, which provide the backdrop for the Glyptothek's café. On fine days the café spreads out into the courtyard beyond, making it one of the most charming and unusual cafés in Munich.

In each room of the Glyptothek are black-and-white photographs showing the interior as it appeared before its ornately painted walls were destroyed during the Second World War. The bare brick walls seen today might look sympathetically 'ancient' to our eyes but they are not as they were meant. Similarly, the plain stone statues from the Temple of Aphaia may appear to have always looked that way but evidence suggests that at one time they too were vividly painted. A small wooden model of part of the Temple of Aphaia in Room VII shows just how vivid those sculptures may once have looked.

After Prussian court architect Karl Friedrich Schinkel, Leo von Klenze was the greatest proponent of the neo-Classical movement in 19th century German architecture. Together with Ludwig I he was responsible for planning Munich as the new Athens. His other works in the city include the Alte Pinakothek, the Ruhmeshalle, parts of the Residenz, and much of Ludwigstrasse, which demonstates Ludwig's great affinity with the Italian Renaissance. It is on Königsplatz, however, that the neo-Classical effect is strongest, where Klenze was responsible not only for the Glyptothek but also the Propyläen, a monumental gateway built on the west side in 1854–1862. As early as 1815 Ludwig and Klenze had planned the buildings on Königsplatz to each represent one of the architectural orders of ancient Greece: the Glyptothek had been graceful Ionic and so the Propyläen was sturdy Doric (its original pediment sculptures are displayed on the platforms of the Königsplatz U-Bahn station). Klenze would probably also have designed the southern side of the square too had he not had a temporary rift with his sometimes truculent patron, resulting in the architect Georg Friedrich Ziebland being asked to design an exhibition hall that today houses the National Collection of Antiquities (Staatliche Antikensammlungen) (see no. 34). Completed in 1848 it takes the form of a temple in the Corinthian-style, the third and final of the Greek orders.

Another building designed by Leo von Klenze for King Ludwig I, which like the Glyptothek lost its painted plasterwork during the Second World War, is All Saints' Court Church (Allerheiligen-Hofkirche) on Marstallplatz. Recently restored as a venue for cultural events its bare brick walls offer the same warmth and peace as the Glyptothek. Immediately adjacent is the easy-to-miss Cabinet Garden (Kabinettsgarten), with its pretty flower beds and modern water rills.

Other places of interest nearby: 32, 34, 35, 37, 38, 40

40 How Munich Might Have Looked

Maxvorstadt, the *Ehrentempel* foundations on Königsplatz
U2 Königsplatz; Bus 20, 21, 27

Between 1933 and 1945 Munich, together with Berlin, Hamburg, Nuremberg and Linz, was designated a "City of the Führer of the Reich". Such cities were to be completely redesigned architecturally, in Munich's case as the centre of party administration and the 'Capital of the Nazi Movement' (Hauptstadt der Bewegung). Of the many plans for this transformation very few ever left the drawing board: had they done so Munich would look very different today.

Adolf Hitler intended to place the architect Paul Ludwig Troost (1878–1934) in charge of the rebuilding of Munich. Troost had already proved himself worthy of the task through his refurbishment of the Brown House on Brienner Strasse, Hitler's apartment on Prinzregentenplatz, and the designing of the House of German Art (Haus der Deutschen Kunst) on Prinzregentenstrasse (see nos. 41, 44 & 53). His lean, neo-Classical approach to architecture, using little ornament but with elements of modernity, was seen as the ideal of National Socialist architecture.

Not surpisingly Troost had also been tasked with designing the most important offices of the Reich leadership *(Reichsleitung)* in Maxvorstadt. This extensive building project involved the construction of the *Führerbau* at Arcisstrasse 12 (Hitler's official seat in the city and where the Munich Agreement was signed in 1938) and the near-identical NSDAP Administration Building at number 10 (today Meiserstrasse). Between the two buildings, on either side of Brienner Strasse, were the so-called *Ehrentempel* (Temples of Honour), a pair of colonnaded structures designed by Troost to contain the coffins of the sixteen "martyrs of the movement", who died during Hitler's failed Beer Hall Putsch of 1923. The ensemble was made complete by the paving over of Königsplatz, which stretched out in front of the party buildings and temples, to form a gigantic Nazi forum and ceremonial parade ground (see no. 40).

Troost died unexpectedly in 1934 and after the war his work was thoroughly de-Nazified; most notably the *Ehrentempel* were demolished leaving only their foundations visible. Abandoned and forlorn they now provide the perfect location at which to reflect not only on the way in which the Nazis subverted architecture for their own political aggrandisement but also on how Munich might have looked had the German war effort not prevented further building.

In 1938 the architect Hermann Giesler (1898–1987) was made 'Architect General for the Capital of the Movement'. In direct competition with his rival Albert Speer in Berlin Giesler adopted Troost's existing plans for the city but increased their scale enormously. As in Berlin the focal point of this entirely unrealised scheme was to be a pair of intersecting boulevards (or Axes), lined with a series of huge party and public buildings. The East-West Axis would be the most important, stretching six kilometres along Landsberger Strasse, from Karlsplatz out to a proposed SA Forum and motorway junction on the

The former Führerbau on Arcisstrasse, once Adolf Hitler's official seat in Munich

edge of the city. At its junction with the Friedensheimer Brücke a new railway station was planned with a colossal dome, inside which the Frauenkirche would easily have fitted. The existing station was to be demolished and replaced by a towering Monument to the Movement over 300 metres high. The 2.5-kilometre-long stretch of boulevard between these two points would be called the Great Axis on which would be built the world's largest opera house. In front of the new station and forming a 93-metre-high gateway to the Great Axis the architect Ernst Sagebiel planned two tower blocks, one an office for the central publishing house of the NSDAP, the other a "Strength through Joy" hotel.

Equally imposing would have been the North-South Axis, leading from a "City of Soldiers" down to a Sports Forum on the Theresien-

All that remains of Hitler's Ehrentempel on Königsplatz

wiese (see no. 31). Other projects included the New Odeon in the Hof-garten, the House of German Architecture opposite the existing House of German Art, the paving of Odeonsplatz as another parade ground, and the construction of a monumental NSDAP Chancellery on Gabels-bergerstrasse (parallel to the Alte Pinakothek). Farther along Gabels-bergerstrasse, at its junction with Türkenstrasse, even Hitler's mauso-leum, based on the Pantheon in Rome, had been planned, linked by a bridge to a forum for party meetings on the opposite side of the road. In reality, the dictator's pitiful remains were cremated long after the war by the Russians and dumped without ceremony into the waters of the Elbe.

Other places of interest nearby: 32, 33, 34, 38, 39, 41

41 The Fate of the Brown House

Maxvorstadt, the former site of the Brown House
(Braunes Haus) on Brienner Strasse
U2 Königsplatz; Tram 27

In 1988 work began on the removal of the 22 000 granite paving slabs that had covered Königsplatz since 1935, when Adolf Hitler had converted the square into a ceremonial parade ground and venue for celebrating the Nazi cult. One of the stone slabs is preserved in the Münchner Stadtmuseum (Munich City Museum) on St.-Jakobs-Platz. The Allies had ordered that all Nazi monuments in Munich be removed as long ago as 1946 but by the time of the de-Nazification of Königsplatz some commentators felt such acts were beginning to draw a dangerous veil over Munich's former role as the 'Capital of the Nazi Movement'

(Hauptstadt der Bewegung). Accordingly, members of the city's left-leaning council proposed a bill to create a Documentation Centre for the History of National Socialism (NS-Dokumentationszentrum), in order to establish a permanent and historically-defined link between the city's present and past. The vacant site they suggested at Brienner Strasse 45, just off Königsplatz, was a controversial one, since it was here between 1931 and 1937 that the Nazi Party (NSDAP) had their national headquarters.

Nicknamed the Brown House (Braunes Haus), after the colour of the nascent Nazi Party's uniforms, Hitler and his supporters moved here after outgrowing their original headquarters at

The Brown House (Braunes Haus) on Brienner Strasse in 1935

Only a street lamp marks where the Brown House (Braunes Haus) once stood, with the former Führerbau beyond

Schellingstrasse 50 (see no. 46). The imposing villa, called originally the Barlow Palace, was sold to them by the widow of William Barlow, an English wholesale merchant. It was converted into offices by Paul Ludwig Troost (1878–1934), Hitler's preferred architect at the time, and financed by the wealthy industrialist Friedrich 'Fritz' Thyssen (1873–1951). Over the door was the motto "Deutschland, Erwache" (Germany, awaken). It was in the Brown House on June 30th 1934 that Hitler interrogated Ernst Röhm, the leader of the *Sturmabteilung* (Stormtroopers), whom he suspected of plotting a coup. Röhm was later murdered in Munich's Stadelheim prison.

In 1937 Hitler moved around the corner from the Brown House to the specially-constructed *Führerbau* on Arcisstrasse; overlooking Königsplatz this was now the ceremonial and bureaucratic heart of Nazi Munich. The Brown House was retained by the party for administrative purposes and also to house the so-called *Blutfahne*, or Blood Flag, carried during Hitler's abortive Beer Hall Putsch of 1923. The

"Brown House", before 1933

Ruin of the "Brown House" and northern "Pantheon", April 1945

Archive photos of the Brown House (Braunes Haus) on an information panel on Königsplatz

blood-spattered flag had subsequently been transformed into a macabre sacred relic.

The Brown House was largely destroyed during Allied bombing in January 1945 (together with the so-called Black House, directly across the road, which once housed the pro-Nazi Papal Embassy). The rubble was cleared away in 1947 leaving only its backfilled cellar and some battered steps fronting the pavement. Unmarked, the vacant plot has remained this way ever since, although it features on the information board at the corner of Brienner Strasse and Arcisstrasse.

Not until December 2005 did the Bavarian state authorities finally give their approval to use the site for the new documentation centre. The decision, part of a growing desire in German cities to focus not only on memorials to the victims of Nazi persecution but also on the places where those crimes were perpetrated, was delayed while conservative state officials attempted unsuccessfully to suppress the project, fearful that it would raise awkward questions about their own political traditions. Forever tainted, this seemingly anonymous plot of land is the perfect location for the centre, designed as it will be to combat ignorance about Munich's darkest chapter. Although Hitler may not have spent much time in the Brown House the building remains important because it is where the Nazi Party operated for much of the 1930s.

Other places of interest nearby: 32, 33, 40, 42

42   An Unusual Shopping List

Maxvorstadt, a tour beginning with Otto Pachmayr
at Theresienstrasse 33
U2 Theresienstrasse, U3, U4, U5, U6 Odeonsplatz; Tram 27

Although the city high streets of Europe all look somewhat similar these days, being dominated by the same powerful brands, Munich has managed to retain a healthy number of independent specialist retailers. These bastions of local colour, manned by knowledgeable staff with a passion for their products, can be found not only in Old Town (Altstadt) but also in the suburbs, where this tour begins.

Those with a thirst should head to Otto Pachmayr's drinks company at Theresienstrasse 33. Mineral water manufacturers since 1867 the company still occupies its original premises, the walls of which are adorned with old advertisements and carbonating equipment. Pachmayr still manufacture their own brand of lemonade, as well as offering a soda siphon re-filling service.

A couple of roads away at Luisenstrasse 68 can be found Die Puppenstube, where since the early 1970s proprietor Gertraud Stadler has been restoring antique porcelain dolls in her workshop, as well as selling puppets to children, puppeteers, and collectors.

Staying in the Maxvorstadt but moving southwards we find Kremer Pigmente at Barer Strasse 46. A true specialist the shop stocks a thousand different powdered paint pigments,

Old carbonating equipment in Otto Pachmayr's drinks
company on Theresienstrasse

developed over thirty years for use by artists and art restorers.

Further south again and still in the suburbs is Tonnadel-Paradies Friedrich Gleich, tucked away in a courtyard at Landwehrstrasse 48. Another specialist it stocks every type of record player needle. The walls of this fascinating shop are lined with tiny compartments containing needles and other audiophonic components, as well as a collection of old radios and gramophones.

Moving into Old Town (Altstadt) now there is Romi Senn-Hodel at Kreuzstrasse 5, a tiny gallery of original Jugendstil and Art Deco stained and etched glass windows dating from the period 1880–1930. Everything on display is for sale having been restored in the company's workshop in Hausen.

A family of porcelain dolls in Die Puppenstube on Luisenstrasse

Eastwards, at Sendlinger Strasse 62, the Tea House is a tea drinker's paradise, boasting 750 sorts from around the world, including everything from classic First Flush Darjeelings to 25 year-old aromatic Formosan Oolongs. Quite different but no less specialised is Seilerei Kienmoser, along the road at Sendlingerstrasse 36. Well concealed inside a courtyard the shop specialises in rope.

In the southern reaches of Old Town can be found D'Original Oberbayerische Kräuter- & Wurzel-Sepp at Blumenstrasse 15. Founded in 1887 this traditional herbalist always has a small queue of customers awaiting both products and knowledge, its walls filled with containers of herbs for preparations and teas. Little to look at from the outside the shop can be identified by the smell of herbs wafting down the street.

Parallel to Blumenstrasse is Müllerstrasse where at number 39 can be found the antique toy specialist Spielart, a must for anyone nostalgic about their childhood with its tin toys, train sets, model soldiers, and vintage games.

An antique medicine cabinet in the Orlando Apotheke on Ledererstrasse

Our tour of unusual shops finishes in the very heart of Munich, amongst the big brand names and fast food restaurants. Geknöpft & Zugenäht Ludwig Beck at Burgstrasse 7 is a modern, magnificently well-stocked draper's shop filled with ribbons, buttons, yarns, and coloured threads. Similarly with a nod to the past is the Orlando Apotheke at Ledererstrasse 4, our final port of call. A seemingly normal chemist it reserves one of its windows for a tiny apothecary museum, including pill-making equipment, mortars and pestles, medicine bottles, and a wooden cabinet with draws labelled for different plant-based medicaments.

Other places of interest nearby: 32, 40, 41, 42

43 Drinking in the History

Maxvorstadt, Alter Simpl at Türkenstrasse 57
U3, U6 Universität; Tram 27

Two of Munich's most historic and storied watering holes are to be found in Maxvorstadt, just one road away from each other. The first, Alter Simpl at Türkenstrasse 57, opened its doors in 1903 and is where the city's intellectuals and creatives gathered to exchange ideas in the years before the First World War. Cabarettists, artists, writers, and thinkers were all habitués (see no. 48). Most of them were readers of the satirical magazine *Simplicissimus*, founded in 1896 by publisher Albert Langen (1869–1909), which explains why framed pages of *Simplicissimus* hang on the walls today. The magazine's distinctive logo of a dog breaking its chains represented the freedom of expression expounded within its pages (see page 229). By arrangement with the publisher an abbreviated version of the name, together with a suitably modified version of the logo (the dog now clutching a Champagne bottle), was adopted by the Alter Simpl for its own logo.

Alter Simpl was closed by the Nazis during the Second World War because of its patrons' obvious left wing tendencies. The building was severely damaged during air raids, during which its façade as well as the large skylight and stage that once existed to the rear were destroyed (these can still be made out in old photographs displayed in the back room). Fortunately, the damaged parts of the building were renewed in the 1950s, albeit in a far plainer style, and connected by a narrow corridor with ornate plastered cornices, which is all that remains of the original fabric. After serving for a while as a nightclub the Alter Simpl eventually re-emerged as a meeting place for a broad mix of people, from artists and students to business people and tourists. All congregate here for good conversation and no-nonsense food and drink.

Just around the corner from Alter Simpl, at Schellingstrasse 54, stands the venerable Schelling-Salon, a Viennese-style café-restaurant that has been in the same family since it opened in 1872. It was founded by Fridoline and Silvester Mehr, local entrepreneurs who also managed a canteen at the Ostbahnhof. With the Schelling-Salon they profited greatly from the horsedrawn trams carrying thirsty mourners to and from the Old North Cemetery (Alter Nordfriedhof) on nearby Arcisstrasse, which had opened in 1868. In 1911 Engelbert Mehr took over the business becoming the city's youngest restaurateur. He famously

refused to let Hitler use the premises for his early political activities, forcing the future dictator to relocate to the Osteria Bavaria restaurant, a few doors along at number 62 (today an Italian restaurant). Those that *were* allowed through the doors included the likes of Lenin, Bertolt Brecht, Rainer Maria Rilke, Wassily Kandinsky, Henrik Ibsen, and Franz Marc.

The Schelling-Salon was lucky to survive the Second World War intact since the editorial offices and printing works of the *Völkischer Beobachter* (Nationalist Observer), the official NSDAP newspaper, were closeby at Schellingstrasse 39–41, and were targetted specifically during Allied air raids. Many of the books produced by the party's Central Publishing House (Franz Eher Verlag) were printed here, including ten million copies of Hitler's *Mein Kampf*. The last issue was dated 30th April 1945, the day the Americans entered the city, and typically featured an article on the "successful" German defence of Munich, the 'Capital of the Nazi Movement'. The issue was never distributed.

The customers at the Schelling-Salon today transcend the boundaries of age, from students playing on the half dozen billiard tables, to elderly couples enjoying a romantic dinner.

Other places of interest nearby: 42, 44, 45, 46

44 Scars of Remembrance

Maxvorstadt, the 'Scars of Remembrance' memorial
at the corner of Ludwigstrasse and Schellingstrasse
U3, U6 Universität

Unlike Berlin, the urban fabric of Munich reveals very few physical traces of the widespread destruction wrought by the Second World War. This is partly because there were far fewer house-to-house battles than in the Reich capital, and partly because the damage inflicted by Allied air raids was subsequently erased through one of Germany's most conservative reconstruction plans. It is today difficult to imagine that by the end of the war nearly half of the city lay in ruins. In August 1945, following the American occuption, Munich's city council opted in favour of a tradition-orientated reconstruction, one which would preserve the old street-grid and historical city centre. Unlike other German cities, Munich had been little altered by industrialisation, and so its post-war reconstruction has preserved the cosy feel of the 19th century royal city.

With such wholesale reconstruction in mind, a Europe-wide art project called 'Scars of Remembrance' was undertaken in 1993–1995 by the political artists Andreas von Weizsäcker and Beate Passow. Their aim was not to erect traditional war memorials in central locations, but rather to create more modest installations from existing war-damaged fabric, often in less obvious places. As such, these artworks not only jolt passers-by into recalling the brutal conflict that occurred there, but through their novelty retain the power to surprise. Books pierced by bullets in a Czech town archive; artillery marks on a bridge in the Netherlands; bomb-damaged trees in Belgium; a bullet-strafed wall in a Viennese backstreet. All these poignant testaments to the world's greatest conflict have been screened with glass by the artists and labelled with the same phrase in the language of the respective country: 'Scars of Remembrance'.

Munich has three such 'Scars' (Wunden der Erinnerung). The first can be found at the corner of Ludwigstrasse and Schellingstrasse, in the wall of the library of the Ludwig-Maximilian University (Ludwig-Maximilians-Universität), where the White Rose resistance group distributed their anti-Nazi leaflets (see no. 45). The red bricks of the wall have clearly been shattered by a bomb blast or automatic gun fire.

A 'Scars of Remembrance' memorial on the corner of Ludwigstrasse and Schellingstrasse

Munich's second 'Scar' can be found on Arcisstrasse, outside the western façade of the Old Pinakothek (Alte Pinakothek), which itself carries significant scars from the Second World War. The bronze sculpture of a horse and tamer has been preserved complete with numerous un-repaired bullet-holes, again reminding the onlooker of the violence of war.

The third 'Scar' is at the Haus der Kunst (formerly the Haus der Deutschen Kunst) (1937) at Prinzregen-tenstrasse 1, the only art gallery erected during the period of the Third Reich, and financed by the likes of BMW, Volkswagen, Siemens, and Krupps (the original donor plaque is displayed in the entrance hall). Designed by Hitler's preferred architect Paul Ludwig Troost (1878–1934) the building typifies the repetitive, and poorly-proportioned neo-Classical style favoured by the Nazi Party. Spared serious damage from bombing raids it was pockmarked with gunfire and shrapnel holes, one of which has been left visible behind a pane of glass to the rear of the building.

It is interesting to compare the impact these installations have on passers-by with the city's more traditional memorials, such as the official Munich War Memorial (Münchener Kriegerdenkmal) on the eastern edge of the Hofgarten. Located in a sunken courtyard in front of the Bavarian State Chancellery (Bayerische Staatskanzlei), formerly the Army Museum, it was erected in 1924 to commemorate the victims of the First World War but is now dedicated to the dead of both World Wars. The memorial consists of the sculpture of a young

The 'Scars of Remembrance' memorial outside the Old Pinakothek (Alte Pinakothek) on Arcisstrasse

dead soldier covered by a huge stone inscribed "They will rise again". More modern is the memorial to the victims of National Socialism at the eastern end of Maximiliansplatz, which takes the form of a symbolic prison cell containing an eternal flame of freedom. Alongside it is a modest memorial to the Roma and Sinti victims of Nazi aggression.

Other places of interest nearby: 43, 45, 46

45 Memorials to the White Rose

Maxvorstadt, the White Rose Memorial Site (DenkStätte
Weiße Rose) in the Ludwig Maximilian University (Ludwig-
Maximilians-Universität) at Geschwister-Scholl-Platz 1
U3, U6 Universität

Most Munich visitors will know something about brave Sophie Scholl (1921–1943) and the White Rose *(Die Weiße Rose)*, a non-violent resistance group in Nazi Germany consisting of five students from the University of Munich together with their philosophy professor. The group was responsible for an anonymous leaflet campaign, lasting from June 1942 until their arrest in February 1943, calling for active opposition to the Hitler regime. After interrogation by the Gestapo they were sentenced to death and executed. Motivated primarily by their Christian values the members of the White Rose became icons of post-war Germany.

Fewer visitors will be aware of the excellent White Rose Memorial Site (DenkStätte Weiße Rose) at Geschwister-Scholl-Platz 1, a square named in honour of Sophie and her brother Hans. It is housed in a room beyond the atrium of the Ludwig Maximilian University (Ludwig-Maximilians-Universität), where one of the final chapters in the short life of Sophie Scholl was played out.

Before visiting the university a detour should first be made to Franz-Josef-Strasse 13, where a wall plaque marks the building in which the Scholls lived as students. It was from here on 18th February 1943, inspired by a recent anti-government protest in the congress hall of the Deutsches Museum on Museumsinsel, that they carried a suitcase full of leaflets to the university. Following in their footsteps the visitor will find an unusual memorial outside the main door of the university in the form of ceramic leaflets, incorporated into the cobblestones as if they had been dropped.

Once inside the university building the Scholls left stacks of leaflets in the hallways for students to find after their classes finished. With still some to spare Sophie took the last stack and flung it into the air over the atrium. Witnessing this the university porter notified the police and the siblings were arrested along with fellow White Rose member, Christoph Propst. Witnesses to the event remarked on how peaceably they went.

A visit to the nearby memorial room takes up the story now, with

A pavement memorial outside the Ludwig Maximilian University (Ludwig-Maximilians-Universität) remind the passer-by of brave Sophie Scholl

how the three were taken for interrogation to Gestapo headquarters in the former Wittelsbacher Palais at Brienner Strasse 20 (the building occupying the site today carries a plaque to this effect). Afterwards they were transferred for trial to the Palace of Justice (Justizpalast) on Priel-mayerstrasse, where they were found guilty and sentenced to death. They were executed by guillotine the same day in Stadelheim Prison at Stadelheimer Strasse 12, where a memorial can be found. Afterwards they were buried towards the rear of the adjacent Perlacher Forst Cemetery (Friedhof am Perlacher Forst). The location of the grave (73-1-18/19) is marked clearly on the plan at the main entrance.

In 1996 a black granite cube was placed at the northern edge of the Hofgarten in memory of Sophie Scholl and the White Rose, and is inscribed with some of their words.

Also interrogated in Gestapo headquarters on Brienner Strasse was Johann Georg Elser (1903–1945), who in 1939 made a solo attempt on Hitler's life in the Bürgerbräukeller on Rosenheimer Strasse (the site is today occupied by the Hilton Hotel and the Gasteig München cultural centre). Suspected by Goebbels of being part of a British Secret Service operation, Elser was arrested and imprisoned in Sachsenhausen concentration camp in readiness for a show trial. When Germany's defeat was imminent Hitler personally ordered Elser's execution in Dachau.

Other places of interest nearby: 43, 44, 46

46 An Innocent Address?

Maxvorstadt, former Nazi Party headquarters at
Schellingstrasse 50
U2 Theresienstrasse, U3, U6 Universität; Tram 27

There are many unremarkable buildings in Munich that played an important part in the rise of the Nazi Party. Some are private addresses, such as the apartment house at Knöbelstrasse 38 where SS Chief Heinrich Himmler was born, and the villa at Zuccalistrasse 4 where head of the SS Security Service Reinhard Heydrich lived. Others are public buildings, for example Karolinenplatz 2, from where Gertrud Scholtz-Klink's National Socialist Women's League urged German women to breed for the Führer. These and many similar addresses are unmarked today but it would be dangerous to forget them entirely. As the philosopher George Santayana (1863–1952) once famously said, "Those who cannot remember the past, are condemned to repeat it".

Perhaps the most important of these hidden addresses is Schellingstrasse 50, since it was here that the Nazi Party had its headquarters from 1925 until 1931. Even before moving to Schellingstrasse, however, the nascent party had occupied two other easily-forgotten addresses in Munich. The first was a small rented room in the former Sterneckerbräu beer hall at Tal 54 (now number 38); it was used by the German Workers' Party (Deutsche Arbeiterpartei or DAP) after Adolf Hitler joined their ranks in late 1919 (the premises are now shops) (see no. 12). In January 1920 the party moved headquarters to Corneliusstrasse 12, where a month later it was re-named the National Socialist German Workers' Party (Nationalsozialistische Deutsche Arbeiterpartei or NSDAP). Membership of the Nazi Party increased dramatically during this time and in November 1923 they attempted to oust the government in Munich in the face of ruinous inflation brought on by war reparations.

Hitler's so-called Beer Hall Putsch failed to provoke the nationwide anti-government revolt he had hoped for: instead, the Nazi party was declared temporarily illegal, its offices on Corneliusstrasse closed down (and subsequently demolished), and Hitler imprisoned. Despite being found guilty of high treason, a crime punishable by death, Hitler was released in December 1924 and immediately set about securing new premises for his party. It was now that Hitler's personal photographer Heinrich Hoffmann (1885–1957) offered the party a dozen rooms in his studio at the back of Schellingstrasse 50. Today a residential building, yet still marked with a battered stone eagle above the doorway, it was here that Hoffmann took many studio pictures of Hitler perfecting his demagogic style. It was through Hoffmann that Hitler was introduced to the seventeen-year old Eva Braun, who was employed as a studio assistant.

The Nazi Party was relaunched in February 1925 at the Bürgerbräukeller on Rosenheimer Strasse, from where the failed Putsch had begun in 1923. As membership grew once again the party began organising itself across Germany, and several new affiliated organisations opened offices at Schellingstrasse 50. These included the *Sturmabteilung* (SA or Stormtroopers), the *Schutzstaffel* (SS), and the *Hitlerjugend* (Hitler Youth).

This innocent-looking building on Schellingstrasse was once the headquarters of the Nazi Party

Then in September 1930 the Nazi Party received 18.3% of the votes in the Reichstag elections making it the country's second most powerful political party. The following year the Nazi Party relocated once more, this time to the Brown House on Brienner Strasse, where Hitler became Chancellor of Germany (see no. 41).

Other places of interest nearby: 43, 44, 45

47 Schwabing's Green Oasis

Maxvorstadt, the Old North Cemetery
(Alter Nordfriedhof) at Arcisstrasse 45
U2 Josephsplatz

As Munich's population grew during the second half of the 19th century, so the need for more burial grounds increased too. To create extra building space and improve sanitation, old city centre cemeteries were cleared and replaced by larger ones out in the suburbs. Munich today has 29 cemeteries of varying sizes, many of them having been laid out by city architects such as Arnold Zenetti (1824–1891) and Hans Grässel (1860–1939).

Typical for the time was Zenetti's Old North Cemetery (Alter Nordfriedhof) on Arcisstrasse, created between 1866 and 1868 with room for 7000 Catholic and Protestant grave plots. In 1933, however, Hitler's architects planned to connect Isabellastrasse and Luisenstrasse, which terminated either side of the cemetery, in order to create a long avenue running up from the Nazi forum on Königsplatz (see no. 40). Indeed, burials were prohibited after 1939 because Hitler also wanted to build himself a new townhouse here.

Severely damaged during Allied air raids the Old North Cemetery never re-opened. Hitler's plans never came to fruition and it was subsequently converted into an unusual public park, which today provides an oasis of green in busy Schwabing. Behind the high brick perimeter walls visitors might be surprised to see children playing happily among the headstones, groups of relxed picnickers, sunbathers seeking shade beneath the trees, and joggers doing their rounds. Although by 1939 only 800 graves had been occupied many of them were marked with ornately decorated monuments, which are still well worth looking at. Zenetti himself, however, whose architectural legacy also included several Munich hospitals, the cattle market, and part of the sewer system, is ironically not buried here but rather in the Old South Cemetery (Alter Südfriedhof) on Thalkirchner Strasse, which the Old North Cemetery was created to replace (see no. 68).

A fine example of a cemetery by Hans Grässel, who in 1914 was awarded a civil class *Pour le Mérite* for his efforts, can be found farther out of the city on Ungererstrasse. The North Cemetery (Nordfriedhof) is far larger than Zenetti's cemetery, and more formal in its design. Enclosed by a low stone wall it is laid out symmetrically, with a grid of

Art and nature in the Old North Cemetery (Alter Nordfriedhof) on Arcisstrasse

pathways lined by large, shade-giving trees. It typifies the formal 'City of the Dead' concept, against which Grässel would later rebel with his naturalistic Waldfriedhof ('Forest Cemetery') (see no. 69). The graves, which tend to be less elaborately marked than those in the Old North Cemetery, include several Third Reich-era incumbents, notably Traudl Junge (1920–2002), who as a young secretary took down Hitler's last will and testament in the Berlin *Führerbunker* before his suicide, Eduard Dietl (1890–1944), one of Hitler's favourite generals, who was the first soldier to receive the oakleaf cluster *(Eichenlaub)* to his Iron Cross for bravery, Paul Ludwig Troost (1878–1934), Hitler's preferred architect in Munich (although the family name has been erased from the gravestone), and Max Wünsche (1915–1995), a member of the Leib-standarte SS Adolf Hitler, the dictator's personal bodyguard regiment.

It is interesting to note that in May 1945 the US Army created a temporary internment camp at the North Cemetery to hold 114 high-ranking Nazis awaiting trial. Among the prisoners were Hitler's personal photographer Heinrich Hoffmann, Munich's former mayor Karl Fiehler, and NSDAP regional leader Karl Lederer. In late 1948, with the dena-zification process completed, the camp was dissolved and all trace removed. All quiet today, a noticeboard in the cemetery lists more than fifty songbirds that can be heard here.

Other places of interest nearby: 46, 48

48 When Munich Shone

Schwabing-West, former artists' apartments at
Ainmillerstrasse 32, 34, and 36
U3, U6 Giselastrasse; Tram 27; Bus 53

It is sometimes difficult to grasp that a few short decades before Hitler dominated Munich's political and cultural stage the city had been an important centre for freethinking Modernism. As a means of coming to terms with the increasingly secularised, industrialised and urbanised nature of late 19th century society, certain Munich artists and writers turned away from prevailing creative forms, in favour of some highly original practices of their own.

The geographical focus for this new movement was the suburb of Schwabing, a former village older than Munich itself, which was incorporated into the city in 1891. Schwabing had already been linked physically to Munich with the construction of Ludwigstrasse during the reign of Ludwig I, King of Bavaria (1825–1845). Stretching northwards from the Feldherrnhalle to the Siegestor it was lined with monumental institutions, including the Ludwig Maximilian University (Ludwig-Maximilians-Universität) (1840), the Bavarian State Library (Bayerische Staatsbibliothek) (1843), and the Academy of Fine Arts (Akademie der Bildenden Künste) (1884). Between the 1890s and 1914 the area became popular not only with students and academics but also with artists, resulting in a brief golden age for the city. It was a time when as Thomas Mann wrote in his novella *Gladius Dei* (1902) "München leuchtete" (Munich shone).

Walking around the area now it is clear that the days of *la vie bohème* are long gone, the writers and artists having since moved away to cheaper areas such as Haidhausen. However, there are still certain addresses where with a little imagination the ghosts still linger, such as the Café Altschwabing at Schellingstrasse 56, the Schelling-Salon at Schellingstrasse 54, and the Alter Simpl at Türkenstrasse 57 (see nos. 25 & 43). For the purposes of this chapter we will focus on just one street, Ainmillerstrasse, where three of Schwabing's most creative inhabitants lived and worked a century ago.

The first, the artist Paul Klee (1879–1940), lived at Ainmillerstrasse 32. Rather than a traditional wall plaque, the site is memorialised by the artist's name being painted on the pavement, together with the dates he lived here (1906–1921). Klee, who had two studios in Schwabing, was

A painted sign on Ainmillerstrasse marks the former home of the artist Paul Klee

not only a painter, but also an undogmatic teacher and an inspiring author on art. After leaving Munich he held noteworthy exhibitions in Paris and New York.

Next door at number 34 a bronze plaque identifies where the Poet Rainer Maria Rilke (1875–1926) lived between 1918 and 1919. Together with other talented local writers, such as playwright Frank Wedekind (1864–1918) and novelist Thomas Mann (1875–1955), who wrote his first great novel *Buddenbrooks* in Schwabing, Rilke contributed to the satirical, anti-authoritarian weekly magazine *Simplicissimus*. Old copies can still be found in the fascinating antiquarian bookshops of Maxvorstadt, for example Antiquariat Hammerstein at Türkenstrasse 37, Heinrich Hauser at Schellingstrasse 17, and Antiquariat J. Kitzinger at Schellingstrasse 25. Incidentally, the doomed English poet Rupert Brooke (1887–1915) was drawn to Munich in early 1911 in order to translate the works of Wedekind into English.

The third former incumbent of Aimillerstrasse is artist Wassily Kandinsky (1866–1944), who between 1908 and 1914 lived at number 36, together with the Expressionist painter Gabriele Münter (1877–1962). Again a bronze plaque now marks the spot. Initially influenced by the Impressionists, Russian-born Kandinsky turned later to pure

Old copies of Simplicissimus adorn the window of Antiquariat Hammerstein on Türkenstrasse

and vigorous abstraction, using bright colours and geometric shapes to elicit an emotional response. In 1911 he established the group *Der Blaue Reiter* (The Blue Rider) together with fellow Expressionist Franz Marc (1880–1916), who lived at Schellingstrasse 33. The group, which also included Paul Klee, Gabriele Münter, Marianne von Werefkin (1860–1938), Alfred Kubin (1877–1959), Alexej Jawlensky (1864–1941) and August Macke (1887–1914), were encouraged by the artistic unshackling of the *Jugendstil* movement, which was transforming the appearance of certain streets in the area (see no. 81).

It was Kandinsky who put Schwabing's cultural importance into a broader context when he described the suburb as "a spiritual island in the great world, in Germany, mostly in Munich itself". That spirituality was inevitably dimmed after the First World War.

Other places of interest nearby: 47, 81

49 Climbing Rubble Mountains

Schwabing-West, the Luitpoldhügel in Luitpoldpark
U2, U3 Scheidplatz; Tram 12

Walking around central Munich today one could be forgiven for thinking that the city escaped significant destruction during the Allied air raids of the Second World War. This is an illusion. More than seventy air raids were made on Munich, not only because it was the 'Capital of the Nazi Movement' (Haupstadt der Bewegung), but also because it was an important centre for the German armaments industry (see no. 72). When the Americans entered the city on 30th April 1945 they found almost half of the city in ruins: 3.5 million incendiary and explosive bombs had destroyed 81500 homes leaving 300 000 people homeless. In August, however, the new city council voted for a reconstruction of the inner city in "its old form". This resulted in the old façades being retained, and new structures built behind them. Thus, Munich looks today much as it did a century ago.

Before work could begin, however, an estimated five million cubic metres of rubble had to be cleared from the streets. As in Berlin and other German cities, the task of sifting through the rubble and retaining anything reuseable fell initially to women; by the end of the war Munich's population had been reduced by about 40000, and of those remaining the fittest were female (most men were either dead, wounded, or else in captivity). Aged between 15 and 65 they were conscripted as so-called 'Rubble Women' *(Trümmerfrauen)* to salvage bricks, timbers, and girders for reuse. A common sight on the streets until the 1950s they were at first paid with little more than handfuls of potatoes but eventually received food rations.

It soon became clear that the sheer volume of rubble was too large to process. The solution was to dump it at selected locations around the city and in so doing create rubble mountains *(Trümmerberge)*, which would later be landscaped. In a flat city such as Munich the existence of these geographical anomalies is today all too apparent.

Of the two largest rubble mountains in Munich, the 37 metre-high Luitpoldhügel is perhaps the more interesting. Concealed beneath a thin layer of earth and grass lie approximately one million cubic metres of rubble. At its highest point, reached by a series of paths winding through the trees, there stands a cross with the following inscription: "Pray and remember those who died under the mountains of rubble." A fine over-

A simple cross stands at the summit of the Luitpoldhügel, a manmade rubble mountain

view of the city skyline is available from the nearby viewing platform.

To the south of the hill is the peaceful English-style Luitpold-Park, with its main entrance on Karl-Theodor-Strasse. Here stands a tall obelisk inscribed as follows: "This column and grove of ninety lime trees are to commemorate the gratitude felt by the city of Munich on the 12th March 1911, the ninetieth year in the life of His Royal Highness, the Prince Regent Luitpold of Bavaria, then in the 25th year of his reign." Popular with the people Luitpold had deposed his nephew King Ludwig II (after he was declared insane in 1886) and then ruled as regent for his mentally ill nephew Otto I, King of Bavaria (1886–1913). Today, the park contains the Bamberger Haus, a pavilion containing a café and gallery, which was itself damaged in the war and subsequently restored. There is also a charming wayside shrine at the corner of Karl-Theodor-Strasse and Brunnerstrasse, its icon of Mary and Jesus adorned with candles and artificial roses.

Immediately west of Luitpoldpark is Olympiapark, where Munich's other great rubble mountain stands. The Olympiaberg is even larger than the Luitpoldhügel and is said to also contain rubble extracted during the construction of the city's U-Bahn system. Covering 87 hectares it is more open than the Luitpoldhügel and has been completely landscaped with paths, patches of woodland, and grassy slopes. From the top there is a magnificent vista of the former Olympic facilities below, as well as the site of the annual open-air Tollwood music festival, which was inaugurated in 1988.

50 A Private Museum for Contemporary Art

Bogenhausen, the Goetz Collection (Sammlung Goetz)
at Oberföhringer Strasse 103 (note: this private collection
is open by appointment only, tel. 0049-89-9593969-0,
www.sammlung-goetz.de)
U4 Richard-Strauss-Strasse then Bus 188 to Bürgerpark
Oberföhring

Munich is renowned for the wide-ranging subject matter of its many fine art collections. They are housed in an equally eclectic array of gallery buildings, constructed in styles ranging from neo-Classical (Glyptothek, Schack-Galerie, and Haus der Kunst) and neo-Renaissance (Alte Pinakothek), through to Italianate (Lenbachhaus Art Gallery) and postmodern (Neue Pinakothek and Pinakothek der Moderne). Probably the most unusual of all, however, is the Goetz Collection (Sammlung Goetz), a privately-owned museum of contemporary art that is tucked away in the residential district of Oberföhring, far from the cultural heart of central Munich.

The stunning and frankly unexpected building that houses the Goetz Collection was completed in 1993 to a design by the Swiss architectural firm of Jacques Herzog and Pierre de Meuron, renowned for their work at London's Tate Museum of Modern Art, as well as Munich's own Allianz Arena. Working together with art collector Ingvild Goetz (b. 1941), the architects conjured up a simple but intriguing minimalist construction of two identically-sized rectangular boxes stacked on top of one another, facing away from the nearby road towards a garden. The upper portions of the boxes are formed by a band of opaline-white, translucent glass. These bands imbue the building with an intriguing physical lightness.

The upper box is birch wood, whereas the lower one is concrete, sunk into the ground so as to leave only its glazed zone visible. This was necessary because building regulations restricted the height and footprint of the building.

From the outside the upper box appears to be floating without suitable structural support. In reality, it is supported invisibly by a slender U-shaped concrete support at either end of the building, one of which contains the staircase connecting both exhibition floors. Adjacent to the staircase, and seemingly suspended at ground floor level, is a com-

This striking building houses the Goetz Collection (Sammlung Goetz), a museum of contemporary art in Oberföhring

bined entrance hall, office, and library, matched at the other end of the building by a technical and depot room.

Of the exhibition spaces themselves, the upper floor contains three, almost square rooms. The high interior walls are finished ascetically with natural white plaster, which helps concentrate the viewer's attention on the exhibits themselves. The glass bands, meanwhile, create a soft and even distribution of glare-free daylight, whilst remaining high enough to prohibit any distracting view of the outside world. The basement follows similar principles yet appears much bigger than its modest 24.2 by 8 metre plan, affording the maximum number of viewpoints from which to view the exhibits. The slight feeling of disorientation here is purely intentional and aimed at dissassociating the viewer from the familiar world outside.

The collection itself encompasses contemporary art in all media, from the 1960s up to the present, including drawings, paintings, graphics, sculptures, and photographs, video and film work, room-sized installations, and multi-channel projections. Twice a year Goetz exhibits works taken from her own collection, by artists such as Matthew Barney, Mike Kelley, and Thomas Zipp. Goetz has been quoted as saying: "I always collect the younger generation on principle." Her exhibitions predominantly focus on the development of individual creative expression, helping reinforce her appointed aim of stressing the autonomy and creative strength of art, and of promoting artists who place our social reality in question. She thus uses contemporary art to correct preconceived thoughts and views, both aesthetically and politically, believing that "the collector that buys works which personally jar and engage him creates, through his collection, a new total work of art." No stranger to controversy Goetz had her residence permit revoked in Zurich in 1969 after publicly criticising Switzerland's supplying of arms to Angola.

In 2000 the Munich-based architect Wolfgang Brune, in consultation with Herzog and de Meuron, converted and extended a former storage area adjacent to the museum to create a media zone called BASE103. Connected to the main building by a felt-lined passage it is used specifically for the museum's film inventory.

Parallel to the subject matter of the exhibitons is the Goetz Collection's extensive library of around 6000 volumes, focussing on the art of the second half of the 20th century and the early years of the 21st. It is an invaluable resource for students fortunate enough to undertake research in this unique building.

51 Where Thomas Mann Lived

Bogenhausen, the Thomas Mann Villa at Poschingerstrasse 1
(note: the villa is not open to the public)
Tram 16, 18 or Bus 54 to Herkomerplatz, then walk down
Gustl-Waldau-Steig onto Poschingerstrasse

Unlike the western bank of Munich's River Isar, which is lined with retaining walls and busy roads, the eastern shore is gently sloping, with dense woodland concealing attractive old buildings. One of these is the so-called Thomas Mann Villa at Poschingerstrasse 1, where the author lived between 1914 and 1933. Recently reconstructed, the history of the villa speaks eloquently not only of Mann himself, but also of the times in which he lived.

Thomas Mann (1875–1955) was born in 1875 in Lübeck the second son of a grain merchant. Following his father's death in 1891 the family relocated to the Munich suburb of Schwabing, where Mann worked briefly for an insurance company, before entering university to study literature and art. During this period he also wrote for the satirical magazine *Simplicissimus* (see no. 48). Thereafter Mann devoted himself exlusively to writing and in 1901 aged just twenty-five he published his first major novel, *Buddenbrooks*. Before being banned and burned by Hitler the book sold over a million copies in Germany alone. Its success, together with that of succeeding works such as *Der Tod in Venedig (Death in Venice)*, enabled Mann to purchase his newly-built riverside villa, where he lived with his wife Katia and their six children. Three storeys high, with a library and French windows opening onto a large garden, it was every inch the typical German bourgeois cultured home.

Mann's second great novel, *Der Zauberberg (The Magic Mountain)*, was published in 1924, and in 1929 he was awarded the Nobel Prize for literature. The first volume of his tetralogy *Joseph und seine Brüder (Joseph and his Brothers)* followed in 1933, the same year that he exiled himself to Switzerland in response to Hitler becoming chancellor. From there he moved in 1938 to America, where he would eventually write such works as *Doktor Faustus (Doctor Faustus)* and *Der Erwählte (The Holy Sinner)*. Ostracised in the city he once lauded for its freedom, Mann looked on as his

Thomas-Mann-Allee is named
in honour of the famous author

The Thomas Mann Villa near the river in Bogenhausen has been re-built

villa was expropriated without compensation and used by the SS for its maternity home *(Lebensborn)* programme. Damaged during the Second World War the ruins were eventually restituted back to Mann in 1948. He revisited Germany one last time in 1949 and then returned to Switzerland from where he sold the villa in 1952.

Between 1953 and 2002 another building was erected on the site of Mann's villa but in 2006 this was torn down. In its place a new building was constructed privately, which bears the outward appearance of Mann's original villa. The riverside road was also re-named Thomas-Mann-Allee in the author's honour.

Of Thomas Mann's six children, all of whom became literary and artistic figures in their own right, Erika (1905–1969) and Klaus (1906–1949) caused the greatest stir. In 1933 they founded the anti-Fascist cabaret *Die Pfeffermühle* (The Peppermill) in a Munich cellar, reopening it in America after fleeing there to avoid prosecution.

Thomas-Mann-Allee continues northwards as Heinrich-Mann-Allee, in honour of Thomas Mann's older brother. Heinrich Mann (1871–1950) was exiled from Nazi Germany in 1933 because of his literary attacks on the authoritarian stance of Wilhelmine German society. He is remembered for the adaptation of his novel *Professor Unrat* into the film *Der Blaue Engel (The Blue Angel)* (1930) starring Marlene Dietrich.

Other places of interest nearby: 52

52   Three Brave Men of God

Bogenhausen, memorial to Alfred Delp at the Church of
St. George (Kirche St. Georg) at Bogenhausener Kirchplatz 1
U4, U5 Max-Weber-Platz, then Tram 16 to Sternwartstrasse

The names of Sophie and Hans Scholl, together with the other members of the White Rose *(Die Weiße Rose)* student resistance movement,
usually spring to mind when thinking of those who protested against
the Nazi regime in Munich (see no. 45). However, there were others too,
notably three brave men whose Christian values forced them to speak
out.

The first was the Jesuit priest Alfred Delp (1907–1945), who studied
philosophy and theology in Munich and was ordained in 1937. In 1941
he became rector of the charming Late Baroque (Rococo) Church of St.
George (Kirche St. Georg) on Bogenhausener Kirchplatz, from where he
preached against the Nazis. His private rooms soon became a meeting
place for fellow sympathisers. In 1942 he was introduced to the Kreisau
Circle (Kreisauer Kreis), a political resistance group formed around Hel-
muth James Graf von Moltke (1907–1945), after whose estate in Silesia
the group was named. Together they created a vision of a German con-
stitution based upon Christian social principles, and from 1943 onwards
they focussed on active regime change. After von Moltke was arrested
the group gravitated towards Claus Schenk Graf von Stauffenberg
(1907–1944), who very nearly succeeded in killing Hitler with a briefcase
bomb on 20th July 1944. Eight days later Delp was arrested and found
guilty of high treason. On 2nd February 1945 he was executed in Berlin's
notorious Plötzensee prison, his last words whispered to the prison's
chaplain being, "In half an hour, I'll know more than you do." Today,
there is an epitaph to Alfred Delp on the west façade of the Church of
St. George, as well as a memorial outside the church gate. Numerous
schools across Germany are also named in his honour.

Another brave Jesuit priest was Rupert Mayer (1876–1945), who
spoke out against the Nazis in the Church of St. Michael (Michaelskirche) at Neuhauser Strasse 6 (see no. 6). Mayer was a well-known face
in Munich after the First World War having been the first battlefield
chaplain to be awarded the Iron Cross for bravery. His first anti-Nazi
outburst came in 1923 during an NSDAP party meeting at the Bürger-
bräu beer hall. The topic was "Can a Catholic be a National Socialist?"
and Mayer stunned the audience by saying: "You have applauded me

too soon, because I will tell you clearly that a German Catholic can never be a National Socialist." Despite being banned from his pulpit by the Nazis in 1936 Mayer continued to speak out and was sentenced to several months imprisonment. In 1939 he was sent to the Sachsenhausen concentration camp near Berlin, and spent the rest of the war under house arrest at Ettal Monastery, south of Munich. The Nazis kept him alive because they feared making a martyr out of him. The strain on the priest was too much, however, and he suffered a fatal stroke shortly after the war whilst giving a sermon back in his old church. Like Delp, several schools were named after him, and in 1987 he was beatified by Pope John Paul II. His tomb can be found in the lower church of the Bürgersaalkirche at Neuhauser Strasse 14, alongside a bronze bust worn smooth by the touch of visiting pilgrims.

A memorial to the priest Alfred Delp outside the Church of St. George (Kirche St. Georg) in Bogenhausen

A third man of courage was the journalist Fritz Gerlich (1883–1934). A convert to Catholicism he was editor-in-chief between 1920 and 1928 of the newspaper *Münchner Neueste Nachrichten*, in which he voiced openly his opposition to Nazism on Christian grounds. This he continued to do from 1930 onwards in the pages of *Der Gerade Weg* (The Straight Path), a Catholic weekly. After Hitler became Chancellor in 1933 Gerlich was arrested and sent to the concentration camp at Dachau, where he was executed during the Night of the Long Knives, a far-reaching purge by the Nazis of their political opponents. A memorial plaque has been erected at the corner of Sendlinger Strasse and Färbergraben, where Gerlich was arrested, by the *Süddeutsche Zeitung*, which superceded the *Münchner Neueste Nachrichten* in October 1945.

Other places of interest nearby: 51, 53

53 Geli, Eva and Unity

Bogenhausen, Adolf Hitler's former apartment at
Prinzregentenplatz 16
U4 Prinzregentenplatz; Bus 54

A tour of Munich addresses where the dictator Adolf Hitler once resid-
ed makes for an chilling thematic tour, made all the more interesting
by incorporating some details of three women who touched his life here
during the 1920s and 30s.

Our journey begins at Schleissheimer Strasse 34, where Hitler first
lived after arriving in Munich from Vienna in May 1913; it was here
that he volunteered for the Bavarian Army in August 1914 (a plaque
recording his time here was removed in 1945). After the First World
War Hitler returned to Munich, where from 1918 until 1920 he lived in
his regimental barracks at Lothstrasse 29; during this time he joined
the German Workers' Party (Deutsche Arbeiterpartei or DAP), which
in 1920 became the National Socialist German Workers' Party (Nationalsozialistische Deutsche Arbeiterpartei or NSDAP). After being dis-
charged from the army in March 1920 Hitler moved to Thierschstrasse
41, where he lived in the first floor flat of his landlady until 1929 (again
a wall plaque once existed here). During this period he orchestrated the
Beer Hall Putsch of 1923 (for which he was imprisoned), wrote *Mein
Kampf*, and in 1925 relaunched the NSDAP, or Nazi Party.

Hitler's last Munich residence, from 1929 until his death in 1945,
was a 9-bedroom apartment on the second floor at Prinzregentenplatz
16. Today a police station, the ground floor once contained quarters for
Hitler's SS guards, whilst the first floor was given over to guest rooms;
in the basement were kitchens together with an extensive air raid shelter installed in 1942. Of the many episodes that took place here during
Hitler's time, including Mussolini's visit in 1937 and Neville Chamber-
lain's in 1938, the strangest undoubtedly concerns Hitler's half-niece,
'Geli' Raubal.

Angelika Maria Raubal (1908–1931) arrived in Munich in 1927 to
study medicine, living in a pension that stood at Königinstrasse 43.
Earlier the same year her widowed mother, Hitler's half-sister, had
become housekeeper at the Berghof, Hitler's mountain retreat near
Berchtesgaden. After meeting Raubal there Hitler became entranced
by her carefree manner and the pair began accompanying each other
in Munich. Rumours of an affair soon began to circulate. From August

Adolf Hitler's former apartment on Prinzregentenplatz is now a police station

1928 to November 1929 Hitler rented an apartment for Raubal next to his own on Thierschstrasse, after which he installed her in his new residence on Prinzregentenplatz. On 19th September 1931, whilst Hitler was on his way to Hamburg, Raubal was found dead in her room at the back of the building, with Hitler's Walther pistol at her side. Still a mystery today, numerous theories for her death exist, from suicide over Hitler's jealous possessiveness and his forbidding her to visit Vienna, to murder on Hitler's orders because she had become pregnant by him and was a dangerous embarrassment.

It is possible that Raubal committed suicide because Hitler, or 'Uncle Alf' as she called him, had begun to direct his affections towards the seventeen-year-old Eva Braun (1912–1945). Born in her family's Munich home at Isabellastrasse 45, Braun became Hitler's mistress for twelve years and eventually his wife for one day. With little interest in politics and never a Nazi Party member she remained quite unknown to those outside Hitler's inner circle until after the war. Braun first met Hitler in October 1929, whilst working as a secretary to Heinrich Hoffmann, Hitler's official photographer, whose shop was at Schellingstrasse 50 (see no. 46).

It is often forgotten that Braun's eventual suicide with Hitler in the Berlin *Führerbunker* was her third attempt at taking her own life. The first was in November 1932, when she was found with a bullet in her neck in the family apartment at Hohenzollernstrasse 93. A desperate attempt to gain Hitler's undivided attention she tried again in May 1935, this time with an overdose of sleeping pills. To avoid any

The home of Eva Braun from 1936 until her death in Berlin in 1945

further scandal Hitler rented a flat for her at Widenmayerstrasse 42, where she lived from August 1935 until March 1936, when he used proceeds from the sale of Hoffmann's publicity photos to buy her a villa at Wasserburger Strasse 12 (now Delpstrasse). One of the first houses in Munich to contain a television set it remained in Braun's possession until 1945.

Another female admirer to come within Hitler's sphere was the aristocratic Englishwoman Unity Valkyrie Mitford (1914–1948), who arrived in Munich in 1934 to attend a finishing school at Königinstrasse 121. Intrigued by her middle name, her penchant for black clothes, and the fact that she had allegedly been conceived in the town of Swastika, Ontario, where her aristocratic family had gold mines, Hitler invited her to his table at the Osteria Bavaria at Schellingstrasse 62. Many meetings followed and Hitler even provided her with an apartment at Agnesstrasse 26. In April 1935 Mitford instigated a lunch at Hitler's house on Prinzregentenplatz with Sir Oswald Mosley, the leader of the British Union of Fascists. Mitford's sister, Diana, would marry Mosley in 1936 in the Berlin home of Nazi propaganda minister, Joseph Goebbels, with Hitler in attendance.

Unity Mitford often stressed to Hitler the need for good relations between their two countries and was deeply upset when Britain was forced into declaring war on Germany. As a result she shot herself in the head in the Englischer Garten. Severely wounded she was hospitalised on Hitler's orders in a clinic at Nussbaumstrasse 20, where she remained in a coma despite Hitler visiting twice. Returned to England in 1940 she never fully recovered and died of meningitis in 1948.

Other places of interest nearby: 52, 54

54 Bombproof Munich

Bogenhausen, the former civilian air raid shelter
on Prinzregentenstrasse
U4 Prinzregentenplatz; Bus 54

On the morning of 5th August 1933 sirens and bells were sounded across Munich heralding a simulated air raid during which a squadron of low-flying aircraft dropped a payload of harmless paper bombs. At the subsequent debriefing it was emphasised that a real air raid would have destroyed much of the inner city, together with many of its inhabitants.

Seven years later, in May 1940, British bomber command began its own aerial war on Germany by bombing the Ruhr valley. In June the same year Munich was attacked because of its importance to the German armaments industry (see no. 72). Although the city was initially spared heavy bombardment, since it lay at the limit of the Allied bombers' range, the perceived threat prompted a crash air raid shelter-building programme across Germany. Requiring an estimated 200 million cubic metres of concrete it was the largest building project in history.

In 1942 the British started using longer-range aircraft, and from spring 1944 American bombers regularly attacked Munich during the day, while the British bombers continued after dark. With access to their own personal bunkers top-ranking Nazi officials had little need to worry during such raids (see no. 64). Everybody else, however, had to take their chances in one of the city's thirty or so overcrowded civilian air raid shelters *(Luftschutzräume)*. Victim to more than seventy raids, on the night of 25th April alone 870 000

The former civilian air-raid shelter on Prinzregentenstrasse

incendiary devices were dropped on Munich, creating a fire that could be seen from as far away as the Alps.

By the end of the war Munich's air raid shelters remained unharmed amidst the smouldering rubble of the city, and most of them are still standing today. A typical example can be found at the corner of Blumenstrasse and Corneliusstrasse, in the southern part of Old Town (Altstadt). With walls 1.3 metres thick and a roof two metres thick this square-shaped shelter could hold 750 people. It is interesting to note that it is decorated with unnecessary architectural details, including a balustraded entrance and a red-tiled roof. This made it not only difficult to identify from the air, but also served to reassure the local populace that all was well.

Similar examples to the Blumenstrasse shelter can be seen at Müllerstrasse 7, Quellenstrasse 2, the corner of Ungererstrasse and Crailsheimstrasse, and on Albert-Beyerle-Platz. An equally sturdy, octagonal variant stands on Anhalter Platz, Schleissheimer Strasse, Sonnwendjochstrasse 54a, and in front of the S-Bahn station at Allach (see no. 72).

Most unusual is a row of apartments terminated by square-shaped air raid shelters on Prinzregentenstrasse, filling the north side of the street between Wilhelm-Tell-Strasse and Brucknerstrasse. This complex was constructed by the National Socialists as a housing experiment in preparation for their unrealised 'Neue Südstadt' estate of 14 500 apartments, which they planned to build between Ramersdorf and Giesing. It remains the only housing complex completed as part of Hitler's projected large-scale re-development of Munich.

After the war some of Munich's shelters were used as hostels for displaced persons, although most were eventually abandoned or else adapted as cold stores, archives and equipment rooms because of their constant internal temperatures. An exception is the octagonal shelter at the corner of Claude-Lorrain-Strasse and Sachsenstrasse, which has been very successfully converted into apartments.

The word *Bunker*, incidentally, only entered general parlance in Autumn 1940, and correctly describes a strengthened military position and *not* a civilian shelter. The smallest bunker held just a couple of men and was known as a *Kugelbunker* because of its spherical shape: a fine example can be seen in the courtyard of the Münchner Stadtmuseum (Munich City Museum) on St.-Jakobs-Platz.

A so-called Kugelbunker in the Münchner Stadtmuseum (Munich City Museum)
on St.-Jakobs-Platz

Munich contains very few reminders of the Cold War. At Hessstrasse 120, however, on
the western border of Schwabing, there is a former civilian shelter constructed to support more than 3000 people in the event of a nuclear attack. Maintained until the late
1990s the shelter lies deep underground and offered 12000 square metres of living
space. Later converted to office space for the Emergency Disaster Response Centre it
is today also used by the city's fire service.

Other places of interest nearby: 52, 53

55 Homage to the Humble Potato

Berg am Laim, the Potato Museum (Kartoffelmuseum) in the
OTEC-Haus at Grafinger Strasse 2
S1, S2, S3, S4, S6, S7, S8 Ostbahnhof; U5 Ostbahnhof

"In the morning round, at noon mashed and in the evening cut – that is the way it should be – this is healthy", noted the great German poet Goethe about the humble potato. It seems fitting therefore that a German city should be home to a Potato Museum (Kartoffelmuseum), just around the corner from Munich's Ostbahnhof at Grafinger Strasse 2. It is the world's only museum devoted exclusively to the social, political, and artistic impact of this important vegetable. Opened in 1996, the year before the 350th anniversary of the introduction of the potato into Germany, it is a private collection managed under the auspices of the Otto Eckart Foundation (Stiftung Otto Eckart), Eckart being the former chief of Pfanni Werke, a potato products company.

Munich is home to Europe's only Potato Museum
(Kartoffelmuseum)

The museum very cleverly takes what could be seen as a dull subject and breaks it down into eight very digestible thematic sections, beginning in the first room with the history of the potato, from being an object of veneration for the Incas of Peru, to its subsequent 'discovery' by Christopher Columbus. Also mentioned here are King Frederick the Great of Prussia, who introduced the potato into Germany during the 18th century, and Benjamin Thompson, Count of Rumford (1753–1814), who not only promoted the potato in Munich but also laid out the city's English Garden (Englischer Garten). Thereafter follow sections illustrating the natural history of the potato, its harvesting, and its marketing. It is interesting to note that there are over a thousand varieties of potato worldwide, and that the German word *Kartoffel* is derived from *tartuffuli*, since the Italians thought originally that the potato was a truffle.

Wine, beer, vinegar, and schnaps can all be made from potatoes

The fifth room in the museum is particularly interesting because it details the many uses to which the potato has been put, extending far beyond that of a simple table vegetable: vinegar, beer, coffee, schnaps, bread, cheese, sausage, paper, soap, candles, and gas – to name but a few! Even more surprising, in the next room, is a display of curious and novel items that have taken the potato as a source of inspiration, including decorations formed by wrapping potatoes in silver foil, which adorned Berlin's first Christmas tree in 1755, and even a potato-shaped telephone!

The penultimate room is entitled *Fürstenspeise und Arme-Leute-Essen* (Food for sovereigns and nourishment for the poor) in which can be seen a single table set for both parties. As such it reminds us of the potato's long European journey from royal delicacy to paupers' dish, emphasising the broad-based popularity and versatility of this most important of arable crops. The museum concludes in the corridor with a rotating display of contemporary potato-related art drawn from its extensive holdings of oil paintings, water colours, photographs, and arthouse images.

For those wishing to visit further unusual museums in Munich consider the Alpine Museum (Alpines Museum) (see no. 14), the Toy Museum (Spielzeugmuseum) (see no. 16), and the German Hunting and Fishing Museum (Deutsches Jagd- und Fischereimuseum) (see no. 7). Most obscure of all is the Meter Museum (Zählermuseum) at Franzstrasse 9, which contains over 700 electricity meters from Thomas Edison's first electrolytic model of 1881 through to the modern electronic meters of the 1980s.

Other places of interest nearby: 26

56 An Almost Forgotten Airport

Trudering – Riem, the former Munich-Riem Airport on
Olof-Palme-Strasse
U2 Messestadt-West

The control tower of the former Munich-
Riem Airport

In 1992 Munich's former international airport at Riem was closed and the site transformed into a vast exhibition area, the Neue Messe München (New Munich Trade Fair Centre). Boasting a covered area of 200 000 square metres it now plays host to major international events. Visiting the site today it is all too easy to forget that an airport was ever here, never mind one that had served 12 million passengers.

To retell the story of the Munich-Riem Airport we leave the Messestadt-West U-Bahn station and walk northwards along Olof-Palme-Strasse, passing between the trade centre on the right and a stunning modern watergarden on the left, now home to a surprising abundance of wildlife (in one of the ponds is the artwork *Gran Paradiso* (1997) by Stephan Huber, consisting of two rows of scale model mountains). At the end of the street we are confronted by all that remains of the old airport: a red-brick control tower, and to its left the original arrivals hall, the so-called *Wappenhalle* (Hall of Emblems). Both structures are now protected monuments.

In 1936, Reich Aviation Minister Hermann Göring ordered that new airports be constructed in Berlin, Munich and Stuttgart. The project was handled by the office of architect Ernst Sagebiel (1872–1970), with Berlin-Tempelhof Airport becoming the largest building in Europe. Munich's new airport, replacing the 30-year old airfield at Oberwiesenfeld (now the site of the Olympic Village), followed similar lines and was located near the village of Riem. Along an extensive oval-shaped airfield the airport building stretched for 1.7 kilometres in a slight curve. In the centre of the building was the 13-metre high arrivals hall still standing today.

One of the most modern airports in the world the first plane landed at Munich-Riem on 25th October 1939, signalling the start of both civil and military air traffic here. In April 1945 the squadron of fighter ace Major General Adolf Galland was also stationed here, equipped with the new Me 262, the world's first jet-powered fighter. Shortly afterwards Allied air raids reduced much of the airport to ruins.

The airport arrivals hall of the former Munich-Riem Airport

Munich-Riem Airport was restored after the war and in 1948 became the first airport in Germany to be used for civil aviation. Unfortunately, the airport made the headlines again on 6th February 1958, when a charter plan crashed soon after take-off. Known subsequently as the Munich Air Disaster it cost the lives of 23 passengers, including eight members of Britain's Manchester United football team.

The runway at Munich-Riem Airport was lengthened on several occasions, with a final extension to 2804 metres in 1969. However, it had become apparent as early as 1963 that unlimited extension was impossible and that eventually Riem would be closed and a new airport built elsewhere. Despite a bomb attack on passengers bound for Israel in 1982, and the realisation that its taxiing system was no longer efficient, Riem Airport struggled on until the night of 17th May 1992, when the entire operation was moved to a new location near Erding (named after former Bavarian minister-president Franz Josef Strauss).

Until 1995, when work began on the construction of the trade fair centre, the airport's remaining facilities were used as an unusual concert venue, where the last concert of rock band Nirvana was staged in 1994.

57 A Curious Stone in the Forest

Ramersdorf – Perlach, the Sweden Memorial Stone
(Schweden-Gedenkstein) in the Truderinger Wald
S4, S6 Trudering or U2 Trudering then Bus 194 Nauestrasse

Concealed in the Truderinger Wald, a forest in Neuperlach on Munich's eastern edge, there stands a curious stone. Not listed in any guidebook the stone can be found by taking Bus 194 from the Trudering U-Bahn station, as far as Nauestrasse. From here a track called Breites Geräumt leads directly southwards into the forest, a place of surprising natural beauty. The second track on the left leads shortly to the stone (to the right is a disused quarry, now an idyllic, reed-fringed lake, well-stocked with fish).

Taking the form of a slender column atop a square-shaped base the stone carries a small plaque at its base, which informs the passer-by that it is called the Schweden-Gedenkstein, or Sweden memorial stone (on maps it is sometimes marked 'General Horn Schwedensäule'). The plaque also reveals that the stone is a replica, the original, dating from around 1500, having been removed in the 1950s to the courtyard (Marstallhof) of the Münchner Stadtmuseum (Munich City Museum) on St.-Jakobs-Platz.

Exactly why the column was first erected here remains a mystery. Perhaps it was a border marker, a wayside memorial to some forgotten tragedy, a plague cross, or even a reminder that Holy Roman Emperor Charles V attended a hunt here in 1530? How the column got its name is even more mysterious, a persistent local rumour being that it marks the grave of the soldier and politician Gustav Horn. Horn was one of the most able military commanders of the Swedish King Gustavus Adolphus (1594–1632), who during the period of the Thirty Years War (1618–1648) elevated his kingdom from a mere regional power to one of the great powers of Europe. That Horn in reality died in 1657 and is buried in Stockholm has done little to dispel this fanciful legend.

Whatever the truth about this curious stone it serves to remind us of an important and sometimes bloody period in Bavaria's history. The Thirty Years War had been sparked by an anti-Catholic uprising of Protestants in Prague in 1618. Against this backdrop in 1623 Maximilian I, Duke of Bavaria (1597–1623) was made a Prince Elector *(Kurfürst)* (1623–1651), in return for his support of the Catholic League of the Habsburg Holy Roman Emperor. Despite such an alliance by 1630

Gustavus Adolphus had begun pushing into northern Germany, where he soon consolidated the Protestant position. Meanwhile, at the First Battle of Breitenfeld (1631) he engaged and defeated a Catholic army that was laying waste to his allies in Saxony. Together with the French he now made plans for the invasion of the rest of the Holy Roman Empire, and in March 1632 invaded Bavaria.

Forcing the withdrawal of his Catholic opponents at the Battle of Rain and occupying Munich marked the highpoint of the campaign of Gustavus Adolphus. With the countryside ravaged Maximilian sued for peace. Fortunately Gustavus Adolphus was so impressed by the Wittelsbach's city palace, the Residenz, that he spared Munich from destruction, in gratitude for which Maximi-

This curious stone stands in a forest in Neuperlach

lian erected the column to the Virgin Mary in Marienplatz. After Gustavus Adolphus was killed at the Battle of Lützen Maximilian opted for a pro-French policy that would colour Bavarian politics until German unification in 1871.

58 An Experimental Brewery

Ramersdorf – Perlach, the Forschungsbrauerei at
Unterhachinger Strasse 76
S7 Perlach; Bus 55

Munich is probably as famous for its rich brewing heritage as anything else, and the city offers any number of beer halls and beer gardens in which to sample these liquid delights. For something a little different, however, why not take a trip out to the suburb of Perlach, where along-side the S-Bahn line, amongst market gardens, a family-run micro-brewery offering its own distinctive beers.

In 1930, after 25 years spent working in the brewing business, mas-ter brewer Gottfried Jakob realised his dream of opening a private ex-perimental brewery (Forschungsbrauerei) at Unterhachinger Strasse 76. His goal was to develop new brewing technologies and thus produce better quality beers, whilst still adhering to the *Reinheitsgebot* brewing law of 1516 restricting the ingredients to only barley malt, yeast, hops, and water. The results were tried and tested by local patrons in a small bar attached to the brewery. Through his numerous writings and pat-ents Jakob was able to pass on the results of his research to his succes-sors, and it is this unique heritage that makes a visit to the Forschungs-brauerei so special today.

Now managed by Stefan Jakob, the founder's grandson, the For-schungsbrauerei easily matches the beers produced by Munich's brew-ing giants, whilst electing to remain small and unaffected by mass production. It offers a pair of unique, high-quality beers, namely the wonderfully hoppy Pilsissi-mus (5.2%), a light, golden-yellow lager beer *(Helles)* with a fine head of foam, and the famed St. Jakobus Blonder Bock (7.5%), a full-bodied, honey-coloured strong beer *(Doppelbock)*. The latter by tradition can be served a week before the city's *Starkbierzeit* (Strong Beer Season) officially opens on 19th March (St. Jo-seph's Day) (see no. 30).

Beer at Perlach's Forschungsbrauerei is only served in
Keferloher ceramic tankards

Beer at the Forschungs-brauerei is served in Kefer-loher ceramic tankards, made in Keferloh in Grasbrunn, Upper Bavaria; they are designed specifically to keep the beer cool and to allow it to retain its freshness (the inclusion of salt in the firing process enables carbonic acid to remain longer in the beer). The beer can be enjoyed either in the cosy Bräustüberl (in which the very first beers were sampled), or the leafy beer garden in the lee of the brewing tower, which contains several large copper brewing vats. The traditional planting of broadleaved Chestnut trees in beer gardens is said to keep not only the customers cool but also the beer cellar below.

The brewing tower at the Forschungsbrauerei bears the name of its most famous beer

Food is available at the Forschungsbrauerei too, its kitchen offering a fine selection of traditional Bavarian specialities. These include *Surhaxn* (marinated pork knuckle with *Weinkraut* (baked Sauerkraut with added wine)), *Münchner Tellerfleisch mit Meerrettich* (braised beef with horseradish), and whole chicken grilled freshly to order. There are also a wide variety of snacks *(Brotzeiten)* on offer, including *Obatzter* (a spicy Bavarian cream cheese served with pretzels *(Brezeln)* and radishes), *Presssack* (jellied meat), *Leberkäse* (steamed, finely-chopped pork), *Bauernspeck* (farm-house-style smoked ham), *Leberwurst* (spiced liver sausage), and *Brathering* (smoked herring). Cheers and Guten Appetit!

59 Secrets of Ramersdorf – Perlach

Ramersdorf – Perlach, a tour beginning with the Church
of St. Maria Ramersdorf (Kirche St. Maria Ramersdorf)
at Ramersdorfer Strasse 6
U5 Innsbrucker Ring, U2 Karl-Preis-Platz; Bus 55

Far from Munich's Old Town (Altstadt), and even its inner suburbs, the district of Ramersdorf – Perlach does not see too many tourists. Those that do stray this far will probably do so by U-Bahn, alighting at either the Innsbrucker Ring or the Karl-Preis-Platz stations. From here a brisk walk takes the traveller directly into the former village of Ramersdorf. Bypassed by the busy roads now surrounding it the village has remained an oasis of calm, in what is today a bustling and industrialised suburb.

The pilgrimmage Church of St. Maria Ramersdorf
(Kirche St. Maria Ramersdorf)

Our first port of call, alongside the ubiquitous village maypole on Ramersdorfer Strasse, is the Church of St. Maria Ramersdorf (Kirche St. Maria Ramersdorf). In use since the 15th century it is one of the oldest pilgrimage churches *(Wallfahrtskirche)* in Bavaria. Initially pilgrims made their way here to worship a relic of the Holy Cross that is kept in a precious monstrance. However, since 1465 another object of veneration has been a figure of the *Madonna Enthroned* carved by the renowned Munich craftsman Erasmus Grasser (c.1450–c.1515) (see no. 19). The exterior of the church still retains its original Gothic character, whilst the interior has been re-worked in the

Ramersdorf is home to Germany's first National Socialist housing estate

Baroque style, as have the stucco-adorned Gothic cloisters. After walking around the tiny graveyard surrounding the church pay a visit to the nearby Alter Wirt, an inn with a leafy beer garden once frequented by pilgrims on the road between Salzburg and Augsburg.

Directly in front of the Alter Wirt is busy Rosenheimer Strasse, on the opposite side of which lies another of the area's secrets. The Ramersdorf Housing Estate, bounded by Chiemgaustrasse, Wilramstrasse, Hohenaschauerstrasse, and Rosenheimer Strasse, was unveiled in 1934 to coincide with Munich's German Housing Exhibition. Called originally Mustersiedlung, or 'model estate', it was the result of an architectural competion announced in 1932 to construct well-built, reasonably-priced family homes for the German people. Under the guidance of the Munich City Officer for Housing and NSDAP member Guido Harbers, more than twenty architects participated in the project resulting in the construction of 192 houses. As such it was the first National Socialist model estate in the German Reich. Unfortunately for Harbers his dream that the houses would provide the blueprint for future housing across the country was never realised, as construction was eventually deemed too expensive. The Ramersdorf Housing Estate is today a listed historical monument, its unaltered façades and large gardens (planned originally to encourage self-sufficiency) protected for posterity.

Southeast of the estate, and best reached by Bus 55, is the New South Cemetery (Neuer Südfriedhof), on Hochäckerstrasse in the former village of Perlach. Opened in 1977 to supplement the Perlacher Forst Cemetery (Friedhof am Perlacher Forst) it offers little in the way of historic monuments or famous graves, its most celebrated incumbent being Lou van Burg (1917–1986) (Section 305, Plot 1, Grave 140), who began his stage career in 1950s Paris performing with the likes of Josephine Baker. During the 1960s and 70s he gained television fame as 'Onkel Lou', the presenter of *Der Goldene Schuss* (The Golden Shot), but was fired after revelations of an affair with his assistant.

More interesting to the historian is the fact that the oldest evidence for man's activity in Perlach was uncovered in the cemetery, in the form of a Celtic ritual centre dating back to 500BC. In the 7th century AD a cemetery was established between nearby Weddigenstrasse and Schmidbauerstrasse, suggesting the presence of Perlach's first settlement there. By the 18th century the village was large enough to warrant a new Baroque church, which still stands on Pfanzeltplatz today.

Our tour finishes at the Forschungsbrauerei at Unterhachinger Strasse 76, a family-run brewery renowned for its unique beers and traditional Bavarian cooking (see no. 58).

60 On the Right Tracks

Ramersdorf – Perlach, the MVG Museum at Ständlerstrasse 20
S5, S6, U2 Giesing then walk or take half hourly historic
museum bus; Tram 17 Schwanseestrasse

Most people interested in Munich's transport history visit the Deutsches Museum Verkehrszentrum at Theresienhöhe 14a, with its steam locomotives, motorbikes and racing cars. Less well known but of equal interest is the MVG Museum at Ständlerstrasse 20, the official museum of the Münchner Verkehrsgesellschaft (Munich Transport Company).

Suitably located inside part of the company's main workshops, which were erected in 1918, the MVG Museum illustrates primarily the history of Munich's tram network and includes fifteen historic trams. There are also two buses and a solitary U-Bahn carriage. A pair of rare Munich trolleybuses have also been acquired and are undergoing restoration. Inside the light and airy exhibition hall the various vehicles are superbly displayed, along with related artefacts such as signals, uni-

Trams and buses in the fascinating MVG Museum

Visitors can climb aboard this historic tram at the MVG Museum

forms, and models. It is commendable for a specialist museum that all the labelling is in both German and English.

Other exhibits include a selection of maintenance and emergency vehicles *(Dienstwagen)*, including a snowplough, which are painted orange so as to distinguish them from the traditional white and blue livery of the rest of the fleet. In the smaller rooms alongside the main hall can be seen the contents of a former tram workshop at Westend-strasse, in which replacement parts for older trams were until recently hand-crafted. There is also a reconstructed blacksmith's workshop dating back to 1934. To give an idea of how modern trams are maintained, a service trench beneath one of the vehicles can be visited. A curious little display nearby is a glass-topped cabinet containing examples of axle breakages! The sole U-Bahn carriage contains a simulator that allows visitors to experience driving a train for themselves (see no. 82).

The MVG Museum is manned entirely by enthusiasts, who are also responsible for restoring the vehicles at weekends. During the week the same workshops are bustling with MVG engineers working on present-day rolling stock.

The Munich tram system today consists of 10 lines, 95 cars, 71 kilometres of track, and 148 stops. Despite declining somewhat during the 1980s this clean and efficient transport system is expanding once again. It is interesting to note that in Munich the word 'Trambahn' is used rather than the usual 'Strassenbahn'. The oldest motorised tram on display in the museum is number 256, which was built in 1899. Restored to full working order to celebrate the centenary of the inauguration of the Munich tram system it still sometimes takes to the streets, together with a horse-drawn tram.

A replica of a horsedrawn tram can be seen in the U-Bahn station at Max-Weber-Platz, reminding passers-by that between 1882 and 1899, when the system was electrified, Munich's first horse-drawn tram line passed this way. The tram depot that once stood here had space for 54 cars and stables for 180 horses, the latter converted subsequently into office space. The U4/U5 U-Bahn line arrived here in 1988, connecting the western suburbs of Laim and Westend with the city centre and the eastern suburbs of Haidhausen, Bogenhausen, Ramersdorf, Berg am Laim, and Neuperlach.

Alongside the MVG Museum is a building containing the headquarters of the Friends of the Munich Tramway Museum (Freunde des Münchner Trambahnmuseums) as well as the Society for Tramway History (Gesellschaft für Trambahngeschichte). Their library contains 3500 books about trams and trains.

On Saturdays and Sundays between May and September the MVG offers guided city tours on its trams. They depart from a special tram stop at Sendlinger Tor at 11am, 12am, 1pm, and 2pm. For further details visit www.mvg-mobil.de.

61 Wartime Memories in the East Cemetery

Obergiesing, the East Cemetery (Ostfriedhof) at the corner
of Tegernseer Landstrasse and St.-Bonifatius-Strasse
U4, U5 Max-Weber-Platz then Tram 15, 25 Ostfriedhof;
Tram 17

Munich's East Cemetery (Ostfriedhof), on the gentle slopes of the Nock-herberg, began life as a burial ground for the suburb of Au. Throughout the 19th century it was expanded into a general city cemetery, its graves laid out along a classic formal grid-pattern of avenues and paths. Today, this 'city of the dead' is home to more than 35 000 graves, including a handful of celebrities, such as neuroanatomist Dr. Bernhard von Gudden (1824–1886), who was found drowned in Lake Starnberg alongside his patient Ludwig II, King of Bavaria (1864–1886). Also interred here is Austrian actress Barbara Valentin (1940–2002), dubbed the German Jayne Mansfield and remembered for her relationship with the singer Freddie Mercury, and Ludwig Franz Hirtreiter (1939–1999), better known as the balladeer Rex Gildo.

Unfortunately, the East Cemetery also has a much darker side, one which dates back to the time of the Third Reich. It is a little-known fact that during Hitler's tenure as Chancellor of Germany 3996 concentration camp victims were cremated here. Many were from the camp at Dachau just outside Munich, which opened in March 1933 and remained in continuous operation until its liberation in April 1945. The first camp on German soil it was the model for all those that followed.

Another little-known fact about the East Cemetery is that in 1946, by an ironic twist of fate, the bodies of a dozen German war criminals, hung as a result of the Nuremberg Trials, were also brought here for cremation. They included Hitler's onetime successor and Luftwaffe commander Reichsmarschall Hermann Göring (1893–1946), head of the High Command of the Armed Forces Field Marshall Wilhelm Keitel (1882–1946), German Foreign Minister Joachim von Ribbentrop (1893–1946), and SS leader and Chief of Security Police Ernst Kaltenbrunner (1903–1946), the highest ranking Nazi official to stand trial. Whereas today there is a modest memorial to their victims outside the crematorium, their own remains were tossed without ceremony into the River Isar so as not to give sympathisers the chance of establishing a grave cult.

The crematorium at the East Cemetery (Ostfriedhof) in Obergiesing

Others who carved out a career under the Nazi flag were more fortunate in being given conventional graves at the East Cemetery. For obvious reasons their locations are not amongst the noteworthy listed at each entrance. They include nightfighter ace Werner Streib (1911–1986), SS General Johann Rattenhuber (1897–1957), and SS Major General Julius Schaub (1898–1967), who had participated in the Munich Putsch in 1923 and was Hitler's loyal adjutant from 1940 onwards; after the war Schaub managed a pharmacy in Munich until his death in 1967. Also buried here are the actors Joe Stöckel (1894–1959) and Wastl Witt (1882–1955), both of whom had roles in *SA-Mann Brand (Storm Trooper Brand)* (1933), the first feature-length Nazi propaganda film (see no. 63).

One grave that should perhaps be listed is that of Rudolf Christoph Freiherr von Gersdorff (1905–1980), tucked away in the north-eastern part of the cemetery (Grave field 152, row 1, plot 12a). As with all municipal cemeteries in Germany the graves of the East Cemetery are subject to "resting periods", that is their upkeep is guaranteed for between 25 and 50 years if paid for in advance. If payment is not renewed the grave will be levelled and re-used; exceptions occur if the grave is that of someone considered notable, in which case the state will maintain the grave if necessary. Gersdorff's is such a grave, the burial record in

The grave of Rudolf Christoph Freiherr von Gersdorff, who attempted to assassinate Hitler in 1943

the cemetery office stamped clearly in red ink "Bekannte, Berühmt" (Known, Famous). The reason for this is that Gersdorff attempted unsuccessfully to assassinate Hitler.

A highly decorated officer in the Wehrmacht, Gersdorff took part in the invasion of Poland, the Battle of France, and the invasion of the Soviet Union. Increasingly at odds with Nazi Party crimes against humanity, notably Hitler's order to murder all Red Army political commissars among Soviet prisoners of war, Gersdorff joined a close circle of sympathisers based around Colonel Henning von Tresckow. On 21st March 1943, Gersdorff placed two timer bombs in his coat pockets and accompanied Hitler around an exhibition of captured Soviet weapons in Berlin, intent on killing the dictator and himself. Quite unexpectedly Hitler cut the tour short and Gersdorff missed his opportunity. Transferred back to the Eastern Front Gersdorff's activities were never discovered by the Gestapo, and he became one of the few German military anti-Hitler plotters to survive the war. His colleague Tresckow described the importance of such acts as being " to prove to the world and for the records of history that the men of the resistance dared to take the decisive step".

Other places of interest nearby: 27

62 On the Trail of Rare Animals

Untergiesing – Harlaching, the Hellabrunn Zoo (Tierpark
Hellabrunn) at Tierparkstrasse 30
U3 Thalkirchen; Bus 62

Munich's zoo, the Tierpark Hellabrunn, was established in 1911 and
was the first in the world to display its species by continent. Within
each area the animal enclosures and pavilions are designed to replicate
as closely as possible the natural environment of the species. Covering an area of 3.6 square kilometres the zoo is located on the banks of
the River Isar and is watered by a winding stream, the Auer Mühlbach.
With its many trees and tranquil groves the Tierpark Hellabrunn is undoubtedly one of the most beautiful zoos in the world.

Most visitors, especially families with children, will probably want
to head straight for the usual favourites: the lions and tigers, elephants
and rhinos, chimpanzees and penguins. And who can blame them!
However, it should not be forgotten that the Tierpark Hellabrunn is
also world renowned for its breeding programme of lesser-known animals threatened with extinction. A great way to escape the crowds is to
track down some of these rare animals.

Our tour begins at the zoo's Isar Gate, reached easily from the
Thalkirchen U-Bahn station. Follow the path straight ahead into the
European section, where on the right-hand side can be found a small
herd of Persian or Mesopotamian Fallow Deer *(Dama mesopotamica)*.
Once found across southern Europe and northern Africa there is a debate whether this gentle creature is a sub-species of the European Fallow Deer or an entirely separate species. Certainly it shares the chestnut brown coat and white speckles of its European counterpart but it
is also larger and has differently-shaped antlers. Hunted extensively it
can now only be found wild in western Iran and Israel.

Crossing the river ahead take the next right turn to find an enclosure containing Przewalski's Horse *(Equus (ferus) przewalski)*, known
also as the Asiatic or Mongolian Wild Horse. Pronounced '(p)she-vahl-
skee' it is named after General Nikolai Przhevalsky (1839–1888), an explorer and naturalist employed by the Russian Tsar. In 1881, after hearing rumours of the existence of a stocky wild horse with erect mane and
a black stripe on its back, the general was sent to Central Asia to look
for it. By 1900 fifty-four foals had been captured for aristocratic and
zoo collections throughout Europe. During the 20th century the native

A herd of rare Przewalski's Horse at the Hellabrunn Zoo (Tierpark Hellabrunn)

population of the horse declined rapidly due to hunting, lack of water, harsh winters, and grazing competition from domestic flocks. After the last wild herd was reported in Mongolia in 1967 a foundation to save the horse was set up in the Netherlands. Today's global population of about 2000 horses has been bred from captive animals descended from the original imported foals, some of which have been successfully released back into the wild.

In the next enclosure on the left-hand side can be seen a definite European rarity, namely the Alpine Ibex *(Capra ibex)*. Known in German as the *Steinbock* it is an excellent climber and inhabits the snowline above the forests of the European Alps. Long considered a mystical animal, almost all its body parts and even its excrement were once sought as cures for various illnesses and as ingredients for magic potions. By the early 19th century it had been hunted close to extinction although subsequent protection programmes have ensured a wild population today of about 30 000.

Follow the stream southwards, past the Rhinoceros and Tapir, into the Asian section to find the Kiang *(Equus kiang)*, the largest of the wild asses and a native of the high Tibetan plateau. Once held to be a subspecies of the Onager, or Asiatic Wild Ass, it is now classed as a distinct

The Alpine Ibex is another rarity at the Hellabrunn Zoo (Tierpark Hellabrunn)

species. With its chestnut coat and face, and white underside, legs and muzzle, it still exists in small numbers in northern Nepal along the Tibetan border.

We finish our safari by turning left through the beer garden (only in Munich!) and then crossing the stream into the African area, to find the elegant Mhorr Gazelle *(Gazella dama mhorr)*, a sub-species of the Dama Gazelle *(Nanger dama)* but now extinct in the wild. Like the Dama Gazelle it inhabited the Sahara desert, migrating north and south during the dry season; its rust-coloured coat and white underside provides perfect desert camouflage. Despite an ongoing breeding programme there are still only about 150 captive Mhorr Gazelle worldwide.

From this point the Flamingo Gate in the north-east corner of the zoo can be reached by walking northwards, past the lions, elephants, monkeys, and aquarium.

Other places of interest nearby: 65, 66, 67

63 Behind the Scenes at Bavaria Film

Geiselgasteig, the studios of Bavaria Film at Bavariafilmplatz 7
U1 Wettersteinplatz then Tram 25 Bavariafilmplatz

Until 1919 Munich's first film studio was located in the city's Karlsplatz (Stachus) area, after which the company Münchner Lichtspiel-Kunst (Emelka, for short) founded a studio for making silent films in Geiselgasteig, just outside what is today the city's southernmost district of Untergiesing – Harlaching. With electric lighting still in its infancy the company built a studio entirely of glass, in order to make full use of the available natural light; unfortunately, this structure was destroyed during a violent storm in the 1920s and was replaced by a conventional studio building, which itself has long since vanished. Emelka itself didn't last much longer since it went bankrupt in an attempt to upgrade its facilities for sound pictures. Now long forgotten, it was during these early days that Alfred Hitchcock came here to direct his first ever film, *The Pleasure Garden* (1925).

In September 1932 the facility was bought up and re-invented as Bavaria Film Ltd. Within a few months Hitler's Nazi Party began to intervene in the film industry as part of their so-called *Gleichschaltung*, the cultural harmonisation of all aspects of German life in line with National Socialist ideology. Not long afterwards, on 14th January 1933, the Bavaria Film production *SA-Mann Brand (Stormtrooper Brand)* was premiered in Munich, the first feature-length Nazi propaganda film. Taking the Nazis' "time of struggle" as its theme it featured 1600 extras.

Three months later, the premiere of the film *Hitlerjunge Quex (Hitler Youth Quex)*, sub-titled "A film about the sacrificial spirit of German youth", took place at the studios in the presence of Hitler himself. Up until the end of the Second World War the studios continued making similar films (although many more were made in Berlin), as well as so-called *Heimat* films, a genre used to promote a traditional and nostalgic German way of life. The oldest extant stages on the site today (numbers 4 and 5) were erected during this period (1943). They can be seen as part of the studios' 90-minute Filmstadt (Film City) guided tour. A combination of history and hands-on activities the tour, which was inaugurated in 1981, should provide something of interest to young and old, German and non-German alike.

From July 1945 a news programme for the Allied occupied zones was produced at the studios under the direction of the US army. The studios subsequently became popular with American directors because the facilities they offered were relatively cheap to rent. Films from this period include Stanley Kubrick's story of trench warfare *Paths of Glory*

The Marienhof street set at the Bavaria Film studios

(1957), starring Kirk Douglas, Billy Wilder's *One, Two, Three* (1961), and *The Great Escape* (1963), with Steve McQueen; for the latter film, an authentic prisoner-of-war camp was built in the woods surrounding the studios.

Dubbed 'Hollywood on the Isar', Bavaria Film is today one of the leading film production companies in Europe, generating both feature films as well as television series, the sets for several of which are included on the tour. There are two full-sized streets, one of which provides the backdrop for Germany's longest-running soap opera, *Marienhof*; the other is called 'Munich Street' and is a versatile generic set that has been used in many German productions; its variety of façades (from working class Haidhausen tenements to bourgeois Schwabing villas) are constructed in a '9'-shaped ground plan so as to provide as many corners – and hence photo opportunities – as possible.

International productions at Bavaria Film have included Gene Wilder's *Willy Wonka & the Chocolate Factory* (1971), *The Never Ending Story* (1984), the first real-life *Asterix & Obelisk* film (1999), *Perfume* (2006), and *Der Untergang (Downfall)* (2004), a dramatisation of Hitler's last days, for which the dictator's bunker was re-built in studio 12, one of the five biggest sound stages in Europe. Less well-known is the cult science fiction film *Enemy Mine* (1985), which was the first film to be directed by Wolfgang Petersen, who went on to make *The Perfect Storm* (2000) with George Clooney. In between he directed what is arguably his finest film, *Das Boot* (1981), about the crew of a U-Boat during the Second World War.

The story of the making of *Das Boot* is perhaps the most fascinating and unusual aspect of the Filmstadt tour, since so much of the original set is still here. It is a little-known fact that nowhere during the

This replica submarine interior provided the backdrop for the film Das Boot

entire film does a *real* submarine actually appear. The scenes on board the fictional U-96 were filmed using either a 57 metre-long replica of an interior, created from original plans of a Type VIIC German submarine, or else a series of stand-alone conning towers and variously-scaled models, which can be found dotted around the park. Walking the full length of the replica interior is unforgettable and enables one to sense something of the claustrophobia and discomfort endured by the 52 man-crew of such craft during the Second World War. The only real Type VIIC submarine still in existence, the U-995, can be seen at Laboe, near Kiel on the Baltic coast, where it forms part of a memorial to the naval dead of all nationalities.

Those interested in vintage cinemas in Munich should visit the Theatiner Filmkunst in the Theatiner Passage at Theatinerstrasse 32, which has been screening arthouse films since its opening in 1957, the Filmtheater Sendlinger Tor at Sendlingertor Platz 11, in business since 1913, and the Museum-Lichtspiele-Filmtheater at Lilienstrasse 2, which opened in 1910 inside a converted varieties theatre; it is famous for having screened The Rocky Horror Picture Show every week for almost three decades. Oldest of all is the Gabriel Filmtheater at Dachauer Strasse 16, which opened in 1906, making it possibly the world's oldest.

64 The Führer's Hidden Headquarters

Pullach, the former Führer Headquarters 'Siegfried'
on Heilmannstrasse
S7 Grosshesselohe Isartalbahnhof

In recent years a growing desire to identify Munich's former Nazi sites has prompted several tour companies to offer Third Reich history tours to visitors and locals alike (see page 230). There is one such site, however, located in the quiet town of Pullach, just outside the southern boundary of the city, that has clung on to its secrets.

Pullach is not on many tourists' itineraries and yet it has played a significant part in German history since the early 1930s, when Martin Bormann, then Head of Staff to Adolf Hitler's deputy Rudolf Hess, purchased several private properties here. In tandem with the construction around Königsplatz of the most important offices of the NSDAP *Reichsleitung* (Reich leadership) there was a need to find a secure out-of-town location for housing the party elite.

On a 68-hectare site at Pullach, just south of Promenadeweg, between Heilmannstrasse and the main Munich railway line, Roderich Fick, one of Hitler's favoured architects and later Reich Architect of Linz, was commissioned to create a suitable estate. Around a rectangular green he planned a series of simple, well-proportioned one- and two-family homes, accessible from a private loop road called Sonnenweg. The houses all faced inwards and were shielded from Heilmannstrasse by head-high walls, leaving only their red-tiled roofs showing. Near the southern end of the estate, which was built in 1937–1938 and named Reich Housing Estate Rudolf Hess (Reichssiedlung Rudolf Hess), was the *Stabsleiterhaus* (Residence of the Head of Staff), a villa with public rooms on the ground floor and the private residence of Martin Bormann and his family above. Until the completion of the official NSDAP party buildings on Arcisstrasse in 1937, Hess directed the Nazi Party from here (see no. 40).

During the Second World War, the Organisation Todt was instructed to build twenty official Führer Headquarters *(Führerhauptquartiere)* across Europe, from where Hitler and the Command of the Wehrmacht could oversee their military operations. Of the fourteen that were completed the most famous are the Wolfsschanze ('Wolf's Lair') in former

East Prussia (from where Hitler directed his doomed Soviet offensive in 1941), the Berghof at Obersalzberg near Berchtesgaden (where he met with foreign and domestic officials), and the Führerbunker in Berlin (where he committed suicide in April 1945). Far less well-known is the one built between March 1943 and November 1944 at Pullach, under the codename "Siegfried". Located in the woods directly east of Heilmannstrasse, the site had been earmarked by Bormann, now Head of the Party Chancellery following the defection of Hess, as an alternative command post for Hitler in the event of the Obersalzberg being bombed.

Although Hitler never used the Führer Headquarters 'Siegfried', it was kept fully operational until the very end of the war. The main feature was a command shelter alongside Heilmannstrasse, made from 25 000 cubic metres of reinforced concrete. Measuring 70 by 20 metres, and with a ceiling three metres thick, it contained thirty rooms and had its own emergency power supply. In the woods beyond the shelter were dotted various administration buildings, vehicle parks, and barracks buildings, most of which are no longer standing. The compound as a whole was accessed from the north via Promenadeweg, and was connected to the main railway line by its own spur, enabling Hitler's private 'Führer Train' to get as close as possible.

In late March 1945 the families of Munich's Nazi Party leaders evacuated the Pullach estate, and at the end of April the Americans occupied the entire area. Having sustained very little damage during the war, the buildings were initially used as accommodations for troops and displaced persons, as well as a makeshift prison camp. Between autumn 1945 and 1947 the Civilian Censorship Division, an organisation for censoring letters, was based here, which then made room for the clandestine Organisation Gehlen.

During the Second World War Reinhard Gehlen (1902–1979) had been a Major-General in the Wehrmacht and played a minor role in the abortive Stauffenberg plot to assassinate Hitler. He also served as chief of intelligence-gathering on the Eastern Front, and was subsequently recruited by the United States military to set up a spy ring directed against the Soviet Occupation Zone (from 1949 the GDR) – and the Soviet Union itself. Pullach's out-of-town location, as well as its existing self-contained infrastructure, made it the ideal home for the staff and families of this new organisation.

In 1955 Organisation Gehlen was officially handed over to the Federal Republic of Germany, and in April 1956 it became the nucleus of the newly-created Federal Intelligence Service (Bundesnachrichtendi-

Unlike other streets in Pullach, Heilmannstrasse conceals a secret

enst). Gehlen remained its president until his retirement in 1968, and with the end of the East-West standoff the service turned instead towards gathering intelligence about terrorism, the arms trade, and drug trafficking.

All this helps explains why Heilmannstrasse today is lined with security walls topped with barbed wire, security cameras, and signs threatening huge fines for those attempting to take photographs. For much of the street there is little to see although the sense of being somewhere politically sensitive is palpable. Continuing southwards towards sleepy Pullach itself, the walls give way to a series of buildings on the righthand side which were built as vehicle repair workshops for the "Siegfried" site. A right turn here along Margaretenstrasse, which leads eventually to the railway station at Pullach, permits the only real glimpse of Hitler's former headquarters, in the shape of a rusty iron door by the side of number 17, which leads via a concrete strengthened staircase down to another command shelter. Even here photography is *strictly* forbidden.

Between 2003 and 2011 the Federal Intelligence Service was gradually relocated to new offices in Berlin, although a few employees remain in Pullach.

65 Surfing in the City

Thalkirchen – Obersendling, surfing on the Floßlände
U3 Obersendling or U3 Thalkirchen, then Bus 135 Floßlände
(Mar–Oct only) or walk

It came as a great surprise to this author to discover that landlocked Munich, which lies several hundred miles from the nearest ocean, has become something of a mecca for surfers! Whilst the city obviously cannot offer conventional sea surfing opportunities, wherein the surfer rides individual waves as they roll inexorably towards the shore, it *is* able to provide several so-called 'standing river waves'. These are permanent, fixed-location waves created when water is chanelled through a manmade artificial weir. Whilst river surfing is not quite as dynamic for those participating, it is ideal for training and lends itself perfectly as a spectator sport, since many popular sea surfing techniques and manoeuvres, including 'aerials', 'cutbacks', '360s', and 'floaters', can be seen close-up. Indeed it is no coincidence that internationally recognized surfers Quirin Rohleder and Tim Pelz began their careers in Munich.

There are two locations in Munich where this unusual sport can be experienced. The most central venue is alongside the Haus der Kunst on Prinzregentenstrasse, at the southern edge of the English Garden (Englischer Garten), where surfers have congregated since the early 1970s. It is here through the arches of a 19th century road bridge that a culverted tributary of the Isar emerges in a cold and raging torrent from beneath the city, on its way northwards to rejoin the main river. Not without reason is it called the Eisbach, or 'Ice Stream'.

Until recently a sign clearly forbade swimming or any other water sports on the Eisbach, following a series of injuries and one fatality. Munich's surfers are quick to point out, however, that the fatality occurred farther downstream, and that many of the injuries sustained are the result of amateurs trying their luck without wearing the proper equipment. As a result the local police have long turned a blind eye, and in 2010 surfing on the Eisbach was finally legalised. The river surfers now queue up on the riverbank to ride the 'standing wave', created by three rows of concrete blocks lying just 40 centimetres beneath the surface. Since the Eisbach is a mere 5 metres wide at this point only one surfer can ride the wave at a time, usually for about 10–20 seconds, before being swept away downstream. The blocks, incidentally, were

Surfing on the Eisbach

placed here in the 1970s by civic engineers in an attempt to weaken the flow of water.

Munich's second 'standing river wave' is located on the Floßlände, a swift-flowing tributary of the Isar canal, which forms the Maria Einsiedel-Hinterbrühl Island in Obersendling. The wave can be found near the camp site on Zentralländstrasse, at the end of a sloping concrete race beneath an arching modern bridge. It rears up here because of a sudden change in the shape of the concrete, enhanced by wooden boards added by the surfers themselves. A series of sluices used to regulate the flow of water to a power station farther downstream determines the size of the wave. Since 2001 the climax of the riversurfing season has been celebrated here with the Munich Surf Opens, an event that attracts many riversurfing greats of both sexes, including Mick Höllerer, Gerry Schlegl and Robert Beetz, and Manu Wagner, Isabelle Biehl and Heidi Lammerer.

During the summer months another extraordinary sight can be witnessed on the Floßlände. The name itself means 'Raft Landing' and indeed in former times log-built rafts were used here to transport cargoes. The rafts can still be seen today, however the cargo now consists predominantly of boisterous males, enticed aboard by the prospect of beer and rousing brass band music (see page 230). The sight of them hurtling down one of the sluices clutching their tankards and brass instruments is unforgettable!

Other places of interest nearby: 62, 66

66 A Passion for Bavarian Baroque

Thalkirchen – Obersendling, the Asam-Schlössl at
Maria-Einsiedel-Strasse 45
U3 Obersendling or U3 Thalkirchen, then Bus 135 or walk

It was Ferdinand Maria, Elector of Bavaria (1651–1679), who imported the Baroque style of art and architecture from Italy into Bavaria.
More precisely it was his wife Henriette Adelaide of Savoy (1636–1676),
whose father was an Italian duke. At her behest the architect Agostino
Barelli (1627–1687) was brought from Italy to design Munich's Theatinerkirche, the first large Baroque building north of the Alps (see
no. 6). In turn the Wittelsbach court architect Josef Effner (1687–1745)
was greatly influenced by the new style and became the first local architect to create a distinct form of Baroque architecture peculiar to Bavaria. This 'Bavarian Baroque' reached its zenith in a series churches
built by the renowned Asam brothers.

In 1733 the sculptor and stuccoist Egid Quirin Asam (1692–1750)
purchased a house for himself, the so-called Asamhaus at Sendlinger
Strasse 34. Immediately next door, at number 32, he built a church
with his brother, the fresco painter Cosmas Damian Asam (1689–1739).
Dedicated to St. Johann-Nepomuk it is more commonly known as the
Asamkirche and was completed in 1746. Usually choked with tourists
the church is surprisingly narrow (just under 9 metres wide) and yet
despite this limitation the brothers managed to install one of their
trademark *theatrum sacrum* interiors here, an overwhelming mix of architectural, sculptural, painting, and lighting effects. It must be seen to
be believed!

Far less showy than the Asamkirche, and generally free of tourist groups, is the Asam-Schlössl at Maria-Einsiedel-Strasse 45, which
Cosmas Damian Asam chose as his country residence in 1724. Having
purchased this 17th century building he set about converting the second
floor into a studio, illuminated by a large semi-circular window. The
highlight of the building, which was named Maria-Einsiedel after a
Swiss pilgrimmage church the brothers had decorated, is its façade. Cosmas Damian covered every inch of it with his own paintings, restored
versions of which can be seen today. With the Asamkirche the brothers
sought to render such extravagant façades in three-dimensional form.

The Asam-Schlössl today contains a restaurant with a beautiful garden to the rear.

Back in Munich's Old Town (Altstadt), fans of Baroque will enjoy visiting the Church of St. Peter (Peterskirche) at Rindermarkt 1, the Church of the Holy Spirit (Heiliggeistkirche) at Tal 77, the Bürgersaalkirche at Neuhauser Strasse 14, and the Church of the Holy Trinity (Dreifaltigkeitskirche) at Pacellistrasse 6. There are Baroque palaces worth looking at too, for example Palais Preysing at Residenzstrasse 27, Palais Porcia at Kardinal-Faulhaber Strasse 12, and Palais Seinsheim at Prannerstrasse 7.

The Church of St. Anne (Damenstift St. Anna) at Damenstiftstrasse 1 is especially

The painted façade of the Asam-Schlössl, which is today a restaurant

unusual because of its wall paintings, which were restored after the Second World War in sepia, the reason being that the only photographs available of the original paintings were black and white! The realistic group of full-size *Last Supper* figures to the left of the altar are probably copied from Spanish originals and were re-discovered in the cellar by a cleaning lady.

We finish at the Abbey Church of St. Anne (Klosterkirche St. Anna) at St.-Anna-Strasse 19. Built to a design by Johann Michael Fischer in 1727–1733, and with an interior by the Asam brothers, it was Munich's first Late Baroque (Rococo) religious building. Only a street away from bustling Maximilianstrasse it remains an oasis of calm in this part of the city. Such places are rare and found usually only in the suburbs: an example is the glorious Rococo Church of St. Michael (Michaelskirche) at Johann-Michael-Fischer-Platz 2 in Berg am Laim.

Other places of interest nearby: 62, 65

67 The Jewish Stones Speak

Sendling, the Old Jewish Cemetery
(Alter Israelitischer Friedhof) at Thalkirchner Strasse 30
U3 Brudermühlstrasse

The history of Munich's Jewish community stretches back almost as far as the city's own founding, since when the Jews have played an indispensible part in the city's history, despite pogroms, expulsion, and extermination (see no. 29). An unforgettable way to experience the community's history is to visit the city's two Jewish cemeteries. Whilst the gravestones here speak eloquently of the achievements of Munich's Jews, the abandoned aspect of the cemeteries today speaks poignantly of the loss of a generation.

We begin at the Old Jewish Cemetery (Alter Israelitischer Friedhof) at Thalkirchner Strasse 30, Munich's first official Jewish cemetery opened in 1816. Following their expulsion in 1442 the Jews had filtered back to Munich in 1763, where their legal status was recognised by royal edict in 1813. The official establishment of the Jewish Community (Israelitische Kultusgemeinde) in 1815 prompted construction of the cemetery. Surrounded by a high brick wall and covering 2.5 hectares the cemetery contains approximately 6000 graves, several of which are those of so-called 'Court Jews', ennobled for their services to the Bavarian court. Its peace is rarely disturbed since the cemetery is only open a few precious days a year for guided tours given to the city's Volkshochschule (Community College), Bildungswerk (Association for Adult Education), and other institutions (for details contact the Jewish Community, tel. 089 20 24 00-100). The rest of the time just a handful of elaborate funerary monuments can be glimpsed at through the iron gates on Thalkirchner Strasse, dotted about beneath the swaying Cypress trees.

In 1848 Munich's Jews gained the right to vote. With the abolition in 1861 of limits placed on the number of Jews permitted to reside in each district the community increased in size, and in 1880 many Eastern Jews arrived in the wake of pogroms in Russia. Inevitably, the Old Jewish Cemetery could no longer cope and in 1908 it was replaced by the New Jewish Cemetery (Neuer Israelitischer Friedhof) at Garchinger Strasse 37. Open to the general public but fairly well concealed this is undoubtedly one of the most beautiful and affecting cemeteries in Munich.

The New Jewish Cemetery represents the highs and the lows of Munich's 19th and 20th century Jewish communities. A spacious six hectares in size it was designed by the architect Hans Grässel (1860–1939), in line with his new ideas about forest cemeteries (see no. 69). Within a couple of years of its opening the community reached an all time high of around 9000 members. However, by 1944 only seven members of the community were left alive in Munich, the rest having emigrated, or else been deported to the concentration and death camps by the Nazis. This extermination robbed the cemetery of its regular visitors, many of the older graves having been untended ever since.

Just inside the main entrance to the cemetery there is a fine ceremonial hall designed by Grässel, the interior

Graves in the Old Jewish Cemetery (Alter Israelitischer Friedhof) in Sendling

of which can be glimpsed through its glass doors. Immediately opposite is a mass grave for Jewish soldiers who gave their lives for the German 'Fatherland' during the First World War; eight stones are inscribed with the names and ranks of those buried here. Beyond are several memorials to the many Jews murdered between 1933 and 1945. Their flat surfaces are stacked with pebbles ('memory stones') left by visitors; the tradition is thought to be an ancient Bedouin custom, the stones being used to mark out graves in the shifting desert sands. The oldest graves of the cemetery are to be found hereabouts too, their headstones poking up out of the verdant moss and ivy. To the rear of this part of the cemetery can also be found the grave of Kurt Eisner, the assassinated founder of Munich's short-lived Bavarian Soviet Republic (see no. 3).

Detail of a gravestone in Munich's New Jewish Cemetery (Neuer Israelitischer Friedhof)

It is interesting to note that some headstones carry signs symbolising the derivation of the deceased's name. Cohen, for example, meaning priest in Hebrew, is represented by a pair of blessing hands; similarly Levi, meaning a priest's assistant, is represented by the jug used to wash the priest's hands. The farthest reaches of the cemetery are reserved for more recent burials, which have been made here since Munich's Jewish Community was re-established after the Second World War. To date 7500 of the cemetery's total of 10 000 graves have been filled.

The overgrown appearance of both cemeteries is due only in part to the absence of mourners since the traditional Jewish view is that a cemetery is a cultic homeland and a place of eventual physical resurrection, whose peace must in no way be disturbed. Trees are therefore only cut when they present a danger, and no headstone is ever removed, even if it appears to have been abandoned.

Just inside the southern entrance to the Brudermühlstrasse U-Bahn station, near the New Jewish Cemetery, there is a large, circular iron object, which many people use to extinguish their cigarettes. Far from being an ashtray this curious object is a pair of grindstones, taken from a mill which stood nearby until it burnt down in 1897. The mill was founded originally as Ekolf's Mill (Ekolfsmühl) in the late 13th century, and re-developed by a group of Franciscan brothers in 1577, after whom the mill was subsequently re-named. An engraving of the mill, both before and during the fire, can be seen on an information board.

Other places of interest nearby: 62

68 The Heroic Farmers of Sendling

Sendling, St. Margaret's Church (Margaretenkirche) on
Sendlinger Kirchplatz
S7, S20, S27 Harras; U6 Harras; U3, U6 Implerstrasse

One of the bloodiest episodes in Munich's history occurred in what is today the peaceful district of Sendling. To the rear of the old parish church of St. Margaret (1711–1712) on Sendlinger Kirchplatz there is a fresco by the painter Wilhelm Lindenschmidt the Elder (1806–1848) entitled *Die Sendlinger Bauernschlacht 1705* ('The Farmers' Battle of Sendling 1705'). The violent scenes played out in the fresco cast the on-looker's mind back to the turbulent reign of Maximilian II Emanuel, Elector of Bavaria (1679–1726).

Known as the 'White Knight', Maximilian is remembered not only as a popular leader and as a patron of the arts, but also for his military ambitions and his attempts to become involved in the Austrian Succession. To achieve this he allied himself with the Habsburg court in Vienna and took part in the defence of that city in 1683, during which the Ottoman Turks were finally repulsed. As a result Maximilian was awarded the regency of the southern Netherlands. Soon embroiled in the Wars of the Spanish Succession he swapped allegiances and in 1702 made an alliance with Louis XIV of France.

However, in 1704 the Franco-Bavarian army was defeated by Habsburg troops and Maximilian was forced to flee to France, unable to return to the Elector's throne until a peace treaty was signed in 1714. Meanwhile, Bavaria endured a decade of harsh Austrian rule during which protests by desperate peasants were bloodily suppressed. It is one of these protests from 1705 that is depicted in the Sendling fresco.

Referred to in the history books either as Sendlinger Mordweihnacht ('Sendling Murder Christmas') or Sendlinger Blutweihnacht ('Sendling Blood Christmas') it is recorded that a thousand protesting farmers and other peasants were massacred here by Austrian troops. A further seven hundred were taken prisoner, many of whom were later executed, whilst on the Austrian side only about forty soldiers were reported wounded.

Of the dead some eight hundred were buried in a mass grave at the scene (now occupied by the church), over which a monument was

raised in 1830. Adorned with a gilded sword and wreath the monument records how the farmers died for "Fürst und Vaterland" (elector and country). Several hundred more were buried in the Old South Cemetery (Alter Südfriedhof) on Thalkirchner Strasse 17, just outside the city's Sendling Gate (Sendlinger Tor). Occupying a narrow triangular plot defined by Thalkirchnerstrasse, Pestalozzistrasse and Kapuzinerstrasse, the cemetery began in 1563 as a burial ground for paupers and plague victims but after the city churchyards were closed around 1800 it became Munich's main cemetery. A monument to the victims of the Sendling massacre can be seen there today.

The fighting farmers of Sendling depicted in a fresco at St. Margaret's Church (Margaretenkirche)

The Old South Cemetery, which has been a public park since 1944, is worthy of a visit since it is the last resting place of many of Munich's notable 19th century scientists and artists. They include physicist Georg Ohm (1789–1854), the father of the electrical circuit, and optician Josef von Fraunhofer (1787–1826), the creator of the world's finest optical glass; Alois Senefelder (1771–1834), the inventor of the lithographic printing process; the Bavarian court architect Leo von Klenze (1784–1864), who designed the Propyläen and the Glyptothek on Königsplatz, the Alte Pinakothek on Barer Strasse, as well as the Ruhmeshalle on Theresienwiese; the sculptor Ludwig von Schwanthaler (1802–1848), creator of the colossal *Bavaria* statue in front of the Ruhmeshalle; and the Romantic and Biedermeier artist Carl Spitzweg (1808–1885), whose work hangs in the Lenbachhaus Art Gallery (Galerie im Lenbachhaus). A map at the entrance to the cemetery shows clearly their location.

69 The First Forest Cemetery

Hadern, the Waldfriedhof at the junction of Graubündener-strasse and Forst-Kasten-Allee
U3 Fürstenried-West

Most of the great European city cemeteries of the late 19th century were laid out as imposing 'cities of the dead', their plans strictly defined by a rigid grid-pattern of paths and grave plots, with the mausolea of the wealthy placed very much centre-stage (see nos. 47 & 61). A complete break with these practices came in 1907, when the German architect Hans Grässel (1860–1939) opened a very different kind of cemetery in Munich's south-western suburbs. Termed a Waldfriedhof, or 'forest cemetery', all straight lines have been sacrificed in favour of winding paths, the dead of all classes mingling happily side-by-side amongst the trees. As such, Munich's Waldfriedhof is considered Europe's first true forest cemetery.

The re-location of munich's cemeteries during the second half of the 19th century, from cramped city churchyards out into the suburbs, was deemed necessary as sanitation improved, population increased, and more building space was required. However, the move inevitably brought with it a dissassociation of the burial ground from the church building itself, with the result that new cemeteries became more like parks. To regain some symbolic strength, Grässel used influences from early Christian and Byzantine architecture in the funerary chapels and other structures he installed in his forest cemetery. Both buildings and graves are dotted artfully amongst carefully planted groves creating a contrived yet wholly convincing connection between nature and death. Thus, the main feature of the cemetery is no longer individual monuments but the natural setting and tranquil mood of the cemetery as a whole. Grässel's ideas later inspired not only other German forest cemeteries but also the Skogskyrkogården, a UNESCO world heritage cemetery outside Stockholm.

The Munich Waldfriedhof is divided into two main sections, namely the Old Section (Alter Teil) to the north, and the New Section (Neuer Teil) to the south. Altogether it covers an area roughly the same size as Munich's Old Town (Altstadt), making it impossible to explore in a single visit. To get a good flavour, however, it is recommended to enter the cemetery from the south (at the junction of Graubundener-strasse and Forst-Kasten-Allee) and walk northwards (to the exit at

Munich's Waldfriedhof was Europe's first forest cemetery

the junction of Würmtalstrasse and Fürstenriederstrasse). Keeping to the paths on the righthand-side affords the opportunity to see a rich variety of graves, including those of several celebrities.

The first is Leni Riefenstahl (1902–2003), probably the most controversial film director of the 20th century, whose grave can be found in Group 509. After serving as a ballerina during the early 1920s in the films of director Arnold Fanck she sacrificed the chance of going to Hollywood in favour of becoming a director in her own right. She established herself fully with *Triumph of the Will* (1935), a commissioned record of the 1934 Nuremberg Nazi Party rally, and *Olympia* (1938), which helped promulgate the notion of Aryan physical supremacy at the Berlin Olympic Games of 1936. Despite inventing many camera effects used today her apparent Nazi sympathies saw her shunned by the mainstream film industry after the war.

Just beyond the Riefenstahl grave there is a vast Italian War Cemetery (Cimitero Italiano), its serried ranks of simple headstones presided over by a fluttering Italian flag. Most of those buried here met their end in 1945.

Moving northwards there will be seen amongst the trees numerous special groupings of graves, the most interesting of which are those of Muslims, their headstones all pointing towards Mecca, and the rows of identical metal crosses marking the resting places of generations of Catholic sisters and priests.

In Group 212 can be found the grave of author Michael Ende (1929–1995), whose book *The Neverending Story* was successfully adapted for cinema; his grave is suitably adorned with several open books sculpted in copper.

From here until the exit there are any number of trackways winding off amongst the trees, each lined with the graves of the famous and the forgotten, one of which contains the cemetery's architect Hans Grässel himself. Another contains German scientist Werner Heisenberg (1901–1976), whose former home at Hohenzollernstrasse 110 is today marked by a wall plaque. Heisenberg was instrumental in the development of atomic physics and was awarded the Nobel Prize in Physics in 1932 for his development of quantum mechanics. He was later appointed director of the Kaiser Wilhelm Institute in Berlin, where the atom was first split in 1938 on a simple wooden table that can be seen in Munich's Deutsches Museum on Museumsinsel. After the war

The mausoleum of Carl Krone, the famous circus director, contains a statue of his favorite elephant!

Heisenberg was released without charge having claimed to have deliberately sabotaged the Nazis' efforts to create an atomic bomb.

From the same period in history are the graves of Josef Kammhuber (1896–1986), the first General of the Luftwaffe's 'Night Flights', Paul Hausser (1880–1972), the patriarchal leader of the Waffen-SS, who sought to rehabilitate the organisation after the war, and, by contrast, Professor Kurt Huber (1893–1943), author of the White Rose resistance group's sixth and last leaflet calling for an end to National Socialism, an act for which he was sent to the guillotine (see no. 45). Admiral Alfred von Tirpitz (1849–1930), who is also buried here, transformed the Imperial German Navy from a coastal defence force into a seagoing fleet of battleships, the construction of which heightened tensions with Britain and contributed to the outbreak of the First World War.

Our tour finishes on a lighter note with the mausoleum of Carl Krone (1870–1943), onetime director of Circus Krone, the largest circus in Europe. Inside the mausoleum can be seen a splendid statue of Krone's favourite elephant, Assam.

70 Exploring Little Asia

Sendling – Westpark, the Little Asia (Klein-Asien)
Garden in Westpark (West) on Garmischer Strasse
U6 Westpark

Heading north on the S7 between Harras and Heimeranplatz, passengers with a keen eye might see an abandoned station flash by – a so-called 'ghost station'. It was built to service the IGA 83, the fourth *Internationale Gartenbauausstellung* (International Garden Exhibition), which was held in 1983 in the Westpark on the lefthand side (the U-Bahn stations at Partnachplatz, Westpark, and Holzapfelkreuth were also constructed for the event, which is reflected in their colour schemes).

Westpark was designed by landscape architect Peter Kluska, initially as a site to host the exhibition, and thereafter to be used as a public park. Laid out between 1978 and 1983, on what was once fallow land, it covers an area of 720 000 square metres and extends two kilometres from east to west. Artificial earthworks, as well as 6000 trees and

This Chinese pavilion is one element of Westpark's Little Asia Garden

120 000 shrubs from around the world, help shield the park from busy Garmischer Strasse (and its westwards *Autobahn* connection), which divides the park neatly into an eastern and western section.

Today, the eastern part, Westpark (Ost), is popular with model boat enthusiasts, who frequent its artificial lake, the Mollsee. However, it is to the western part, Westpark (West), that those in search of remnants of the 1983 exhibition should head. Here can be found several intact examples of the exhibition's twenty-three "nation gardens", which were designed by horticultural experts from around the world. Most prominent is the cluster of gardens originating in Asia, preserved thanks to the striking architectural features incorporated into their designs.

A Thai pavilion, or Sala, is an unexpected sight in Munich

Lying on the north shore of an ornamental lake they are today referred to collectively as *Klein-Asien*, or 'Little Asia', and it makes for a sensual and enlightening experience to explore them.

The typically tranquil Japanese Garden was a contribution from the residents of Munich's twin city, Sapporo. Laid out around a shallow lake the garden's pebble beach, wooden walkways, lanterns, and dwarf maples and pines all reflect the Shinto faith of venerating nature. The equally entrancing Chinese Garden was laid out under the watchful eye of six gardeners from Canton. Clumps of rustling bamboo, tinkling waterfalls, and a pair of dragon motif-adorned pavilions make this tiny garden seem like a world of its own. Nearby stands a pagoda constructed piecemeal in Nepal by two hundred craftsmen and then shipped to Germany and reassembled. The pagoda's dark wood is intricately carved, its rooves decorated with tiny bells.

Westpark is also home to a traditional Bavarian log cabin

Of particular interest in Little Asia is a nine-metre-high Thai *Sala*, a traditional pavilion of a type found throughout Thailand, especially in Buddhist temple areas, or *Wats*. Ornately carved they are generally open on all four sides. In Thailand they can have many uses, from rural travellers' rests (*Sala asai*) and riverside boat pavilions (*Sala thaanam*), to large temple meeting places (*Salawat*), where the laity can hear sermons and receive religious instruction. The example in Westpark, which seems to float on the lake in which it is sited, was donated to the 1983 exhibition by a German businessman based in Bangkok, as a mark of German-Thai friendship. The statue of Buddha inside the pavilion was carved in 1994 by the Thai sculptor Nopradal Khamlae, as a symbol of religious and cultural tolerance between peoples. Consecrated in the same year the pavilion was the first public Buddhist shrine in Germany. It is the setting for Munich's Thai New Year celebrations (*Songkran*) each April, as well as the Buddhist Full Moon celebrations in Summer, and the Hindu Festival of Light in October.

For a more traditional European approach to gardening Westpark is also home to a magnificent rose garden consisting of 20 000 individual plants representing some 650 varieties. There is also a charming wooden Bavarian farmhouse, its balcony almost hidden in summer with red geraniums, which was relocated here especially for the 1983 exhibition. It can be found in the eastern part of the garden, not far from a bridge leading into Westpark (Ost).

71 The Castle on the Würm

Pasing – Obermenzing, Schloss Blutenburg on Wiguläus-Hundt-Weg, off Pippinger Strasse
S2 Obermenzing or Tram 17 then Bus 143 Schloss Blutenburg

Schloss Blutenburg ('Blood Castle') stands alone on the banks of the River Würm, to the west of Schloss Nymphenburg. Surrounded by a moat, with trees and meadows beyond, it boasts an idyllic and tranquil setting. This, however, makes it easy to forget the complicated and turbulent times in which it was built.

Initially a hunting lodge it passed to the Wittelsbachs in 1425. During the late 1430s it was converted into a royal residence by Albert III, Duke of Bavaria-Munich (1438–1460), who reigned during the time of Bavaria's Second Partition (1349–1503). The partition came about when the six co-ruling sons of Holy Roman Emperor Louis IV (1328–1347) split Bavaria into Upper and Lower Bavaria. A further partition in 1353 created Bavaria-Landshut and Bavaria-Straubing, and then another in 1392 created Bavaria-Ingoldstadt and Bavaria-Munich. Inevitably the two most powerful duchies, Bavaria-Munich and Bavaria-Landshut, came to blows over succession. Initially it was agreed that in the event of one of the duchies producing no male heir, the duchy *with* a male heir should inherit the other's territory. However, when George, 'the rich', Duke of Bavaria-Landshut (1479–1503) named his daughter his heir in 1503, the decision was rejected by Albert IV, 'the wise', Duke of Bavaria-Munich (1467–1503). The result was the Landshut War of Succession. After two years of bloody fighting the emperor mediated: Bavaria was reunited under Albert with Munich as its capital. In 1506 Albert decreed that the duchy should henceforth pass according to the rule of primogeniture, which it did from 1545 until the end of the Wittelsbach dynasty in 1918.

The history of Schloss Blutenburg continues in 1488 when Duke Albert III's son, Sigismund, Duke of Bavaria-Munich (1460–1467) extended it. Most significantly he added a chapel in the courtyard, which is today the only original part of the building still standing. The chapel was designed by Jörg von Halsbach, the architect of Munich's Frauenkirche, the foundation stone of which Sigismund laid the same year. The frescoes on the exterior of the chapel are among the few surviving examples of Late Gothic mural painting. The interior of the chapel – remember to close the door to stop the swallows entering – features intri-

Lovely Schloss Blutenburg is situated on the tranquil banks of the River Würm

cate rib vaulting and contains several treasures of Late Gothic religious art, including the wooden Blutenburg Madonna and an altar triptych of 1491 painted by Jan Polack (1435–1519). Sigismund died at Schloss Blutenberg in 1501.

Among Schloss Blutenburg's subsequent royal visitors was Henriette Adelaide of Savoy (1636–1676), wife of Ferdinand Maria, Elector of Bavaria (1651–1679). Her mother was a daughter of Henry IV of France and she had a strong pro-French influence on Bavarian politics, prompting an alliance between France and Bavaria against Habsburg Austria, whom Bavaria had initially supported during the first part of the Thirty Years War (1618–1648). Pro-French policy would define Bavarian politics until German unification in 1871.

After being seriously damaged during the Thirty Years War, Schloss Blutenburg was rebuilt in the early 1680s in much the same shape as it appears today. It was here in 1847 that a young dancer called Lola Montez went into hiding, after a much publicized affair with Ludwig I, King of Bavaria (1825–1848), he was forced to abdicate the following year in favour of his son, Maximilian II (1848–1864). Since 1983 Schloss Blutenburg has housed the International Youth Library (Internationale Jugendbibliothek), the largest collection of children's and young people's literature in the world. Founded in 1946 it contains over 400 000 volumes in more than 130 languages and is under the patronage of UNESCO.

72 Relics of the Nazi War Machine

Allach – Untermenzing, a tour beginning at Allach
S-Bahn station
S2 Allach; Bus 160 Allach

From 1933 onwards many of today's prominent German companies played a part in Hitler's secret plans to rearm Germany and conquer Europe, a fact that is hardly surprising since most had little choice and the financial rewards were tempting. They included the car manufacturers Volkswagen, Mercedes-Benz, BMW, and Opel, as well as the aircraft company Messerschmitt, which was responsible for the ME109, the key fighter plane in Hermann Göring's new Luftwaffe. After the war Messerschmitt was absorbed into the European Aeronautic Defence and Space Company (EADS), which today tenders for lucrative contracts with the American airforce. There were many less obvious co-operations too: Aspirin manufacturer Bayer, for example, was part of the IG Farben conglomerate responsible for the Zyklon-B gas deployed in Nazi death camps; a German subsidiary of IBM produced punch cards used to overhaul the census system of newly-invaded countries; Siemens used forced labourers in its factories supplying munitions to the German military; and in 1933 the clothing company of Hugo Boss designed and manufactured black uniforms for Heinrich Himmler's SS, the brown-shirted SA, as well as for the Hitler Youth.

Some of the most important armament factories of the Third Reich were located on the outskirts of Munich, where until 1942 they remained outside the range of Allied bombers. A fascinating trip to discover what remains of this wartime landscape begins by alighting the S-Bahn at Allach, where the station platform affords a clear view of the Krauss-Maffei-Wegmann factory, at Krauss-Maffei Strasse 2. Opened in 1933 and manned by prisoners of war the factory produced thousands of locomotives, tanks, and other armoured vehicles for Hitler's war machine. Lauded as a model company by the German Work Front it is today the leading producer of armoured wheeled and tracked vehicles in Europe. (Directly behind the factory is the former Porcelain Works Allach at Reinhard-von-Frank-Strasse 8, where kitsch Third Reich ornaments were manufactured, samples of which are displayed in the permanent National Socialism exhibition of the Münchner Stadtmuseum (Munich City Museum) on St.-Jakobs-Platz.)

Immediately outside the railway station one is greeted by an octagonal Second World War civilian air raid shelter. It is made to look like a Renaissance tower, replete with balustraded entrance, arched doorway, and steep red-tiled roof, so as to disguise it from the air and to reassure the local populace. From here we take a short stroll northwards along Georg-Reismüller-Strasse and turn right onto Ludwigsfelder Strasse. On the lefthand side at number 11 is the former main warehouse for the Sager & Woerner Construction Company. In 1921 engineer Fritz Todt began working for this company as managing director of its road construction department, and in 1933 he was appointed by Hitler as Chief Planner of the German Motorways. The company profited greatly from ensuing contracts (the first was for the building of the Munich-Salzburg Autobahn), which included Berlin-Tempelhof Airport and part of the *Westwall*, a defensive line in northern France. The company was later transformed into Walter Bau AG and the old site abandoned.

Just before the warehouse is Schöllstrasse, where a little way along on the righthand side, at number 8, can be found a former Junkers Engine Factory, used to produce engines for the Ju 87 *(Stuka)* and Ju 88 fighter-bomber. A hoist to the rear of the building was used to transfer finished engines directly onto awaiting freight trains, from where they were taken to Dessau for final assembly.

Forced labour was supplied to both of these factories from a prisoner of war camp located on nearby Pasteurstrasse. Another forced

This abandoned warehouse in Allach once belonged to the Sager & Woerner Construction Company, responsible for constructing Hitler's Westwall

Engines for Hermann Göring's airforce were once made in this factory

labour camp was set up in the nearby Allach Forest (Allacher Forst), where the BMW Factory II was established to manufacture engines, and latterly jet units, for the Luftwaffe. Some 8000 prisoners worked at the site, which is now owned by the MAN motor and turbine company. (BMW Factory I was located at Lerchenauer Strasse 76 and is still in use today (see no. 80).)

Our tour in Allach ends here but it is worth noting several other former sites of similar interest in Munich, including the Dynamit AG Detonator Factory at the corner of Rosenheimer Strasse and Anzingerstrasse, the IG Farben Detonator Factory at Tegernseer Landstrasse 161, and the Dornier Aircraft factory at Brunhamstrasse 21 in Neuaubing.

73 Royal Pavilions and Golden Sleighs

Neuhausen – Nymphenburg, Schloss Nymphenburg and Schlosspark
S1, S2, S3, S4, S6, S7, S8 Laim or U1, U7 Rotkreuzplatz
then Tram 12, 17 or Bus 51 Schloss Nymphenburg

In 1663 Henriette Adelaide of Savoy gave birth to the heir to the Wittelsbach throne, the future Maximilian II Emanuel. Her husband Ferdinand Maria, Elector of Bavaria (1651–1679), celebrated by commissioning a summer residence at Schloss Nymphenburg. Built in 1664–1675 to a design by the Italian architect Agostino Barelli (1627–1687), the palace and its small decorative garden was subsequently developed in 1714–1726 by Maximilian, now Elector himself (1679–1726).

Working with his court architect Josef Effner (1687–1745), to a design by Dominique Girard, Maximilian created a vast Baroque garden, consisting of a parterre beyond which stretched an axial canal, fed by the River Würm; this was flanked on either side by two groups of six straight avenues, each radiating out from a garden pavilion. In 1800–1823 these formal gardens were radically transformed into a classic English-style landscape park by Maximilian I, King of Bavaria (1799–1825, until 1806 as Elector Maximilian IV Joseph). His garden designer Friedrich Ludwig von Sckell (1750–1823) cleverly integrated some of the earlier Baroque features, including the parterre, canal and pavilions, into a less rigid and more natural design, of lakes, streams, deliberately-placed groves, and far-reaching vistas. The palace building underwent many expansions too, achieving an impressive final length of 650 metres.

We enter the Schlosspark across the Large Parterre, a feature of both the earlier Baroque garden and the later landscape garden, and then cross a bridge over the canal to the right. From here, follow signs to the Magdalenenklause (1725–1728), a garden pavilion designed by Josef Effner. It is noteworthy for being one of the first examples in Europe of a park building designed consciously as a *faux* ruin. Built as a hermitage and chapel for contemplation it takes the form of a shell-lined grotto.

Returning back along the same path, follow signs to the lakeside Pagodenburg (1716–1719), built originally as the focal point for the northern half of the Baroque garden. This building takes the form of an octagonal, two storied tea house with Delft tile decoration on the ground floor, and Chinese wall coverings on the first. It is a fine example of the Chinese style *(Chinoiserie)* popular in the early 18th century. The pavilion's name, incidentally, is derived from the numerous figures of Chinese idols (known as *pagods*), which are incorporated into the decoration.

Behind the Pagodenburg several paths lead to a water lilly pond reminiscent of a scene from a Monet painting. Otherwise, continue along the main path, bearing left along the shore of the lake, taking in Sckell's magnificent North Vista towards the palace. Cross the Central Canal, with its formal view to the palace, and then walk through a meadow with wild flowers, which makes up Sckell's South Vista.

Entering woods notice a statue of Pan sitting over a gurgling spring, and then cross a stream to reach the

Chinoiserie in the Pagodenburg, a teahouse at Schloss Nymphenburg

Badenburg (1718–1721), once the focal point for the southern half of the Baroque garden. Built as a summer palace for Maximilian II Emanuel, the main feature is a unique bathing hall, with gilded water taps, as well as an ornate banqueting hall. The smaller rooms are decorated with Chinese wallpapers. Today, there is a sublime view from the Badenburg across the nearby lake to a magnificently-sited garden temple, the Monopteros, constructed in 1862–1865 to a design by the pioneering neo-Classical architect Leo von Klenze (1784–1864).

Follow the path alongside the river back towards the palace and on the left will be found the Amalienburg (1734–1739), commissioned by Charles Albert, Elector of Bavaria (1726–1745) as a small summer residence and hunting lodge for his wife, Maria Amalia. Designed by the court architect François de Cuvilliés (1695–1768) this single-storey building, notable for its hall of mirrors, is a masterpiece of Late Baroque (Rococo) art. Undoubtedly the most unusual room is the kitchen, with its Chinoiserie-painted ceiling and Delft-tiled walls (see page 231).

Golden sleighs and carriages in the Marstall of Schloss Nymphenburg

That some of the tiling is wrongly assembled suggests that the scenes were received from Rotterdam incomplete.

Once back at the palace don't miss the Royal Sleigh Collection, housed in the Marstall in the South Wing (Südliches Schlossrondell). It contains gilded children's sleighs, hunting sleighs, a court carousel, and King Ludwig II's romantic 'Nymph' and 'Renaissance' sleighs.

Don't miss the huge pumping engine installed in 1808 in the north wing of Schloss Nymphenburg (Nördliches Schlossrondell), used to power the forecourt fountain. Waterpower is also used in the nearby porcelain works (Porzellanmanufaktur Nymphenburg) opened in 1761. Another royal pumping engine is hidden beneath the brick arcade at the eastern end of Galeriestrasse. Dating from the second half of the 19th century it was used to supply the fountains in the Hofgarten.

Other places of interest nearby: 74

74 The Quagga and Other Oddities

Neuhausen – Nymphenburg, the Museum of Man and Nature
(Museum Mensch und Natur) in Schloss Nymphenburg
(North Wing)
S1, S2, S3, S4, S6, S7, S8 Laim or U1, U7 Rotkreutzplatz, then
Tram 12, 17 or Bus 51 Schloss Nymphenburg

Tucked away in the north wing of Schloss Nymphenburg (Nördliches Schlossrondell), the Baroque summer palace commissioned by Ferdinand Maria, Elector of Bavaria (1651–1679), is the fascinating Museum of Man and Nature (Museum Mensch und Natur) (see no. 73). Taken at face value it is a modern and lively natural history collection, renowned for its interactive displays that appeal to visitors of all ages. Its subject matter is broad, from the geological history of planet earth, dinosaurs and biodiversity, to modern themes such as genetic research and nature conservation. Look more closely, however, amidst the flashing

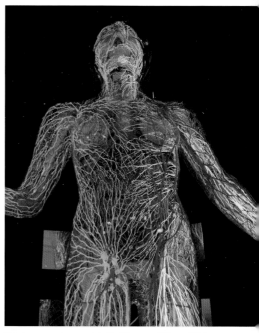

This transparent woman is in the Museum of Man and Nature (Museum Mensch und Natur)

lights and excited school children, and there can be found some rather unusual and perhaps unexpected exhibits.

These include a 50 million-year-old fossilised horse complete with tail hair, a reconstruction of an Archaeopteryx (the earliest bird known to man), a pair of giant Japanese crabs, and a lifesize transparent woman, whose internal organs light up at the touch of a button! There is also a Brown Bear shot in 1834, which until recently was the last wild bear seen in Bavaria: in 2006 an Italian wild bear called Bruno strayed into Bavaria and after making headlines around the world was shot for safety reasons. Bruno was subsequently stuffed and has become one of the museum's most popular exhibits.

Most unusual of all is a stuffed specimen of a Quagga, the now extinct, partially-striped sub-species of the Plains Zebra. This particular example is a female that was acquired in the 1830s, restored in the 1990s, and is now one of only twenty-three stuffed specimens in the world.

It was the Hottentot people (now the Khoikhoi) of the southern African plains, where the Quagga was once the only type of Zebra to be seen, who called this curious creature *Quahah*, referring to its distinctive call. Classified incorrectly in 1788 as a distinct species *(Equus quagga)*, the Quagga differed from the usual Plains Zebra *(Equus burchelli)* in that its body colour was mostly light reddish-brown, the head, neck and forequarters marked with chocolate-brown stripes, and with a dorsal stripe that continued along the full length of the back. The legs and lower parts of the body were cream-coloured or white, and the main was short and upright. The Quagga also differed from the Zebra in being easily tamed. During the 1830s Quaggas could even be found in England, where they served as harness animals, one Sheriff Parkins of London using a pair to pull his carriage around the city!

Unfortunately the Quagga would be extinct before it could be correctly identified as a Zebra sub-species. The wholesale destruction of the Quagga began in the 1840s, as the arrival of the British in southern Africa forced Boer farmers to depart the Cape Colony they had created under the Dutch East India Company. In need of food and tempted by their fatty yellow flesh the Boers hunted down the Quaggas that roamed the plains of southern Africa, retaining a few as guard animals because of their useful call in times of danger. Additionally, the Boers created a booming

Bruno the bear

A rare specimen of the extinct Quagga

business in Quagga hides, which made very durable fruit sacks, shoe leathers, and belts for steam engines.

Slaughtered in their thousands, the Quaggas disappeared sometime during the 1870s. Attempts by various zoos to breed Quaggas came to nought and with the death of the last mare in captivity in Amsterdam Zoo in 1883 the Quagga was declared extinct. Subsequent Quagga sightings were dismissed as aberrantly-marked Plains Zebras or else crosses between feral asses and zebras.

The Quagga story does not finish here though. Although the technology to use recovered DNA for breeding does not yet exist, it is hoped one day to use it to reintroduce the Quagga to the wild. In 1984 the Quagga became the first extinct creature to have its DNA successfully extracted. In the meantime, the Quagga's close relationship with the plains Zebra has led to a programme of selective breeding from Plains Zebra stock, and in 2006 it was reported that creatures looking very much like the extinct Quagga had been produced. Only time will tell whether the Quagga will ever roam the plains of southern Africa again.

Other places of interest nearby: 73

75 A Successful Example of Ecclesiastical Modernism

Neuhausen – Nymphenburg, the Church of the
Heart of Jesus (Herz-Jesu-Kirche) at Lachnerstrasse 8
U1 Rotkreuzplatz; Tram 12; Bus 53

The Church of the Heart of Jesus (Herz-Jesu-Kirche) is
a stunning example of modern architecture

In a quiet residential neighbourhood of medium-rise apartment blocks, not far from Schloss Nymphenburg, there stands one of Europe's most successful examples of ecclesiastical Modernism. The Church of the Heart of Jesus (Herz-Jesu-Kirche) on Lachnerstrasse couldn't look more different from its Baroque counterparts elsewhere in the city, and yet it has endeared itself to its Catholic congregation in much the same way.

The site where the church now stands was originally occupied by a wooden church built in 1899, but in 1944 this was destroyed by fire during an air raid. Subsequently, a second wooden church was erected but this too succumbed to fire in 1994. With the need for a more substantial structure, an architectural competion was announced, which was won by the young Munich firm of Allmann, Sattler and Wappner. Construction of the church began in 1997, and on 2nd November 2000, exactly six years after the second fire, the church was officially opened.

The striking design of the Church of the Heart of Jesus succeeds because it is both structurally inventive (it is made up of two boxes, one inside the other) and liturgically conservative (it marks a return of the bell tower, the ambulatory cloisters of Gothic cathedrals, and of art and iconography). It thus marks a strategic move away from the 'community centre' style of the 1970s, towards a more monumental and mysterious structure. Such new-found confidence appears to fly in the face of dwindling church attendances in the West and the conversion of existing ecclesiastical buildings for non-religious purposes.

The church is laid out on a simple rectangular grid, its two boxes appearing to pull in opposite directions. The outer box is of glass, held together by a delicate framework of steel, the glass itself taking much of the structural load. The inner box comprises a concrete frame with maple wood louvres. The result is an interesting interplay of transparency and opacity between various areas of the two boxes, designed to either open up or else secrete the internal workings of the church.

The most beguiling aspect of the Church of the Heart of Jesus is undoubtedly the deliberate effect that natural light has on the structure, an element to be found in the most ancient places of worship. Quite unexpectedly a shaft of sunlight will penetrate the two contrasting shells to dramatic effect: the louvres cast a forest of shadows at the entrance and directing the light onwards towards the altar. Behind the altar hangs a curtain of woven gold in which is embedded a crucifix, which reveals itself when illuminated by light from an aperture cut through both boxes behind.

A counterpoint to the altar curtain is provided by a pair of 14 metre-high glass doors at the opposite end of the building. Hydraulically-operated they can be swung outwards into the forecourt converting the outer box into a giant portal for the church proper. The space between the two boxes forms a corridor along which visitors can walk or congregate, exactly as they would in the aisles of a Gothic cathedral; the walls of the corridor are hung with images of Jerusalem, which act as stations of the cross.

This most impressive of modern church buildings is finished off with a detached but matching bell tower 37 metres-high. Like the church it comprises a steel-framed glass superstructure with a wooden bell-chamber inside.

76 Outposts of Orthodoxy

Neuhausen – Nymphenburg, the East-West Peace Church
(Ost-West-Friedenskirche) at Spiridon-Louis-Ring 100, off
Rudolf-Harbig-Weg near Olympiapark
U2 Hohenzollernplatz, then Tram 12 Infanteriestrasse,
and walk along Rudolf-Harbig-Weg

In 1829, Ludwig I, King of Bavaria (1825–1848) donated the Church of
the Saviour (Salvatorkirche) at Salvatorplatz 17 to Munich's Greek Orthodox community, as part of a plan to secure a Wittelsbach kingdom in
Greece under his second son, Otto. The Gothic church, with its distinctive slender steeple, had been constructed in the early 1490s to serve as
a funerary chapel for the Frauenkirche, in a new cemetery created just
inside the city walls (the existing cemetery at the Frauenkirche, as well
as that of the Peterskirche, could no longer support Munich's growing
population). Today, the cemetery is long gone but the Church of the
Saviour continues in its role as the focus for the city's Greek Orthodox
community, being the seat of both the *Metropolitan* (diocesan bishop)
of Germany, and the *Exarchen* (Patriarchal deputy) of Central Europe.
The dimly-lit interior contains an unusual mix of Gothic architecture
and Greek Orthodox furnishings, including a gilded *iconostasis* at the
end of the nave, used to conceal the altar from the congregation thus
preserving a sense of religious mystery.

The Greek Orthodox *Metropolis* of Germany, established in 1963,
is the third largest Christian church in Germany, accounting for the
presence of several other Greek churches in the city, for example the
modern Church of All Saints (Allerheiligen-Kirche) at Ungererstrasse
151. Coincidentally, the funerary church of the North Cemetery (Nordfriedhof) across the road is designed in the style of a traditional Greek
Orthodox church.

By contrast, the Russian Orthodox church in Munich is represented by several less monumental structures, including a church on Lin-
colnstrasse next to the Perlacher Forst Cemetery (Friedhof am Perlacher Forst), a small monastery near Schloss Blutenburg on the banks of
the River Würm, and a tiny wooden church at Dachau, just outside the
city, built by Russian soldiers in 1994 to commemorate the 6000 Russian prisoners of war who died at the Nazi concentration camp there.

Most unusual of all is the Russian Orthodox chapel that stands in
its own enclosed garden on Rudolf-Harbig-Weg, just south of Olympia-

Old Father Timofej built the East-West Peace Church (Ost-West-Friedenskirche) entirely by hand

park, on land that each year is used for the Tollwood music festival. The chapel was hand-built by Timofej Wassiljewitsch Prochorow (1894–2004), a Russian emigré who spent much of the Second World War digging coal for the occupying German forces. After losing his horse and cart to retreating Wehrmacht troops in 1943 he claims to have seen a vision of the Virgin Mary, instructing him to leave his family and to travel west to Vienna. This he did and although his plans to erect a chapel in Mary's honour were thwarted he did meet a Russian women there called Natascha, with whom he would spend the next thirty years.

Whilst in Vienna, Timofej experienced a second vision in which he was instructed to go to Munich, where he arrived with Natascha in 1952. They settled in a field called the Oberwiesenfeld (which had been Munich's first airport) alongside a colossal mountain of wartime debris, brought here from the bombed-out city centre (see no. 49). They used some of this debris to construct a small house as well as a chapel, the roof of which was adorned with Russian Orthodox crosses, each with the usual three horizontal members (one for the inscription INRI, one for Christ's hands, and a slanting one for His feet). The chapel was subsequently filled with icons and ornaments, its ceiling lined with silver paper taken from discarded chocolate wrappers.

Inside the Greek Orthodox Church of the Saviour (Salvatorkirche)

Timofej and Natascha lived here peacefully for several decades, in tacit agreement with the authorities regarding their lack of planning permission. In the late 1960s, however, it was suggested the couple be evicted to make way for the site of the 1972 Summer Olympics. Fortunately, thanks to vociferous protests from Munich's citizens and the media, the developers were persuaded to shift their building plans slightly northwards, allowing Timofej's little church to remain standing. By this time it was known as the East-West Peace Church (Ost-West-Friedenskirche), following a third vision (this time in the garden) in which Timofej asked God why the Western Catholic and Eastern Orthodox churches had different calendars? God told him that *neither* Julian nor Gregorian were necessary, as a result of which Timofej united both churches with a new calendar beginning on 1st May.

In the same year as the Olympics, Timofej and Natascha were married but she died just five years later. Forbidden to bury her alongside the church, he erected a symbolic grave there instead, which can still be seen today. On 13th July 2004 'Väterchen Timofej' (Old Father Timofej) died at the grand old age of 110, making him Munich's oldest citizen. He was laid to rest in the nearby West Cemetery (Westfriedhof) (196-2-45) (see no. 77). Although he has gone, his little church remains a unique place of worship and a fitting memorial to the unusual man who created it. A small museum contains photographs illustrating his life and work here, and the surrounding semi-wild garden is alive with roses, bees, and songbirds. The Munich Mayor Christian Ude described this hidden paradise as the city's most loveable illegal building!

77 Some Controversial Graves

Moosach, the West Cemetery (Westfriedhof) at
Baldurstrasse 28
U1, U7 Westfriedhof; Tram 20, 21

Opened just over a century ago the West Cemetery (Westfriedhof) on
Baldurstrasse is Munich's second largest burial ground after the Waldfriedhof (see no. 69). Burials here include the artist Franz von Lenbach
(1836–1904), architect Bernhard Borst (1883–1963), and much-loved
Russian emigré priest, Timofej Wassiljewitsch Prochorow (1894–2004)
(see nos. 35, 76 & 78). However, the cemetery is also the last resting place
of four other characters, who courted controversy in both life and death.

The first is General Hans
Peter Baur (1897–1993) (Group
114-A-29), who served as Adolf
Hitler's personal pilot until the
dictator's suicide in 1945. Something of a war hero Baur shot
down nine enemy aircraft during
the First World War, for which he
was awarded the Bavarian Medal
for Bravery. In 1926 he became
one of the first six pilots of the
newly-founded Lufthansa; it was
shortly after flying his one mil-
lionth kilometer that he was selected personally by Hitler. Act-
ing also as an advisor about air
war policy Baur spent time in the
legendary Berlin *Führerbunker*
with Hitler during the last days
of the Second World War. Baur's
final order was to fly Martin Bormann out of Berlin, but during
their escape attempt on the night
of 1st May 1945 Baur lost sight of
Bormann and was shot and captured by the Russians. One of his
legs was subsequently amputat-

The West Cemetery (Westfriedhof) in Moosach contains
the grave of Adolf Hitler's personal pilot

ed. Over the next decade he was interrogated by the Russians, who suspected he had flown Hitler to safety before the fall of Berlin. Released in 1955 Baur returned to Germany where he wrote his memoirs *Ich flog Mächtige der Erde (I Flew the Powerful of the Earth)* (1956).

Another controversial incumbent of the cemetery is Ernst Röhm (1887–1934), who unlike Baur found himself on the wrong side of Hitler. A German army officer during the First World War Röhm became a close early ally of Hitler, founding the Nazi paramilitary *Sturmabteilung* (Storm Troopers). After Hitler came to power in 1933, however, Röhm and his SA brownshirts were quickly seen as rivals by the German Army and the SS. As a result, Hitler had the SA leadership liquidated during the notorious 'Night of the Long Knives' on 30th June 1934. Röhm himself was murdered in Munich's Stadelheim prison and was buried in a small family grave in the West Cemetery. Having attracted far Right extremists in the past the location of the grave location is not advertised.

A third controversial character is quite different again. Soraya Esfandiary-Bakhtiary (1932-2001) (Group 143-A-17) was known around the world as the second wife and Queen Consort of Mohammed Reza Pahlavi, the last Shah of Iran. She was born in Isfahan, the only daughter of Khalil Esfandiary, a noble of the Bakhtiari tribe who was Iranian ambassador to West Germany in the 1950s. Soraya was introduced to the recently-divorced Shah whilst still at Swiss finishing school, and was married to him in 1951. Amongst the wedding gifts was a mink coat sent by Joseph Stalin. The 2000 guests enjoyed an equestrian circus brought all the way from Rome, together with one and a half tonnes of orchids, tulips, and carnations flown in from the Netherlands.

By 1958 the wedding had disintegrated over Soraya's apparent infertility, with the Shah suggesting that he take a second wife to produce the required heir. On 21st March 1958, Iranian New Year's Day, a weeping Shah announced publically their divorce, and Soraya relocated to France, where she enjoyed a brief career as a film actress. She became companion to film director Franco Indovina (1932–1972) but his death in a plane crash saw Soraya spend the remainder of her life wandering unhappily through Europe, purchasing antiques and appearing at occasional social events. After dying of undisclosed causes in Paris aged 69 Soraya was buried in the West Cemetery alongside her parents and her brother. After her effects were sold at auction for $8.3 million her grave was defaced making newspaper headlines across Europe. Rumours that she was murdered together with her brother, who died a week after her, have never been substantiated.

The last resting place of Soraya Esfandiary-Bakhtiary, second wife of the Shah of Iran

We conclude with another tragic female, Doris Nefedov (1942–1969) (Plot 101, grave 81), a Lithuanian-born pop singer known by the pseudonym 'Alexandra'. As a child her family abandoned their homeland and relocated to Kiel, where Alexandra took up music and dancing. In December 1962 she married Nikolaj Nefedov, with whom she planned to emigrate to America. Unfortunately, after giving birth to a son just six months later, the marriage foundered. But then in 1967 Alexandra was 'discovered' by the music producer Fred Weyrich, and a string of hit records quickly followed. Singing in French, English, Spanish, Russian and Hebrew she toured France and the Soviet Union, and shared the stage with Gilbert Bécaud and Yves Montand. It was not to last, however, and in 1969, after moving to Munich, Alexandra died together with her mother after her white Mercedes collided with a truck. Her son survived the accident leading to suggestions that the crash was deliberate, Alexandra having signed a life insurance policy the week before. Nothing was ever proven, although in 2004 the case was reopened briefly after it was revealed that her lover at the time, Pierre Lafaire, had been an American spy.

Other places of interest nearby: 78

78 A Much Loved Housing Estate

Moosach, the Borstei Housing Estate and Museum at
Löfftzstrasse 10
U1, U7 Westfriedhof; Tram 20, 21

A detail of Bernhard Borst's eponymous
Munich housing estate

Fitted neatly into an angle at the junction of Dachauer Strasse and Landshuter Allee, between Olympiapark and the Westfriedhof, stands one of Munich's least-known but best-loved architectural treasures. The so-called Borstei is a charming Modernist housing estate named after its chief designer, the architect Bernhard Borst (1883–1963).

Born in Baden-Württemberg Borst arrived in Munich as a child and at the age of thirteen found work as a bricklayer. Between 1899 and 1903 he studied at the Royal Building Trade School (Königliche Baugewerkschule), eventually becoming a freelance architect in 1908. As well as assisting the architect August Exter in the design of a terraced housing estate and villa colony in the Munich suburb of Pasing, Borst also founded the technical journal *Baukunst (Architecture)*, which remained in print until 1931. However, his greatest achievement remains the Borstei housing estate, which he created with help from his wife Erna, as well as fellow architect Oswald Bieber.

Borst purchased the land for his estate in 1923. His goal was to find a solution to what he perceived as the problem of modern urban living, namely to incorporate the best features of a detached family home into an apartment, easing the domestic burden on the housewife, and improving the overall well-being of the occupants. Borst initially encouraged fellow architects to submit designs for the estate as part of a competition, but when the winning entries proved too expensive to realise he decided to design the estate himself.

Between 1924 and 1929 he laid out a series of courtyards *(Innenhöfe)* around which he ranged 77 smart apartment blocks. The 773 individual dwellings they contain were thoughtfully but not expensively constructed, using brick instead of concrete, and with Slovenian oak parquet floors, and cork-insulated attics beneath copper-sheathed roofs. The Borstei also featured Germany's first integrated heating and power supply sytem, providing central heating and hot running water, and a level of comfort unknown in Munich at the time.

The Borstei's communal amenities were enviable too, including gardens and children's play areas in the courtyards, and a central laundry that guaranteed clean clothes returned within 24 hours. An array of craftsmen, including plumbers, carpenters, decorators and gardeners, were also at the disposal of the Borstei's fortunate tenants. Together with a selection of shops the built area occupied just over 19 000 square metres, with 70 000 square metres reserved for paths, gardens and recreation areas. During the 1930s the estate attracted the upper middle classes and Borst himself lived here until the Sec-

Gardens and sculptures are important elements in the Borstei Housing Estate

ond World War. During his tenure he organised garden concerts for the inhabitants and carnivals and other celebrations for the children.

A visit to the Borstei today shows it has lost little of its original charm, indeed unlike some modern architecture it has grown more attractive with the passing of time and the advance of nature; quite rightly it is now protected as an area of historical importance. It is surprisingly pleasant to walk from one courtyard to the next, noticing the individual door fittings and the decorative frescoes designed to break up the walls. Most appealing are the gardens with their attendant sculptures, especially the Rose Garden (Rosengarten) between Franz-Marc-Strasse and Hildebrandtstrasse, and the Garden of Peace (Garten der Ruhe) behind Bernhard-Borst-Strasse. The full story of Borst and his philanthropic approach to architecture is given in the little Borst Museum (Borst-Museum), which can be found at Löfftzstrasse 10.

Other places of interest nearby: 77

79 Remembering the Munich Massacre

Moosach, the Munich Massacre memorial at Connollystrasse 31 in the Olympic Village
U3 Olympiazentrum, then walk along Lerchenauer Strasse and turn onto Helene-Mayer-Ring, which leads onto Connolly-strasse

Between 26th August and 11th September 1972 Munich staged the 20th Olympic Summer Games. Triggered by the prospect of so many visitors, the city took the opportunity to reinvent itself. In addition to a reawakening of its self-image, the urban fabric of the city was altered dramatically too, most notably with the construction of Olympiapark, on an area used previously to dump rubble from the Second World War (see no. 49). With its huge Olympic Stadium, sports facilities and entertainment complex (Olympiahalle) the park today attracts five million visitors a year.

These days visitors arrive by U-Bahn but back in 1972 they used the S-Bahn, which had been specifically constructed to facilitate transport to and from the Olympic site. The abandoned arrival station, on a disused rail spur, can still be seen today, at the far end of Werner-Seelenbinder-Weg, alongside Landshuter Allee.

The U-Bahn today arrives at the station Olympiazentrum, not far from the BMW Museum (see no. 80). From here it is a short walk along Lerchenauer Strasse, where a left turn leads onto Helene-Mayer-Ring, and eventually Connollystrasse. We are now in what was once part of the Olympic Village (Olympia-Dorf), erected to house the competitors and their trainers. The simple concrete apartments, used today to provide cheap student accommodation, all appear much the same – with the exception of number 31. A modest memorial plaque outside the front door carries the following inscription in German and Hebrew: "The team of the State of Israel stayed in this building during the 20th Olympic Summer Games ... On 5th September, *[list of names here]* died a violent death. Honour to their memory".

The events of the so-called Munich Massacre, dramatised in a controversial 2005 film by Stephen Spielberg, were originally played out on television screens around the world, courtesy of new satellite technology. With a break in the competition the Israeli athletes were

In 1972 this abandoned S-Bahn station delivered thousands of visitors to Munich's Olympic Games

enjoying a rare night out and went to watch a performance of *Fiddler on the Roof*. Afterwards they headed back to their rooms on Connollystrasse. Settling into bed in the early hours of the morning of September 5th they were blissfully unaware of the eight members of the Palestinian terrorist group Black September approaching the Olympic Village. Wearing ski masks and armed with Kalashnikov rifles and hand grenades the group easily climbed the six-foot high security fence.

Shortly after 4am, Israeli wrestling referee Yossef Gutfreund heard a noise at the door and went to investigate. Opening it he was greeted with the barrel of a submachine gun. Upon hearing the commotion two Israeli athletes managed to escape through the back of the apartment, whilst Gutfreund attempted to bar the door. As the terrorists forced their entry others were less lucky, including the wrestling coach Moshe Weinberg, who was shot in the face, and weightlifter Yossef Romano, who was shot dead. The wounded Weinberg was then coerced into showing the terrorists where more Israelis were staying and a further eight were taken prisoner (including an American competing on the Israeli team).

To back up their demand that more than 200 Palestinians be released from Israeli jails the terrorists now shot Weinberg and dumped

A memorial today marks the apartment on Connollystrasse where the Munich Massacre began

his naked body on the street outside. At this stage the authorities negotiated to move the terrorists and nine hostages by helicopter to a nearby airbase, where a waiting aircraft would take them to Cairo. Upon arrival a rescue was attempted by the West German authorities during which all the hostages, together with five terrorists and one police officer, were killed. Only the events of September 11th 2001 would eclipse the Munich Massacre as the most shocking and outrageous terror attack the world had yet seen.

The München 72 café at Kohlstrasse 11 celebrates the spirit of the Summer Olympics. In warm weather guests sit outside on original seats and vaulting boxes taken from the Olympic stadium. Inside, children play on gymnastic mats, whilst their parents sip coffee at desks from the Olympic Village. The walls are adorned with all manner of Olympic memorabilia, and a vintage television set runs an endless loop of the Games' opening ceremony.

Other places of interest nearby: 80

80 In the Land of BMW

Milbertshofen – Am Hart, a tour of the BMW facilities on
Lerchenauer Strasse and Petuelring
U3 Olympiazentrum

German car manufacturer BMW's longstanding presence in Munich is neither hidden nor little-known, but the way in which it has transformed the landscape of a part of Munich is nothing short of unusual. Based around a series of four highly distinctive, silver-grey structures the BMW site is worth visiting even if you don't like cars!

The Bavarian Engine Factory (Bayerische Motorenwerke – BMW) was founded in 1916 to produce aircraft engines, explaining why the company's distinctive logo depicts what look like moving propellor-blades against a sky-blue background. Production was curtailed in 1919 under the terms of the Versailles treaty and the company turned instead to motorcycle and automobile manufacture. From 1933 onwards, however, the company began fulfilling secret aircraft engine orders from German Army High Command, becoming a vital element in Hitler's rearmament programme. The BMW factory on Lerchenauer Strasse quickly became the largest employer in Munich. By the end of the war the factory was a popular target for Allied bombers, and in October 1945 the Americans ordered what remained of the plant to be dismantled.

After the war BMW once again reinvented itself as an automobile manufacturer, inspired by the post-war success of other former aircraft companies such as Messerschmitt. Exiting the Olympiazentrum U-Bahn station today, the visitor will be in no doubt as to how successful the company has been. Stretching far to the left and right along Lerchenauer Strasse are the steel-grey walls of the company's colossal main factory (BMW Werk München). Here all five generations of the company's famous 3-Series cars have been produced. The factory's working statistics are staggering: 10 000 employees and 700 apprentices from fifty different countries are employed, turning out 800 cars and 1200 engines daily (i.e. 200 000 cars and 300 000 engines each year). To witness firsthand how the factory converts a coil of high grade steel into a finished car take one of the weekday factory tours (in English and German) departing from BMW Welt a little farther along the road.

The curvacious stretched-out façade of BMW Welt (BMW World), which opened in 2007, conceals the company's promotional activities in

The BMW tower viewed from BMW Welt, with the BMW museum on the right

Munich. On the corner with Georg-Brauchle-Ring the building is terminated with an impressive diablo-shaped showroom in which current models are displayed on revolving platforms. Inside the building proper is a distribution centre where excited customers collect their finished cars, driving them away down a special ramp.

BMW Welt is connected to the opposite side of the road by a footbridge, where at Petuelring 130 stands the BMW Museum opened in 1973. Taking the form of a windowless, concrete bowl 41 metres in diameter, it is the work of star Austrian architect Karl Schwanzer (1918–1975). Across five floors connected by a spiral ramp (signifying the continuation of a road within an enclosed space) the museum illustrates the company's history from vintage aircraft and motorcycles to the cars of the future. The structure is counterbalanced by Schwanzer's BMW Tower, unveiled in 1972 to house BMW Group Headquarters. Clad in aluminium the 20-story tower resembles the four cylinders of a car's engine.

Not open to visitors is BMW's Research and Engineering Centre (Forschungs- und Ingenieurzentrum) at Schleissheimer Strasse 418. Directly opposite the building at Knorrstrasse 148 is the former site of the so-called Jewish Housing Estate, the first of the Nazis' holding camps for Jews destined for concentration and death camps. After the camp was emptied BMW installed their own labourers here (see no. 72).

Other places of interest nearby: 79

81 Some Gems of the *Jugendstil*

Schwabing – Freimann, a tour from Leopoldstrasse to
Georgenstrasse
U3, U6 Münchner Freiheit; Tram 27; Bus 53

The late 19ᵗʰ century was a revolutionary period for Munich's artists. Frustrated by the oppressive conservatism of the city's art academies, as well as the domineering control of art patron Franz von Lenbach (1836–1904), many architects, sculptors and painters broke away to participate in a new artistic movement. Inspired by the success of *Art Nouveau* in Paris they rejected backwards-looking Historicism in favour of a dramatically different style characterised by highly stylised organic motifs, flowing lines, and freedom of expression. The group held their first international exhibition in 1893 and in 1896 adopted the name *Jugendstil* ('Youth Style'), following publication of the group's *avant-garde* journal, *Jugend.*

During the same period, Munich was experiencing an unprecedented growth in population, from 100 000 in 1854 to 500 000 in 1900. This created a great demand for new housing and civic architecture, which, combined with the introduction of new industrial processes, gave Munich's architects the opportunity to experiment with their new style. *Jugendstil* buildings were subsequently erected across the city, including several notable public buildings (see no. 23). For a more intimate appreciation of the style, however, a visit to the suburb of Schwabing is highly recommended, since it was to here around 1900 that many of the city's artistic innovators gravitated (see no. 48).

Our tour begins outside the bustling Münchner Freiheit U-Bahn station, where on the western side of the street at Leopoldstrasse 77 can be seen a huge apartment house adorned with many classic *Jugendstil* forms. Built in 1900–1902 to a design by Martin Dülfer the roof line takes the form of a curving tendril, which is echoed by undulating leaf forms on the façade below, a dramatic departure from the neo-Classical gables popular during much of the 19ᵗʰ century (see no. 39). The organic theme is continued at street level by a row of sharply delineated rose tree reliefs, such angular forms being another *Jugendstil* characteristic, mirroring the typeface popular in contemporary art journals.

Walk down Leopoldstrasse (in the direction of the city) and turn right onto Herzogstrasse and then take the fourth left onto peaceful Römerstrasse. Here, at number 11, stands a rather different *Jugendstil*

house, designed by Henry Helbig and Ernst Haiger for a client obsessed by Egyptian culture, hence the pseudo-pharaonic masks worked into the façade. Although *Jugendstil* turned its back on Historicism, Egyptian themes proved to be a novel exception, probably because the country had been explored by Europeans half a century earlier. Other *Jugendstil* trademarks employed here include the bold use of colour, and the sharp verticals, again echoing motifs found in art journals.

Continue down Römerstrasse and turn left onto Ainmillerstrasse, the street on which Kandinsky, Klee and Rilke all lived, where another Helbig and Haiger house can be seen at number 22. Erected in 1899–1900 it was the first residential building in Munich to be given a *Jugendstil* façade and again employs Egyptian-style masks, stylised flowers, and sharp verticals. Most unusual is the frieze depicting Adam and Eve, one of very few pictorial representations on Munich's *Jugendstil* buildings (see page 4). A comparatively subdued *Jugendstil* façade stands next door at number 20.

Walk southwards now along Friedrichstrasse, stopping off at Franz-Joseph-Strasse 19 to see another fine *Jugendstil* façade, this time featuring a pair of golden snakes on one side and a pair of peacocks on the other; the graceful glass doors at street level give on to a delightful garden courtyard. Near the end of Friedrichstrasse, at number 3, there is a different style of *Jugendstil* house. Erected in 1904 its lace-like surface treatment reminds us that *Jugendstil*, like *Art Nouveau*, was not simply an architectural movement, but rather a multi-disciplinary one, in which fashion, painting, sculpture, and literature were all involved.

This tour finishes at the bottom of Friedrichstrasse by turning left into Georgenstrasse, where the Pacelli Palais at number 8–10 permits a direct comparison between Historicism and *Jugendstil*. The right-hand

Munich's first residential Jugendstil façade is on Ainmillerstrasse

half of the building still sports its traditional façade made up of solid but conservative neo-Classical columns, tympana, loggias and sculptures; by contrast, the left-hand side, which was renovated in the early 20th century, carries a pared-down colourful *Jugendstil* façade.

For those interested in seeing other examples of *Jugendstil* art, a visit should be made to the Villa Stuck at Prinzregentenstrasse 60. The painter, sculptor and graphic artist Franz von Stuck (1863–1928) was instrumental in the success of Munich's *Jugendstil*, and his former home and studio now pays permanent homage to his work.

Other places of interest nearby: 48, 82

82 The U-Bahn Began Here

Schwabing – Freimann, U-Bahn monument on Ungererstrasse
outside the Nordfriedhof U-Bahn station
U6 Nordfriedhof

Munich's U-Bahn is neither the oldest (London), the longest (New York City), nor the most used (Moscow) underground electric railway in the world, but as part of a modern integrated transport network, including S-Bahn, trams, and buses, it enables the city's 1.3 million inhabitants to travel almost anywhere. Despite its relative youth the history of the Munich U-Bahn is an interesting one, which offers the city explorer a handful of unusual places to visit.

Plans for an underground railway in Munich date back to the 1930s, when the Nazis forbade the acquisition of new rolling stock for the city's existing tram system in order to demonstrate its "insufficiency". The construction of an underground railway was but one element in their ambitious plans to transform the city into the 'Capital of the Nazi Movement' (Hauptstadt der Bewegung). Consequently, between 1938 and 1941 a tunnel was dug beneath Lindwurmstrasse (between Sendlingertor and Sonnenstrasse) and a platform built at Goetheplatz. As the Second World War intensified, however, construction was abandoned and after the war the reconstruction of the existing but badly damaged tram system took priority.

This modest plaque on Ungererstrasse marks where Munich's U-Bahn began

During the 1950s Munich's capacity for surface traffic became overstretched and it was suggested that some of the existing tram lines be run underground. By 1964 this plan had been dropped in favour of constructing a full underground railway. Construction of the first north-south route began on 1st February 1965, alongside the North Cemetery (Nordfriedhof) on Ungererstrasse, where today a vertical steel girder marks the spot. A plaque records

Brightly coloured panels adorn the walls of the Georg-Brauchle-Ring U-Bahn station

how the Bavarian Prime Minister Dr. Alfons Goppel and the Mayor of Munich Dr. Hans-Jochen Vogel dug the first sod. Stretching between Kieferngarten and Goetheplatz the line opened in October 1971 and is known today as the U6. The 1930s tunnel was incorporated into the system, as was the Goetheplatz platform, which explains why it is a different length to all the other platforms on the line.

When the 1972 Olympic Games were awarded to Munich in 1966 construction work on enlarging the city's U-Bahn network was hastened. The U3 from Münchner Freiheit to Olympiazentrum (where four platforms were installed to cope with the volume of visitors) was opened in May 1972, just ten days after the Munich S-Bahn tunnel through the city centre had been inaugurated. An U-Bahn extension to Harras was opened in 1975, with further stations added in 1983 to service the *Internationale Gartenbauausstellung* (International Garden Exhibition) in Westpark (see no. 70).

Since the early 1980s Munich's U-Bahn network has been expanded continuously and consists today of seven lines, over a hundred kilometres of track, and a similar number of stations. On the U1 some of these stations are worth visiting in their own right, for example Westfriedhof, with its huge aluminium lampshades suspended from

The Westfriedhof U-Bahn station features these huge aluminium lampshades

the ceiling, Georg-Brauchle-Ring, with its multicoloured wall panels by artist Franz Ackermann (b. 1963), and St.-Quirin-Platz, with its steel-and-glass roof pulled intriguingly down on one side, almost to the level of the track. The white-and-blue wave pattern in the tunnel between Am Hart and Frankfurter Ring on the U2 is the only artwork found on the system *outside* of the stations. It is worth noting too that the platforms at Universität, Odeonsplatz, and Goetheplatz on the U3/U6 provide piped classical music to soothe commuters.

Other places of interest nearby: 81

83 Where East Meets West

Schwabing – Freimann, the Freimann Mosque (Moschee
Freimann) and Munich Islamic Centre (Islamisches Zentrum
München) at Wallnerstrasse 1–5
U6 Studentenstadt, then Bus 293 Wallnerstrasse

During the mid-1960s, Germany's previously small Muslim community increased dramatically in size as Turkish and Balkan guest workers *(Gastarbeiter)* were recruited to help with the country's economic revival. They made up for a manpower shortage that resulted not only from the Second World War but also the erection of the Berlin Wall, which blocked the flow of German migrant workers from the east. By the mid-1990s many Turks had decided to make Germany their permanent home and today there are approximately 1.8 million Turks in Germany (out of a total of 3.4 million Muslims), some 120 000 of whom live in Munich.

Despite multiculturalism having been branded a failure in some parts of Europe, it has fared better in Germany. This is partly because it is a much bigger place, and also because few of its urban areas are dominated by a single ethnic group, avoiding the risk of ghettoization. Unfortunately, many Germans have little real contact with their Turkish neighbours, dissuaded in part by radical Islamists in Germany, who wish to prevent the full integration of Turks into German society.

Being initially a temporary population, Germany's Muslims worshipped wherever they could, which meant disused apartments, old factory buildings, and community centres. There are today an estimated 2200 such prayer houses – twenty of which are in Munich – entirely hidden from public view and therefore provoking little racial tension. However, it has recently been acknowledged that Germany's Turkish population is now a permanent one, with a legitimate need for convenient and identifiable, purpose-built places of worship. Whilst the construction of imposing mosques has occurred in Berlin without too much resistance, there has been more opposition in Munich, the heartland of German Catholicism. Two interesting locations illustrate this point well.

A traditional mosque, with a 33 metre-high minaret, has existed in Munich since 1973. A part of the Munich Islamic Centre (Islamisches Zentrum München) the Freimann Mosque (Moschee Freimann) was only the seventh mosque to be built in Germany – and the very first in Bavaria. Located within a leafy walled compound alongside the Schleißheimer Kanal the mosque's domed prayer hall is designed to hold 450 men, with space for a further 100 in the women's gallery. The centre also includes a library and a school. The mosque's construction costs were borne by fourteen Islamic states, with more than half coming from Libya.

The reason why the Freimann Mosque's construction prompted little controversy is two-fold: partly because it is located well to the north of the city centre, alongside a wastewater treatment plant and a former city dump on Wallnerstrasse, and also because at the time of its construction there were not the cultural tensions we see today. The mosque is operated by the Islamic Community of Germany (Islamische Gemeinschaft in Deutschland, or IGD), one of the oldest Muslim organisations in Ger-

Minaret and crescent at the Freimann Mosque (Moschee Freimann) on Wallnerstrasse

many (1958). Despite having been the target of several police raids resulting fom alleged links with Islamic fundamentalism, the mosque hosts open days to which members of all faiths are welcome, in an attempt to bridge religious and cultural gaps.

Meanwhile, south of the city centre in the working-class district of Sendling it was announced in 2004 that a Muslim prayer house, situated since 1989 in an old furniture warehouse on Schanzenbachstrasse, had outgrown itself. Managed by the IGD's legal successor, the Turkish Islamic Union for Religious Affairs (Diyanet İşleri Türk Islam Birliği, or DITIB), which was founded in 1984, it had space for only 130 worshippers but was being used regularly by 700! An application was made by the Turkish community to alter the building but this caused opposition from non-Muslims living nearby. Consequently, plans were drawn up to relocate to a purpose-built mosque on Gotzinger Platz, directly opposite the Roman Catholic Church of St. Korbinian (St. Korbinian Kirche). Although the plans specified a pair of minarets shorter than the steeples of the church, and rooms where non-Muslims could be entertained, there was still local outrage, suggesting that the close proximity of a mosque to a church was seen as a deliberate religious provocation. This seems a pity, since not only had the DITIB staged a large rally in Cologne in 2004 to protest against the use of violence in the name of Islam, but also one of Munich's Turkish community leaders voiced his strong belief that the proximity of the two religious buildings would engender a much-needed dialogue between the two communities. In 2010 DITIB scrapped their plans for the mosque citing financial reasons.

An inscribed standard in the Islamic collection of the State Museum of Ethnology (Staatliches Museum für Völkerkunde) on Maximilianstrasse

To learn more about Islamic culture visit the excellent Islamic collection in the State Museum of Ethnology (Staatliches Museum für Völkerkunde) at Maximilianstrasse 42 (see no. 11). For a taste of modern Turkish life in Munich take a stroll down bustling Landwehrstrasse, with its cafés, restaurants, and shops.

Other places of interest nearby: 84

84 The Sunken Village of Fröttmaning

Schwabing – Freimann, the Holy Cross Church (Heilig-Kreuz-Kirche) on the north side of the Fröttmaninger Berg, near Kreuz-München-Nord (junction of Autobahns 9 and 99)
U6 Studentenstadt, then Bus 293 Wallnerstrasse, then walk along Lottlisa-Behling-Weg following signs to Heilig-Kreuz Fröttmaning

In the far north-eastern corner of Munich, close to the busy A9-A99 Autobahn interchange, stand two of the city's architectural wonders. One is the colossal Allianz Arena, an ultra-modern stadium built for the 2006 FIFA World Cup. In complete contrast, to the east of it, stands the tiny Holy Cross Church (Heilig-Kreuz-Kirche), the oldest completely preserved church in Munich.

The church nestles amidst trees immediately north of the Fröttmaninger Berg, a disused city dump site. It is all that remains of the medieval village of Fröttmaning, which stood here until the mid-20th century on what was the Munich-Freising road. Archaeologists have uncovered even earlier evidence in the form of a blackened circular altar, suggesting the former presence of a Celtic place of sacrifice.

The history of the church itself begins in 815AD, when a wooden building with associated fields was given by the head of the Fröttmaning clan to the Diocese of Freising. The relevant deed of donation (in which the settlement is called Freddamaringun, later Fritmaring) is the oldest document in the Bavarian Public Records Office. The late Romanesque church seen today, which replaced the original building during the first half of the 13th century, comprises characteristically thick walls, arched windows, and a sturdy 18 metre-high tower. An original lime-wash fresco revealed during renovation work in 1981 features the oldest known depiction of Christ in Bavaria. The Baroque ceiling fresco of c. 1740 is from the Asam School and depicts the Byzantine Roman Emperor Heraclius (see no. 66).

The passage of time has seen the little church threatened on several occasions, notably during the 1930s when the nearby motorway interchange was constructed. As originally planned, the Salzburg road running east would have obliterated the church. Fortunately, thanks to the efforts of a local pressure group the road was shifted northwards, and the church saved. The numerous farms that had grown up around it

The Holy Cross Church (Heilig-Kreuz-Kirche) on the Fröttmaninger Berg is Munich's oldest church

were not so lucky, and were swept away in the 1950s to make room for the city dump.

The church was still not secure though and during the 1970s its valuable church treasures and two 15th century bells were stolen. Even as recently as 1984 a plan was mooted to increase the size of the city dump northwards, right up to the walls of the church itself. Vociferous protesters once again won the day.

As the new millennium approached, a citizen's initiative proposed that the church be made an integral part of the new Allianz Arena development area. Accordingly, the site was connected to the Arena park by a road bridge thus guaranteeing it greater security. At the same time an international competition to beautify the Fröttmaninger Berg was announced. In 2004 the commission was given unanimously to Berlin-born artist Timm Ulrichs (b. 1940). Taking the near destruction of the historic church as his inspiration, Ulrichs spent the next two years

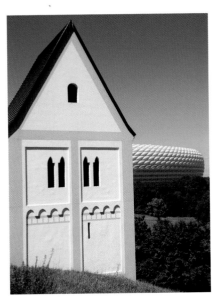

erecting an exact replica of it 150 metres to the south. Constructed this time in concrete it is deliberately half buried in the side of the now landscaped dump. Called *Versunkenes Dorf* (Sunken Village) the result is a cynical work of art, designed to make onlookers reflect on the impermanence of man's labours. As the English poet Percy Bysshe Shelley wrote in his *Ozymandias*: "Look on my works, ye mighty, and despair!"

Other places of interest nearby: 83

This exact replica of the Holy Cross Church (Heilig-Kreuz-Kirche), with the Allianz Arena in the background, was erected in 2004

***

Standing on top of the Fröttmaninger Berg is the perfect place to finish this odyssey, during which some of the more unusual and unsung corners of Munich have been explored. Looking back across the city from this little-visited location allows one to appreciate how far Munich has come since the Second World War, reinventing itself as one of the most vibrant and interesting of European cities. It also gives the satisfied explorer the opportunity to reflect on the myriad achievements (or otherwise) of the many fascinating characters who have chosen to live and work here.

Opening Times

for museums and other places of interest (after each name is the borough)
Correct at time of going to press but may be subject to change.

Abbey Church of St. Anne (Klosterkirche St. Anna), Altstadt – Lehel, St.-Anna-Strasse 19, daily 7.30am–7pm

All Hallows' Church (Allerheiligenkirche am Kreuz), Altstadt – Lehel, Kreuzstrasse 10, daily 8am–8pm

Alpine Museum (Alpines Museum), Altstadt – Lehel, Praterinsel 5, Tue–Fri 1–6pm, Sat & Sun 11am–6pm

Alter Simpl, Maxvorstadt, Türkenstrasse 57, Sun–Thu 11am–3am, Fri & Sat 11am–4am

Asam-Schlössl, Thalkirchen – Obersendling – Forstenried – Fürstenried – Solln, Maria-Einsiedel-Str. 45, daily 11am–1am

Augustinerbräu, Altstadt – Lehel, Neuhauser Strasse 27, Mon–Sat 9am–12pm, Sun 10am–12pm

Augustiner-Keller, Maxvorstadt, Arnulfstrasse 52, beer garden daily 11.30am–12pm, cellars open from 4pm

Basilica of St. Boniface (Basilika St. Bonifaz), Maxvorstadt, Karlstrasse 34, daily 8am–8pm

Bavaria Statue and Ruhmeshalle, Ludwigsvorstadt – Isarvorstadt, Theresienwiese, Apr–mid Oct daily 9am–6pm, Oktoberfest daily 9am–8pm

Bavaria Film Studios (Bavaria Filmstadt), Geiselgasteig, Bavaria-filmplatz 7, guided tours in German Apr–Oct 9am–6pm, Nov–Mar 10am–5pm (English by request)

Bavarian National Museum (Bayerisches Nationalmuseum), Altstadt – Lehe), Prinzregentenstrasse 3, Tue–Sun 10am–5pm (Thu 8pm)

Beer and Oktoberfest Museum (Bier- und Oktoberfestmuseum), Altstadt – Lehel, Sterneckerstrasse 2, Tue–Sat 1–6pm

BMW Museum, Milbertshofen – Am Hart, Petuelring 130, Tue–Sun 10am–6pm; factory tours Mon–Fri 9am–4.30pm

Bogenhausen Cemetery (Friedhof Bogenhausen), Bogenhausen, Kirche St. Georg, Bogenhausener Kirchplatz 1, Nov–Feb daily 8am–5pm, Mar daily 8am–6pm, Apr–Aug daily 8am–8pm, Sep & Oct daily 8am–7pm

Borstei Museum (Borstei-Museum), Moosach, Löfftzstrasse 10, Tue, Thu & Sat 3–6pm

Bürgersaalkirche, Altstadt – Lehel, Neuhauser Strasse 14, lower church daily 8am–8pm; upper church daily 11am–1pm

Café Altschwabing, Maxvorstadt, Schellingstrasse 56, Mon–Fri 8am–1am, Sat & Sun 9am–1am

Café am Beethovenplatz, Ludwigsvorstadt – Isarvorstadt, Hotel Mariandl, Goethestrasse 51, daily 9am–1am

Café Arzmiller, Altstadt – Lehel, Theatinerstrasse 22, Mon–Sat 8.30am–6.30pm

Café Frischhut, Altstadt – Lehel, Prälat-Zistl-Strasse 8, Mon–Sat 7am–6pm

Café Kreutzkamm, Altstadt – Lehel, Maffeistrasse 4, Mon–Fri 8am–7pm, Sat 9am–6pm

Café Luitpold, Maxvorstadt, Luitpoldblock, Brienner Strasse 11, Mon 8am–7pm, Tue–Sat 8am–11pm, Sun 9am–7pm; Café Luitpold Collection (Sammlung Café Luitpold), Palmengarten, Mon–Sat 10am–7pm

Café Tambosi, Altstadt – Lehel, Odeonsplatz 18, daily 9am–1am

Church of Christ the Redeemer (Erlöserkirche), Schwabing – Freimann, Ungerer Strasse 13, Sun Mass 10am

Church of St. Anne (Damenstift St. Anna), Altstadt – Lehel, Damenstiftstrasse 1, daily 8am–8pm

Church of St. Benno (St. Benno-Kirche), Maxvorstadt, Ferdinand-Miller-Platz, Sun Mass 10am

Church of St. Cajetan (Theatinerkirche), Altstadt – Lehel, Theatinerstrasse 22, daily 8am–8pm; crypt Mon–Fri 10am–1.30pm, 2–4.30pm

Church of St. George (Kirche St. Georg), Bogenhausen, Bogenhausener Kirchplatz 1, daily 8am–8pm

Church of St. Johann-Nepomuk (Asamkirche), Altstadt – Lehel, Sendlinger Strasse 32, daily 8am–5.30pm

Church of St. Margaret (Margaretenkirche), Sendling, Sendlinger Kirchplatz, daily 7.30am–7pm

Church of St. Maria Ramersdorf (Kirche St. Maria Ramersdorf), Ramersdorf – Perlach, Ramersdorfer Strasse 6, daily 7.30am–6.30pm

Church of St. Michael (Michaelskirche), Altstadt – Lehel, Neuhauser Strasse 6, Mon–Fri 10am–7pm, Tue–Thu & Sat 8am–7pm, Sun 7am–10.15pm

Church of St. Michael (Michaelskirche), Berg am Laim, Johann-Michael-Fisher-Platz 2, daily 8am–8pm

Church of St. Nicholas at Gasteig (St. Nikolai-Kirche am Gasteig), Au – Haidhausen, Innere Wiener Strasse 1, daily 8am–5pm

Church of St. Peter (Peterskirche), Altstadt – Lehel, Rindermarkt 1, daily 7am–7pm; tower Mon–Fri 9am–6.30pm, Sat & Sun 10am–6.30pm (5.30pm in winter)

Church of the Heart of Jesus (Herz-Jesu-Kirche), Neuhausen – Nymphenburg, Lachnerstrasse 8, daily 8am–7pm

Church of the Holy Spirit (Heiliggeistkirche), Altstadt – Lehel, Tal 77, daily 7–12am, 3–6pm

Church of the Holy Trinity (Dreifaltigkeitskirche), Altstadt – Lehel, Pacellistrasse 6, daily 8am–8pm

Church of the Saviour (Salvatorkirche), Altstadt – Lehel, Salvatorplatz 17, daily 10am–8pm

Dallmayr, Altstadt – Lehel, Dienerstrasse 14–15, Mon–Sat 9.30am–7pm

Deutsches Museum, Ludwigsvorstadt – Isarvorstadt, Museumsinsel, daily 9am–5pm

Deutsches Museum Flugwerft Schleißheim, Oberschleißheim, Effnerstrasse 18, daily 9am–5pm

Deutsches Museum Verkehrszentrum, Schwanthalerhöhe, Theresienhöhe 14a, daily 9am–5pm

Die Puppenstube, Maxvorstadt, Luisenstrasse 68, Mon–Fri 11am–6pm

D'Original Oberbayerische Kräuter- & Wurzel-Sepp, Altstadt – Lehel, Blumenstrasse 15, Mon–Fri 9.30am–6.30pm, Sat 10am–3pm

East Cemetery (Ostfriedhof), Obergiesing, corner of Tegernseer Landstrasse and St.-Bonifatius-Strasse, Nov–Feb daily 8am–5pm, Mar daily 8am–6pm, Apr–Aug daily 8am–8pm, Sep & Oct daily 8am–7pm

East-West Peace Church (Ost-West-Friedenskirche), Neuhausen – Nymphenburg, Spridon-Louis-Ring 100, daily 11am–5pm (closed in bad weather)

Elisabethmarkt, Schwabing-West, Elisabethstrasse, Mon–Fri 10am–6pm, Sat 10am–3pm

Flohmarkt Riem, Trudering – Riem, Neue Messe München, Am Messesee, Sat 6am–4pm (except during trade fairs)

Forschungsbrauerei, Ramersdorf –
Perlach, Unterhachinger Strasse 76,
Mon–Sat 11am–11pm, Sun 11am–
10pm

Frauenkirche, Altstadt – Lehel, Frauenplatz 1, Sat–Wed 7am–7pm, Thu
7am–8.30pm, Fri 7am–6pm; tower
Apr–Oct Mon–Sat 10am–5pm

Friesische Teestube, Schwabing-
West, Pündterplatz 2, daily 10am–
11pm

Geknöpft & Zugenäht, Altstadt –
Lehel, Ludwig Beck, Burgstrasse 7,
Mon–Sat 9.30am–7pm

Geological Museum (Geologisches
Museum), Maxvorstadt, Luisen-
strasse 37, Mon–Fri 8am–6pm, first
Sat each month 10am–4pm

German Hunting and Fishing
Museum (Deutsches Jagd- und
Fischereimuseum), Altstadt – Lehel,
Neuhauser Strasse 2, daily 9.30am–
5pm, Thu until 9pm

Glyptothek, Maxvorstadt, Königsplatz 3, Tue–Sun 10am–5pm (Wed
8pm)

Goetz Collection (Sammlung
Goetz), Bogenhausen, Oberföhringer
Strasse 103, Thu & Fri 2–6pm, Sat
11am–4pm; by appointment only
tel. 0049-89-9593969-0, www.
sammlung-goetz.de

Haus der Kunst, Altstadt – Lehel,
Prinzregentenstrasse 1, daily 10am–
8pm (Thu 10pm)

Hofbräuhaus, Altstadt – Lehel, Platzl
9, daily 9am–11.30pm

Hofgartenbrunnwerk, Altstadt –
Lehel, Galeriestrasse, May–Oct daily
10am–2pm

Holy Cross Church (Heilig-Kreuz-
Kirche), Schwabing – Freimann,
Fröttmaninger Berg, Mon & Fri
9–12am, Tue & Thu 9–12am, 1–5pm

Johannis-Café, Au – Haidhausen,
Johannisplatz 15, Mon, Wed–Sun
11am–5am

Jewish Museum Munich (Jüdisches
Museum München), Altstadt –
Lehel, St.-Jakobs-Platz 16, Tue–Sun
10am–6pm

Käfer, Altstadt – Lehel, Prinzregentenstrasse 73, Mon–Thu
9.30am–8pm, Fri 9am–8pm, Sat
8.30am–4pm

Kremer Pigmente, Maxvorstadt,
Barer Strasse 46, Mon–Fri 10am–
1pm, 2–6pm, Sat 10–12am (closed
Aug Mon & Sat)

Lenbachhaus Art Gallery (Galerie
im Lenbachhaus), Maxvorstadt,
Luisenstrasse 33, Tue–Sun 10am–
6pm

Marionettenstudio Kleines Spiel,
Maxvorstadt, Neureutherstrasse 12,
Thu 8pm

Meter Museum (Zählermuseum),
Schwabing – Freimann, Franzstrasse
9, Wed 9am–12am

Mineralogy Museum (Museum
Reich der Kristalle), Maxvorstadt,
Theresienstrasse 41 (entrance on
Barer Strasse), Tue–Sun 1–5pm

Müller Baths (Müllersches Volksbad), Au – Haidhausen, Rosen-
heimerstrasse 1, daily 7.30am–11pm

München 72, Ludwigvorstadt–Isarvorstadt, Kohlstrasse 11, Tue–Thu
10am–12pm, Fri & Sat 10am–
1.30am, Sun 10am–10pm

Münchner Sanitätsmuseum,
Thalkirchen – Obersendling –
Forstenried – Fürstenried – Solln,
Boschetsriederstrasse 33, open
by appointment only, www.brk-
museum.de

Münchner Stadtmuseum (Munich
City Museum), Altstadt – Lehel, St.-
Jakobs-Platz 1, Tue–Sun 10am–6pm

Munich Chamber Theatre (Münchner Kammerspiele im Schauspielhaus), Altstadt – Lehel, Maximilianstrasse 34–35, box office Mon–Fri
10am–6pm, Sat 10am–1pm

Munich Fire Brigade Museum
(Münchner Feuerwehrmuseum),
Altstadt – Lehel, An der Haupt-
feuerwache 8, Sat 9am–4pm

Munich Puppet Theatre (Münchner
Marionettentheater), Altstadt –
Lehel, Blumenstrasse 32, ticket office
open Tue–Sun 10–12am and one
hour before each performance,
www.muema-theater.de

Museum für Antike Puppen,
Schwabing – Freimann, Gondershauser Strasse 37, Mon & Thu
11am–5pm

Museum of Man and Nature
(Museum Mensch und Natur), Neu-
hausen – Nymphenburg, Schloss
Nymphenburg (North Wing), Tue,
Wed & Fri 9am–5pm, Thu 9am–8pm,
Sat & Sun 10am–6pm

MVG Museum, Ramersdorf –
Perlach, Ständlerstrasse 20, Feb–Jul
every 2nd and 4th Sun in the month
11am–5pm

National Collection of Antiquities
(Staatliche Antikensammlungen),
Maxvorstadt, Königsplatz 3, Tue–Sun
10am–5pm, Wed 8pm

New Botanical Gardens (Botanischer Garten), Neuhausen –
Nymphenburg, Menzingerstrasse 12,
Feb, Mar & Oct daily 9am–5pm, Apr
& Sep daily 9am–6pm, May–Aug
daily 9am–7pm, Nov–Jan daily
9am–4.30pm

New Jewish Cemetery (Neuer
Israelitischer Friedhof), Schwabing
– Freimann, Garchinger Strasse 37,
Nov–Mar Sun–Fri 8am–4pm (Fri
3pm), Apr–Oct Sun–Fri 8am–5pm
(Fri 4pm); visitors must cover their
heads

New Pinakothek (Neue Pinakothek),
Maxvorstadt, Barer Strasse 29, Wed–
Mon 10am–6pm (Wed 8pm)

New Town Hall (Neues Rathaus),
Altstadt – Lehel, Marienplatz 8,
clock chimes Nov–Feb 11am &
12am, Mar–Oct 11am, 12am & 5pm;
tower viewing platform Mon–Fri
10am–7pm, Sat 10am–5pm, Sun
10am–2pm

North Cemetery (Nordfriedhof),
Schwabing – Freimann, Ungererstrasse, Nov–Feb daily 8am–5pm,
Mar daily 8am–6pm, Apr–Aug
daily 8am–8pm, Sep & Oct daily
8am–7pm

Old Catholic Church of St. Willibrord (Alt-Katholische Kirche St.
Willibrord), Altstadt – Lehel, Blumenstrasse 36, Sun Mass 10am

Old Jewish Cemetery (Alter
Israelitischer Friedhof), Sendling,
Thalkirchner Strasse 30, occasional
tours by appointment only, tel.
0049-89-24240021; visitors must
cover their heads

Old Pinakothek (Alte Pinakothek),
Maxvorstadt, Barer Strasse 27, Tue–
Sun 10am–6pm (Tue 8pm)

Old South Cemetery (Alter
Südfriedhof), Ludwigsvorstadt –
Isarvorstadt, Thalkirchnerstrasse 17,
Nov–Feb daily 8am–5pm, Mar daily
8am–6pm, Apr–Aug daily 8am–
8pm, Sep & Oct daily 8am–7pm

Otto Pachmayr, Maxvorstadt,
Theresienstrasse 33, Mon–Fri
9.30am–6.30pm, Sat 9.30am–1.30pm

Palaeontology Museum (Paläonto-
logisches Museum), Maxvorstadt,
Richard-Wagner-Strasse 10, Mon–
Thu 8am–4pm, Fri 8am–2pm; first
Sun of each month 10am–4pm

Paulaner Bräuhaus, Ludwigsvorstadt – Isarvorstadt, Kapuzinerplatz
5, daily 10am–1am

Paulanerkeller, Au – Haidhausen,
Hochstrasse 77, daily 10am–1am

Perlacher Forst Cemetery (Friedhof
am Perlacher Forst), Obergiesing,
Nov–Feb daily 8am–5pm, Mar daily
8am–6pm, Apr–Aug daily 8am–
8pm, Sep & Oct daily 8am–7pm

Pinakothek der Moderne, Maxvorstadt, Barer Strasse 40, Tue–Sun
10am–6pm (Thu 8pm)

Potato Museum (Kartoffelmuseum), Berg am Laim, OTEC-Haus, Grafinger Strasse 2, Fri 9am–6pm, Sat 11am–5pm, Tue–Thu by appointment only, www.kartoffelmuseum.de

Residenz, Altstadt – Lehel, Max-Josef-Platz 3, Apr–mid Oct 9am–6pm, mid Oct–Mar 10am–5pm

Rock Museum Munich, Moosach, Olympiaturm, Spiridon-Louis-Ring 7, daily 9am–6pm

Sammlung Schack, Altstadt – Lehel, Prinzregentenstrasse 9, Wed–Sun 10am–6pm

Schelling-Salon, Maxvorstadt, Schellingstrasse 54, Thu–Mon 10am–1am; closed for summer holidays

Schloss Blutenburg, Pasing – Obermenzing, Internationale Jugendbibliothek Mon–Fri 10am–4pm; chapel Apr–Sep 9am–5pm, Oct–Mar 10am–4pm

Schloss Nymphenburg, Neuhausen – Nymphenburg, Apr–mid Oct 9am–6pm, mid Oct–Mar 10am–4pm; garden pavilions Apr–mid Oct 9am–6pm

Seilerei Kienmoser, Altstadt – Lehel, Sendlingerstrasse 36 (in the courtyard), Mon–Fri 9–12am, 1.30–6pm

Spielart, Altstadt – Lehel, Müllerstrasse 39, Mon–Fri 12am–6pm

State Museum of Egyptian Art (Staatliches Museum Ägyptischer Kunst), Maxvorstadt, Kunstareal, Gabelsbergstrasse 35, Tue–Sun 10am–6pm

State Museum of Ethnology (Staatliches Museum für Völkerkunde), Altstadt – Lehel, Maximilianstrasse 42, Tue–Sun 9.30am–5.30pm

Tea House, Altstadt – Lehel, Sendlingerstrasse 62, Mon–Fri 10am–7pm, Sat 10am–6pm

Tierpark Hellabrunn, Untergiesing – Harlaching, Tierparkstrasse 30, Apr–Oct daily 9am–6pm, Nov–Mar daily 9am–5pm

Tonnadel-Paradies Friedrich Gleich, Ludwigsvorstadt – Isarvorstadt, Landwehrstrasse 48 (in the courtyard), Mon 12am–5pm, Tue–Fri 10am–5pm

Toy Museum (Spielzeugmuseum), Altstadt – Lehel, Old Town Hall (Altes Rathaus), Marienplatz 15, daily 10am–5.30pm

Trader Vic's bar and restaurant, Altstadt – Lehel, Hotel Bayerischer Hof, Promenadeplatz 2–6, daily 5pm–3am

Valentin-Karlstadt-Musäum, Altstadt – Lehel, Isartor, Isartorplatz, Mon, Tue & Thu 11.01am–5.29am, Fri & Sat 11.01am–5.29am, Sun 10.01am–5.29pm

Villa Stuck, Au – Haidhausen, Prinzregentenstrasse 60, Tue–Sun 10am–6pm (first Fri each month 10pm)

Waldfriedhof, Hadern, junction of Graubündenerstrasse and Forst-Kasten-Allee, Nov–Feb daily 8am–5pm, Mar daily 8am–6pm, Apr–Aug daily 8am–8pm, Sep & Oct daily 8am–7pm

West Cemetery (Westfriedhof), Moosach, Baldurstrasse 28, Nov–Feb daily 8am–5pm, Mar daily 8am–6pm, Apr–Aug daily 8am–8pm, Sep & Oct daily 8am–7pm

The Simplicissimus logo on a lantern outside Alter Simpl on Türkenstrasse (see no. 43)

White Rose Memorial Site (DenkStätte Weiße Rose), Maxvorstadt, Ludwig-Maximilians-Universität, Geschwister-Scholl-Platz 1, Apr–Oct Mon–Fri 11.30am–2.30pm, Sat 11.30–2.30pm, Nov–Mar Mon–Fri 10am–4pm

Zum Flaucher, Sendling, Isarauen 8, daily 10am–11pm

Bibliography

GUIDEBOOKS

Eyewitness Travel Guide Munich & the Bavarian Alps (Izabella Galicka and Katarzyna Michalska), Dorling Kindersley, 2008

Wo die Geister wandern – Literarische Spaziergänge durch Schwabing (Dirk Heißerer), Beck, 2008

Stille Winkel in München (Hans Pfitzinger), Ellert & Richter Verlag, 2007

Alte Häuser – Große Namen München (Rudolf Reiser), Stiebner, 2002

Munich, Bavaria & the Black Forest (Andrea Schulte-Peevers), Lonely Planet, 2008

München – Spaziergänge durch die Geschichte einer Stadt (Bernard Setzwein), Klett-Cotta, 2001

ILLUSTRATED BOOKS

München – Kunst und Kultur (Josef H. Biller & Hans-Peter Rasp), Südwest-Verlag, 2005

München. Dichter sehen eine Stadt. Texte und Bilder aus vier Jahrhunderten (Hans-Rüdiger Schwab), Metzler, 1993

Zeitgeister: München Wo Vergangenes Lebt (Various), A1 Verlag, 2006

ARCHITECTURE AND MONUMENTS

Magisches München – Geheime Kraftplätze in der Stadt (Fritz Fenzl), Nymphenburger, 2007

Münchens Lust am Jugendstil – Häuser und Menschen um 1900 (Edda & Michael Neumann-Adrian), Münchenverlag, 2008

Architectural Guide Munich (Various), Reimer, 2008

CHURCH, CEMETERY AND MUSEUM GUIDEBOOKS

Herzog & de Meuron – Sammlung Goetz (Hatje Cantz), Kunsthaus Bregenz, 2003

Magische Kirchen in München (Fritz Fenzl), Stiebner, 2006

Gräber in München (Gerd Otto-Rieke), Alabasta Verlag, 2000

Deutsches Museum Guide (Various), Deutsches Museum, 2005

HISTORY

Streifzüge durch Münchens Kunstgeschicht von der Romanik bis zur Gegenwart (Lothar Altmann), Verlag Schnell & Steiner, 2008

Geschichte Münchens (Richard Bauer), Beck, 2003

München: Die Geschichte einer Stadt (Reinhard Bauer & Ernst Piper), Piper, 1993

Kleine Geschichte Münchens (Reinhard Bauer & Ernst Piper), DTV, 2008

Münchner Stadtgeschichten – Von den Ursprüngen bis Heute (Fritz Fenzl), Stiebner, 2004

Münchens Weg in die Gegenwart: Von Heinrich der Löwe zur Weltstadt (Peter Claus Hartmann), Verlag Schnell & Steiner, 2008

Kleine Kunstgeschichte Münchens (Norbert Huse), Beck, 2004

München 1919–1933 – Stadtrundgänge zur politischen Geschichte (Benedikt Weyerer), Buchendorfer Verlag, 1993

München 1933–1949 – Stadtrundgänge zur politischen Geschichte (Benedikt Weyerer), Buchendorfer Verlag, 1996

HITLER'S MUNICH

Where Ghosts Walked: Munich's Road to the Third Reich (David Clay Large), W. W. Norton & Co., 1998

Hitlers München (David Clay Large), DTV, 2001

Hitler and Munich: A historical guide to the sights and addresses of Munich important to Adolf Hitler, his followers and his victims (Brian Deming), Verlag Anton Plenk, 1988

Hitler's Weg begann in München 1913–1923 (Anton Joachimsthaler), Herbig, 2000

Past Finder – Munich 1933–1945: Traces of German History – A Guidebook (Maik Kopleck), Christoph Links Verlag, 2007

Munich and Memory: Architecture, Monuments and the Legacy of the Third Reich (Gavriel D. Rosenfeld), University of California Press, 2000

Hauptstadt der Bewegung – München 1919–1938 (Viktor Ullrich), Arndt Verlag, 2006

Hunting Nazis in Munich (Joachim von Halasz), Foxley Books, 2006

National Socialism in Munich (Themen Gesichts Pfad) (Various), Landeshauptstadt München, 2007

WEBSITES

www.muenchen.de (Munich's Official Internet Site)

www.muenchen-touristeninformation.de (Munich Tourist Information)

www.best-of-munich.com (Munich Tourist Information, including museums)

www.mvg-mobil.de (Munich Public Transport Network)

www.stattreisen-muenchen.de (Munich City Walks)

www.spurwechsel-muenchen.de (Munich tours on foot, and by bike, tram and bus)

www.munichwalktours.de (Munich Walk Tours)

www.spottedbylocals.com/munich (useful and entertaining city Blog)

www.radiusmunich.com (the original Third Reich walking tour)

www.munich-insider.de (Third Reich and Dachau Concentration Camp Memorial tours)

www.stolpersteine-muenchen.de (Jewish memorial stones initiative)

www.toytowngermany.com/munich (English-language community website for Germany)

www.germany.travel (German Tourist Board)

Rafting on the Floßlände (see no. 65)

Acknowledgments

First and foremost I would like to thank my Viennese publisher, Christian Brandstätter Verlag, for realising the first edition of this book, especially Elisabeth Stein (commissioning editor), Else Rieger (editor), Ekke Wolf (design), Milena Greif (German translation), and Helmut Maurer (maps).

For kind permission to take photographs, as well as arranging for access and the provision of information, the following people are very gratefully acknowledged:

Alex and Daniela (Alter Simpl), Dr. Michael Apel (Museum Mensch und Natur), Beate Bentele & Vivian Dörr (Sammlung Café Luitpold), Stefan Böttcher (Landeshauptstadt München Tourismusamt Fotoservice), Helge Braatz (Bavaria Filmstadt), Café Frischhut, Anette Frankenberger (Kunstbunker Tumulka), Manuel Gatz, Stefan 'Sy' Gebharter, Ingvild Goetz and Nora Wagner (Sammlung Goetz), Dr. Sabine Heym and Günter Graml (Residenz München/Bayerische Schlösserverwaltung), Petra Hammerstein (Antiquariat Hans Hammerstein), Matthias Hansmeier (Müller'sches Volksbad), Renate Herkner, Ulla Hoering, Ignaz-Günther-Haus, Internationale Jugendbibliothek (Schloss Blutenburg), Stefan Jakob (Forschungsbrauerei), Kaffeehaus Altschwabing, Friederike Kaiser and Anke Palden (Deutscher Alpenverein e.V.), Kartoffelmuseum, Sergey Kokasin (Ost-West-Friedenskirche), Konditorei Huber (Ramersdorf), Dusan Krickovic (Westfriedhof), Tom Kristen (Steindruck München), Manuela Krone (www.eye4events. de), Dr. David Leshem (Neuer Israelitischer Friedhof), Thomas Licht & Sebastian Goetz (MVG Museum), Matthias Löffler (BMW Welt), Gabriele Meise and Gabriele Höbel (Münchner Stadtmuseum), Familie Meyer (Schelling-Salon), Ursula Müller, Brigitte Otto (Schloss Nymphenburg), C. Rakowski, Charlotte Knobloch, Carolin Unterreitmeier and Katja Morgenstern (Israelitische Kultusgemeinde München), Johann Rauschendorfer (Deutsches Jagd- und Fischereimuseum), Peter & Evelyn Renda, Ulrich Riegert (Ostfriedhof), Susanna Rusterholz and Catharina Weis (Herzog & de Meuron, Basel), Anna Salewski (Hotel Bayerischer Hof), Wolfgang and Claudia Schelf (Spielzeugmuseum), Ulrich Schindler (Paulaner Bräuhaus), Olaf Schmidt (Johannis-Café), Stefan Schopper, Jörg Schwan (Verlag L. Däbritz/Glyptotheka), Robert Schwandl (www.urbanrail.net), Gottfried 'Gog' Seidl-Carusa, Gertraud Stadler (Puppenstube), Oswalf Telfser (Friesische Teestube), Kristin Teuchtmann, Valentin Karlstadt Musäum, Ludwig Webel (Munich Tourist Office), Daniela Weiland, and Marc Wittwer.

For accommodation and stimulating conversation, Bernd Fischer-Rohn and the staff at the Hotel Max München (Amalienstrasse). Michael Benz in particular extended a very welcome hand of friendship, for which I remain most grateful.

For proof-reading and general advice I would like to thank my old and good friend Hans Kohlenberg.

For invaluable website support, Richard Tinkler.

Finally, very special thanks to my father Trevor for inspiring me to track down unusual locations in the first place – thanks Dad for making it all such fun!

Delft tiles in the Amalienburg at Schloss Nymphenburg (see no. 73)

2nd Revised Edition published by The Urban Explorer, 2014
A division of Duncan J. D. Smith
contact@duncanjdsmith.com
www.onlyinguides.com
www.duncanjdsmith.com

First published by Christian Brandstätter Verlag, 2009

Graphic design: Stefan Fuhrer
Typesetting and picture editing: Ekke Wolf
Revision typesetting and picture editing: Franz Hanns
Maps: © München Tourismusamt
Printed and bound by GraphyCems, Spain

ISBN 978-3-9503662-0-4

The Hundskugel on Hackenstrasse is Munich's
oldest Gasthaus (see no. 21)